DOES PSYCHOTHERAPY
REALLY HELP PEOPLE?

DOES PSYCHOTHERAPY REALLY HELP PEOPLE?

Edited by

JUSUF HARIMAN, Ph.D., FIAEP

Associate Editor, The Australian Journal of Clinical Hypnotherapy and Hypnosis

Associate Editor, The Australian Journal of Transpersonal Psychology

Fellow, The International Academy of Eclectic Psychotherapists

Founder, Limsian Therapy

Founding Editor, The International Journal of Eclectic Psychotherapy

Founding President, The International Academy of Eclectic Psychotherapists

SCHOOL OF
CALIFORNIA PROFESSIONAL
PSYCHOLOGY
LOS ANGELES

CHARLES C THOMAS • PUBLISHER
Springfield • Illinois • U.S.A.

Published and Distributed Throughout the World by

CHARLES C THOMAS • PUBLISHER

2600 South First Street

Springfield, Illinois 62717

© *1984 by* CHARLES C THOMAS • PUBLISHER

ISBN 0-398-05002-3

Library of Congress Catalog Card Number: 84–102

With THOMAS BOOKS *careful attention is given to all details of manufacturing and
design. It is the Publisher's desire to present books that are satisfactory as to their physical
qualities and artistic possibilities and appropriate for their particular use.* THOMAS
BOOKS *will be true to those laws of quality that assure a good name and good will.*

Printed in the United States of America

S–R-3

Library of Congress Cataloging in Publication Data

Main entry under title:

Does psychotherapy really help people?

 Bibliography: p.
 Includes index.
  1. Psychotherapy—Evaluation—Addresses, essays,
lectures. I. Hariman, Jusuf. [DNLM: 1. Psychotherapy,
WM 420 D653]
RC480.5.D58 1984 616.89'14 84–102
ISBN 0-398-05002-3

This book is dedicated to my wife, Polly Hariman, who has been a company in sorrow and a partner in joy. She is the zeal and the meaning of my life. I know I will adore her to the end of my days.

CONTRIBUTORS

GEORGE W. ALBEE, Ph.D., *Professor, Department of Psychology, University of Vermont, Burlington, Vermont, U.S.A.*

DON DIESPECKER, Ph.D., *Founding Editor, The Australian Journal of Transpersonal Psychology, Wollongong, NSW, Australia.*

ALBERT ELLIS, Ph.D., *Executive Director, Institute of Rational Emotive Therapy (Chartered by the Regents of the University of the State of New York), New York City, New York, U.S.A.*

EDWARD ERWIN, Ph.D., *Department of Philosophy, University of Miami, Coral Gables, Florida, U.S.A.*

HANS J. EYSENCK, D.Sc., *Professor, Institute of Psychiatry, London, U.K.*

STANLEY J. GROSS, Ed. D., *Professor of Counseling Psychology, Department of Counseling, Indiana State University, Terre Haute, Indiana, U.S.A.*

RICHARD P. HALGIN, Ph.D., *Assistant Professor, Department of Psychology, University of Massachusetts, Amherst, Massachusetts, U.S.A.*

JOHN A. HATTIE, Ph.D., *Center for Behavioural Studies, University of New England, Armidale, NSW, Australia.*

VIKTOR N. HIRSCH, Ph.D., *Institute of Preventive Medicine, The Methodist Hospital, Houston, Texas, U.S.A.*

MOSHE KROY, Ph.D., *Department of Philosophy, La Trobe University, Victoria, Australia.*

PITTU LAUNGANI, Ph.D., *Department of Social Science, Polytechnic of the South Bank, London, U.K.*

JAMES K. MORRISON, Ph.D., *Private Practice, Latham, New York, U.S.A.*

THOMAS J. NARDI, Ph.D., *Adjunct Faculties; Pace University (Pleasantville); Long Island University at Mercy College, New City, New York, U.S.A.*

WALTER E. O'CONNELL, Ph.D., *Founder, Natural High Actualisation Therapy, Houston, Texas, U.S.A.*

THOMAS D. OVERCAST, Ph.D., *Battelle Human Affairs Research Center, Seattle, Washington, U.S.A.*

MICHAEL R. POLLARD, Ph.D., *Federal Trade Commission, Washington, D.C., U.S.A.*

VICKY RIPPERE, Ph.D., *Institute of Psychiatry, London, U.K.*

H. JANE ROGERS, Ph.D., *Center for Behavioural Studies, University of New England, Armidale, NSW, Australia.*

NOLAN SALTZMAN, Ph.D., *Professor, Department of Anatomy and Physiology, The City University of New York, New York, USA.*

BRUCE D. SALES, Ph.D., *Department of Psychology, University of Arizona, Tucson, Arizona, U.S.A.*

CHRISTOPHER F. SHARPLEY, Ph.D., *Faculty of Education, Monash University, Victoria, Australia.*

PHILIP J. SMITH, Ed.D., *Past Foundation Head, Department of Psychology, Lawley College of Advanced Education, W.A., Australia.*

DANA D. WEAVER, Ph.D., *Department of Psychology, University of Massachusetts, Amherst, Massachusetts, U.S.A.*

PREFACE

In the field of Psychotherapy charlatans are constituted not only by those practising without appropriate qualifications, but more importantly, by those possessing eminent credentials yet holding out as what in reality they are not.

Psychotherapeutic practices are simply businesses and as such there is no compelling reason why they should be excluded from the Trade Practices Act. . . . Increased competition will improve public welfare, as professional societies will then be forced to justify their actions through public-benefit review procedures.

Psychotherapists must regard themselves as servants of their clients, and not behaving like bureaucratic politicians or bosses over them. At the same time, clients are not to be regarded as the passive recipients of treatment effects but must be mobilized in accordance with their avowed goals to participate actively in the processes of therapy. Furthermore, there is in the clients an unlimited source of wisdom — psychotherapists should be pupils of their clients, as well as their teachers. The whole relationship between psychotherapists and their clients can be partially summed up in the analogy: "Psychotherapists are Like the Seeds, and Their Clients are Like the Soil." (Hariman, 1983 a)

The working definition of the term *psychotherapy* adopted here includes, inter alia, all activities involving one or more patients or clients and one or more therapists or facilitators, which are intended to improve a patient or client's feelings of psychological well-being. The term *psychotherapist* refers thus to psychiatrist, psychologist, social worker, and the like practising psychotherapeutic strategies (Hariman, 1983 b). Since psychotherapy as such is not as yet a legally sanctioned profession, it denotes specialisation or quasi specialisation within the professions of psychiatry, psychology, social worker, and the like.

Each paper takes a constructively critical look at the profession of psychotherapy and suggests ways it can be strengthened professionally, but, more importantly, consumerially. That is to say, it looks at ways the consumer's needs can be more appropriately met. The book is therefore vibrantly optimistic in nature. In what follows, there is a brief description of each paper.

- Albee, G. W. *Does including psychotherapy in health insurance represent a subsidy to the rich from the poor?*
  ... since including psychotherapy in health insurance represents a subsidy to the rich from the poor, psychotherapy should reexamine its traditional emphasis on introspection, verbalisation, self-examination, and the development of insight.
- Diespecker, D. *Psychotherapy: Getting what you've got.*
  ... argues that therapists do not have what clients want, they cannot give what clients already have — all the therapeutic tools that they may ever need. Implications for the profession of psychotherapy are outlined.
- Ellis, A. *Must most psychotherapists remain as incompetent as they now are?*
  ... reviews some of the main aspects of therapeutic inefficiency. Specific suggestions for increasing the efficiency of psychotherapy are given.
- Erwin, E. *Is psychotherapy more effective than a placebo?*
  ... argues that psychotherapy is not lacking of evidence of efficacy, but it has not been shown to be more effective than a placebo. Implications for psychotherapy enterprise are discussed.
- Eysenck, H. J. *The battle over psychotherapeutic effectiveness.*
  ... suggests that there is no good evidence to suggest that psychotherapeutic or psychoanalytic treatment of any kind improves the chances of neurotic patients to recover or be cured, when compared with no treatment. Constructive recommendations are made.
- Gross, S. J. *Professional disclosure: Theory, research, and application.*
  ... suggests that professional disclosure is a powerful, if essentially untested tool for expanding consumer knowledge.
- Halgin, R. P., and Weaver, D. D. *Are psychiatrists, social workers, and clinical psychologists really doing their jobs?*
  ... suggest the need to establish professional schools of psychotherapy that are multidisciplinary in nature and would derive their curriculum from relevant aspects of psychiatry, social work, and clinical psychology.

- Hattie, J. A., Sharpley, C. F., and Rogers, H. J. *"Barefoot" psychotherapists: The relative effectiveness of paraprofessionals in mental health services.*
  . . . studies on the relative effectiveness of paraprofessionals in mental health services suggest that empirical investigation of the effectiveness of training procedures should be paramount over accreditation based on traditional academic qualifications.
- Hirsch, V. N., and O'Connell, W. *No laughing matter: The lack of humor in current psychotherapists.*
  . . . suggest that psychotherapists need a crash program on humor if they are to improve their human face.
- Kroy, M. *Psychotherapy and the paradox of service: A transpersonal critique.*
  . . . suggests that a transpersonal revolution is a sine qua non to the elimination of the built-in necessity of failure inherent in the paradox of service.
- Laungani, P. *Do psychotherapies meet clients' perceived needs?*
  . . . poses several issues that every responsible psychotherapist should bear in mind: issues with which most clients seeking therapeutic help are likely to be concerned the most, such as safe-guarding the clients' rights, etc.
- Morrison, J. K. *Eight steps toward protecting the psychotherapy client from "consumer fraud."*
  . . . suggests eight steps toward protecting the psychotherapy client from consumer fraud.
- Nardi, T. J. *Psychotherapy: Cui bono?*
  . . . asks two important questions: For whose benefit? and, To what end? Suggestions for discerning legitimate innovation from idiosyncratic nonsense, the sincere from the insincere, and the competent from the incompetent are made.
- Overcast, T. D., Sales, B. D., and Pollard, M. R. *Applying antitrust laws to the professions: Implications for psychology.*
  . . . reviews recent legal developments applying antitrust principles to selected professional practices such as accreditation, licensing, specialty certification, restrictions on advertising, and fee setting.
- Rippere, V. *Can the taxpayer afford to have the medical establishment go on ignoring ecology?*
  . . . suggests that to the extent that patients' symptoms are due to hypersensitivity to the physical or chemical environment, then

clinical ecology needs to be granted its rightful place in the clinical armamentarium.

- Saltzman, N. *Evolutionary requirements on models of psychotherapy.*
  . . . suggests several evolutionary requirements that will enable psychotherapists to improve their receptivity to their clients' feelings.
- Smith, P. J. *Context and considerations of the education of psychotherapists.*
  . . . raises some major aspects of the problem of the education of professional psychotherapists, especially the aims and the means of obtaining those aims.

As there can be no doubt that the current consumer-oriented legal and social atmosphere is bound to continue to grow (Overcast et al, 1982; Fishman et al, 1982), the book might therefore be crucial for the survival of the profession of psychotherapy. It could be a blueprint for the shape of the psychotherapy of tomorrow.

The book will therefore appeal to all concerned with the survival and growth of the profession of psychotherapy. It is a must for practising counsellors, doctors, psychiatric nurses, psychiatrists, psychologists, and social workers. Researchers and postgraduate students will likewise find the book a rich source of ideas—provoking and stimulating, to say the least. It is an ideal book to be used as a focal point for significant research projects; that is to say, research projects with wide ranging academic, professional, and legal implications.

REFERENCES

Hariman, J. *Reflections: Words of Wisdom.* 1983 a. Unpublished Manuscript.

Hariman, J. (Editor). *The Therapeutic Efficacy of the Major Psychotherapeutic Techniques.* Springfield, Ill: Thomas, 1983 b.

Fishman, D. B., and Neigher, W. D. American psychology in the 80's: Who will buy, *American Psychologist,* 1982, *37*(5), 533–546.

Overcast, T. D., Sales, B. D., and Pollard, M. R. Applying antitrust laws to the professions: Implications for psychology. *American Psychology,* 1982, *37*(2), 517–525.

ACKNOWLEDGMENTS

My greatest debt is to the contributors of this book, all of whom have enabled *Does Psychotherapy Really Help People?* come into being, and particularly to those workers who have patiently acted upon my onerous guidelines.

I am grateful to my beloved parents, brothers, and my darling sister for their loving understanding and support during my recent illness.

Special thanks is due to Doctor Albert Ellis, from whom the title of the book is derived, and Mary C. Cassar, whose sweet tuition has broadened my understanding of the art of communication to an unimaginable extent.

My very dear friends, Doctor Les Carr, Doctor Don Diespecker, and Doctor Philip J. Smith have made me aware of the intricacy of the profession of psychotherapy. Because of them, I came out enlightened.

And last, but not least, Bruno N. Nesci and Irene Moss have taught me much about the finer aspects of legal arguments and interactions. Because of them, I am now capable of going ahead in my life with my chin up, armed with the knowledge that I have a mighty powerful friend: "LAW."

CONTENTS

DOES PSYCHOTHERAPY REALLY HELP PEOPLE?

Chapter 1

DOES INCLUDING PSYCHOTHERAPY IN HEALTH INSURANCE REPRESENT A SUBSIDY TO THE RICH FROM THE POOR?

GEORGE W. ALBEE

ABSTRACT: *Traditionally, psychotherapy has been sought primarily by the affluent. Surveys have found that psychotherapy users come from the higher social classes, are more often female than male, are college educated and/or in one of the professions, and are drawn from the group labeled neurotic or overcontrolled. For the most part they are suburbanites with moderately serious neurotic problems and capable of paying the high cost of frequent sessions. Clearly, the need for help with emotional problems is not limited to the affluent—every survey reports a higher rate of disturbance among the poor. But psychotherapy, with its traditional emphasis on introspection, verbalization, self-examination, and the development of insight, clearly is not a compatible approach to dealing with the problems of poor people, who do not use it much even when it is available and free. Most psychotherapists are heavily clustered in certain census tracts in certain regions of the country, while other areas are barely supplied. These and other considerations suggest that cost-reimbursed psychotherapy under national health insurance may very well make the therapy available at reduced cost to those affluent persons currently among the heaviest users, while the large numbers of poor people not likely to make increased use of the service would increasingly bear its cost.*

Historically, psychotherapy was created for the relief of the emotional problems of affluent clients, and theory and practice in the field reflect this focus on the problems of the affluent. There is no need to recite for this audience the history of the origins of psychoanalysis in Victorian Vienna, but it is instructive to remember that Dr. Freud's first clients were largely middle- and upper-middle-class women suffering

From *American Psychologist*, Vol. 32, No. 9, Sept. 1977. Copyright 1977 by the American Psychological Association. Reprinted by permission of the publisher and author.

from pseudoneurological symptoms that he, as a neurologist, discovered were due to the conversion of unconscious sexual conflicts into mystifying paralyses and anesthesias. In short, the first subjects for psychoanalysis were overcontrolled, neurotic women who were undoubtedly suffering from the sexist, repressive forces characteristic of industrializing societies.

Psychoanalysis has always been prohibitively expensive and therefore available primarily to the rich and especially to the nouveau riche. A recent survey (Marmor, 1975) of the private office practice of psychiatrists in the United States, conducted by the Joint Information Service of the American Psychiatric Association and the National Association for Mental Health, reports as follows:

> The importance of economic factors in access to private psychiatric care is dramatically reflected in figures indicating that, as might be expected, more affluent professional and managerial workers are overrepresented in the private offices of psychiatrists as compared to blue- and white-collar workers. This is particularly true of the more expensive modality of psychoanalytic treatment. A consequence of this fact is that ethnic minorities, and particularly black and Latin American patients, are grossly underrepresented in the private practice of psychiatrists. (p. 39)

But, it will be objected, this is just the purpose of national health insurance—to provide care for everyone and not just for the affluent who now go to private psychiatrists. By extending benefits for coverage to all social class levels, the inability to pay for private care will no longer prevent the poor from getting psychotherapy. This is a naive view. Weihofen has called attention to the double standard of care provided in public tax-supported agencies that, while claiming to be nondiscriminatory, manage to give more attention, to provide better treatment, and to assign more highly qualified therapists to the affluent clients at the expense of the poor. Weihofen (1967) says:

> Because psychiatrists understandably prefer "good" patients—those who are sensitive and sophisticated with social and intellectual standards similar to their own—the poor who become patients frequently get inferior treatment, even in the public clinics that purport not to make distinctions between paying and non-paying patients. A recent survey revealed that even a public clinic excluding those able to pay for private psychiatric care still distinguished its patients by social class. Not only were patients from upper social classes accepted for treatment more often, but their treatment was more apt to be given by a senior or more experienced member of the staff. (p. 2)

In another recent series of studies discussed in a special paper by Bert Brown, Director of the National Institute of Mental Health, it was found that blue-collar auto workers provided with free psychiatric services by their union contract simply failed to make any significant use of this service. They resisted referral to a "shrink" and did not understand the services available.

Let me be so bold as to suggest that the personality characteristics of professional therapists — psychiatrists and psychologists particularly — make them particularly unqualified to provide one-to-one therapy for the poor and the blue-collar class. And similarly, these latter groups do not want or need psychotherapy. The nature of medical education, with its strict admission requirements, its use of a student peonage system, and its authoritarian hierarchical structure — with residency training in psychiatry nearly always obtained on university hospital wards where the patients have Blue Cross or other hospitalization insurance — in short, the entire system of selection and training that produces psychiatrists selects obsessives for survival whose experiences are very largely limited to patients who are members of the middle and upper classes. While most good psychiatric training programs rotate their residents through the back wards of the state hospital, the rotation is usually swift and is drug-therapy oriented.

The training of clinical psychologists is hardly any better in preparing them to work with the poor. As admission to clinical training programs becomes more and more selective and difficult, the lucky few who are admitted are obsessive high-achievers with outstanding academic records and high test scores. In short, they too are obsessives heavily indoctrinated about the importance of time, inner control, and research. Both groups are selected from the upper-middle class, and few of them speak the language, share the values, or understand the problems of the poor.

As Schofield (1964) has pointed out, psychotherapists prefer people with the YAVIS syndrome (young, attractive, verbal, intelligent, and successful). It may be that the training of psychotherapists makes them unsuited for any kind of intervention except one-to-one psychotherapy with middle-class clients. Psychotherapists are themselves drawn from the middle class, are trained with middle-class patients, and are familiar with middle-class problems. Middle-class people tend to be more conscience-laden and guilt-plagued and therefore are more neurotically anxious. The amount of anxiety can often be reduced by individual psychotherapy, and so the process is rewarding and reinforcing to middle-class people. While it may be an oversimplification, there certainly is some epidemiological evidence that neurotic anxiety is less common among the poor. The reality problems of poverty, unemployment, discrimination, poor housing, etc., assume higher levels of urgency than interpersonal relationship problems. Such a formulation would argue that the kind of "mental" outpatient treatment covered in any national health scheme — individual psychotherapy — would be more appropriate and acceptable to the affluent and less utilized by the poor.

Whether the intervention setting is the private office or the community mental health center, the treatment of choice, overwhelmingly, is one-to-one individual psychotherapy. In a study of a group of the nation's best community mental health centers several years ago, Glasscote, Sanders, Forstenzer, and Foley (1964) reported that "psychotherapy is the backbone of treatment." In another study, Rosen, Bahn, Shellow, and Bower (1965) found that adolescents accepted for clinic treatment had to be "preoccupied with self-examination and willing to talk about themselves." This criterion limited service primarily to the middle-class talkers among the teenagers. But because everyone would be paying the bill and only the affluent would have the kind of disturbances for which the treatment was appropriate, once again we see the injustice of everyone paying for help for the few.

In the city with the largest number of psychiatrists, psychologists, and mental health clinics in the nation — Boston — Ryan (1969) found, in a careful survey, that social casework agencies were intervening actively with more emotionally disturbed poor people than were all the psychiatric resources.

Another serious problem involves the geographical distribution of mental health care professionals. Just five states claim the services of more than half of all the psychiatrists in the country. Psychologists are not quite as concentrated as the psychiatrists, but then the majority are not in practice either. There is clearly a significant relationship between the *affluence* of a geographic area or city census tract and the presence of mental health services. At the present time there are few private practitioners in the central city. Even when there are public clinics in the central city, the clientele using them tends to come from the affluent suburbs. Gordon (1965) described the problems involved in getting disturbed poor children through a public-clinic intake process and helping them survive the waiting list. He showed how lower-class children are rejected much more frequently than middle-class children seeking help. One way to accomplish this selection is through the waiting list. Middle-class parents are better able to wait, while poor families are oriented to more urgent, immediate solutions. Also, the higher status agencies have many rigid requirements in defining who will be accepted for treatment. Gordon found that even a child clinic located in the heart of an urban slum attracted most of its clients from suburbia. He found a high correlation between the distance the clients lived from the clinic and the likelihood of their acceptance for treatment!

The distribution of public clinics follows the distribution of mental health personnel. Half of all of the psychiatric clinics in the nation reportedly are in the northeastern states. One survey of more than 2,000 outpatient psychiatric clinics found only·56 of these in rural areas, only 50 of which served children. While one third of all the children in the country live in the rural states, only 4% of the clinics serving children were to be found in these same states.

Senator Edward Kennedy (1975), author of a major national health bill, sounds all of these themes:

> If we were to implement a comprehensive national health insurance program tomorrow, and if we did not change in any way the geographic location of the patient loads of psychiatrists, we would be asking the 86 percent of American families whose earnings are under $20,000 a year to pay the lion's share of the cost of a health care service which is rendered by and large to individuals in families whose incomes are over $20,000 a year. Moreover, we would be asking black families to pay taxes for services only two percent of which go to blacks. And, of course, we would be asking residents of areas of the country which have few psychiatrists available to help pay the bill for other areas of our nation where help can be more easily obtained. (pp. 151–152)

Kennedy sees this public program of mental health care as "contain[ing] the apparent risk of subsidizing services to higher-income citizens directly from tax contributions of middle- and low-income Americans." The really fundamental question, ultimately, is whether persons with the kinds of problems dealt with in outpatient, traditional psychotherapy really are *sick* — whether they truly have illnesses that should be covered by a health insurance plan. Today is not the time to review all of the arguments against a medical or sickness model of emotional disturbance. Let it suffice for me to point out that there is a great deal of evidence to support the position that people have emotional problems in living that are produced by the problems inherent in an industrial civilization and that these problems should not be regarded as illnesses and should not be covered under a national health scheme. I would favor no coverage for any outpatient therapy except in cases of genuine organic illness (Albee, 1975).

REFERENCES

Albee, G. W. To thine own self be true. Comments on "Insurance reimbursement." *American Psychologist,* 1975, *30,* 1156–1158.

Glasscote, R., Sanders, D., Forstenzer, H. M., & Foley, A. R. (Eds.). *The community mental health center: An analysis of existing models.* Washington, D.C.: American Psychiatric Association, 1964.

Gordon, S. Are we seeing the right patients? Child guidance intake: The sacred cow. *American Journal of Orthopsychiatry,* 1965, *35,* 131–137.

Kennedy, E. M. Commentary. In J. Marmor, *Psychiatrists and their patients.* Washington, D.C.: Joint Information Service of the American Psychiatric Association and the National Association for Mental Health, 1975.

Marmor, J. Commentary. In J. Marmor, *Psychiatrists and their patients.* Washington, D.C.: Joint Information Service of the American Psychiatric Association and the National Association for Mental Health, 1975.

Rosen, B., Bahn, A., Shellow, R., & Bower, E. Adolescent patients served in out-patient psychiatric clinics. *American Journal of Public Health,* 1965, *55,* 1563–1577.

Ryan, W. *Distress in the city.* Cleveland: Case Western Reserve University, 1969.

Schofield, W. *Psychotherapy: The purchase of friendship.* Englewood Cliffs, N.J.: Prentice-Hall, 1964.

Weihofen, H. Psychiatry for the poor. *Psychiatric News,* 967, *2*(10), 2.

Chapter 2

PSYCHOTHERAPY:
GETTING WHAT YOU'VE GOT

Don Diespecker

There are many powerful psychotherapeutic challenges, irrespective of the therapist's model. One of them is, "What do you want?" By implication, clients often do not get what they want, and they may never get what they want if that wanted something is held by or "owned" by someone else (even by a therapist!). And it follows that for many who are getting psychopathology that *that* may also be what some want.

Most therapists (i.e. psychotherapists) would probably agree that what matters is that the client initially increases his/her awareness in the short term and in the long term: that she/he is better able to participate creatively in newness and change, for we all coevolve with the living systems that contain us. One might add, "and to become more able to initiate change." The short-term aim is also a widely-held belief by, for example, Gestalt therapists (e.g. Naranjo, 1975). The long-term goals vary with the relative sophistication of therapeutic models.[1]

Let us consider what all of this may mean. A great deal of psychotherapy is a concern with apparent paradox. People come into therapy when they come into an understanding, i.e., a fundamental or underlying belief, that they "need" therapy. The therapist works for the awareness of a metabelief: that the client does not need therapy or the therapist. Why else would a therapist work to assist in healing? Clients also come into therapy when they have tested, to the limit, the patience, caring, and understanding of their loved ones. To struggle within a belief system that echoes the message, "I need help!" is to engage with the challenges of such a system. When therapy is "completed" there will, hopefully, have been a corresponding change in the belief system of the client. The client will no longer believe she/he is dominated by negative beliefs as if they were somehow external to the self.

9

Whatever it is that therapists do, they work, as hired assistants, to influence their clients. If they are at all competent in that endeavour, then not only will the client be influenced, but she/he will again make full use of his/her intuition. The client will be more aware of personal power, of how she makes life-style choices, of knowledge and skills from within. Paradoxically, to be more aware within also means to be able to better appreciate not only one's own interconnectedness—which makes each one of us a truly remarkable system of systems—it means we immediately "know more" about our interconnectedness with everything else that is.[2] The healthy person will experience more fully not only his own wholeness, he will also experience more widely the interconnections, the interrelations, the interdependencies with others, with groups, with societies, and with other living systems. These concepts are more than mere notions or airy psychological constructs: they are fundamental to an understanding of a dynamically changing universe, and to our appreciation of a dynamically changing world view. These concepts are also fundamental to an understanding of the so-called *new physics*.[3] One of the excitements to be experienced for ourselves as systems within other systems is both simple and profound: because we are systemic (as well as magical!) animals, we are not only aspects of the greater whole, but we are the whole! Such a notion is also a transpersonal one.[4] When therapists can unfold and explain this—to "lay it out flat"—then they have begun to work for their own redundancy. As systems of systems within systems, we can never be alone, alienated, or in any way separate from the whole. Being "apart from" is merely an interesting delusion. Not only can the client get what she wants in at least one important respect, but she already has much more than she may yet be aware of.

The Cartesian-Newtonian paradigm has been and continues to be dominant in our (western) science and in our thinking, although that paradigm is now changing and is seen more clearly by greater amounts of people. Because of dualism, for example, and because of mechanism, all of us in the west have grown up in systems that we have seldom perceived as systems. Such powerful sociocultural systems reiterate *ego identity, ownership, competition, materialism,* and *progress.* We have also learned to believe unthinkingly in our individuality. Psychology courses on individual differences, for example, do little more than reassert our fundamental belief in separateness and duality—in other words, our perpetuated belief in delusions. In that sense, such courses may begin to be seen as eloquent conspiracies that catalyse the experiences of alienation and psychopathology. Were we to teach meditation in the schools, rather than competition, the world would no doubt be vastly different. Psychology courses in tertiary institutions are changing—yet they are still conservative enough to reinforce the mind numbing and pathologizing implications of the outmoded Cartesian-Newtonian paradigm. We have yet to encourage the development of university psychology courses on "collective similarities" because we have chosen to ignore that we are holistic and systemic. Thus do we create and perpetuate a left-brain bias in science. Thus we teach halfism instead of holism and instill beliefs in the young that the left-brain concerns (e.g., operationalism, mechanism, reductionism, analysis, logic, and rationality) are to be overvalued at the expense of right and whole brain truths: the holistic, creative, intuitive, synthesizing, i.e., the feminine, rather than the exclusively masculine, the patriarchal rather than the matriarchal.[5] Too much yang, not enough yin. It might help to remember that the earth has an ancient female name: *Gaia*. Thousands of years of patriarchy have given us awesome science and technology, and have led to the false belief that Nature is to be tamed, dominated, and exploited.[6]

Most of our clients may not know of these things. Indeed, most people probably still believe—if they think about it at all—that we are all separate from nature, when it is vital to remember that we each are Nature. These are some of the factors, some of the reasons which explain why persons become clients. They may have been conditioned into believing that they are powerless, or that they are victims. They may be convinced that "society" means "them" or "others."[7] Many counsellors and some therapists may also not appreciate the holistic doctrine, the systems approach. Ignorance may be the polar opposite of awareness. The client can get what she/he wants; it is more than readily available.

Therapists do not have what clients want, because they cannot give what clients already have. Therapists have what they have. What they can offer is assistance of one kind or another. *Assistance* may then be a possibility that already exists in our connectedness to each other. It would be more helpful to clients if therapists would first study and then teach some of the more obvious findings of science, rather than the conventional and conservative delusions that psychology and psychiatry hold.[8] Clients would then more cheerfully know that they are not alone, that they already have all of the therapeutic tools that they may already have: they have their own remarkable selves as therapists, persons, and living systems. And they will begin to believe that complementarity has some meaning: I have free-will, and I am also engaged with others. When I am so engaged, I may be influenced, I will have transactions, and I am always interconnected.

The client cannot get what she/he wants if there is a client belief that therapy can be delivered. We cannot objectively do to, or give to. There is no objective science despite what the behaviorists may believe, any more than there is an objective universe *out there*. A health care system, on the other hand, can be one with which we can all interconnect in the sense that each may interact, transact, and be nourished. The biomedical model—based on the germ theory of disease—has fostered and reinforced the belief that health, therapy, health care, cure, and healing can be "done to," "given to," and "delivered to" the helpless and not—the responsible "victim" of illness and disease. This clever nonsense has encouraged a stupefying belief (for millions of "victims") that the medical profession is an amazingly powerful priesthood, i.e. a hierarchy, which is, of course, also a patriarchy.[9] Clients may not be ready to address the god within; therapists may explain this if they choose to. Therapy (i.e. psychotherapy) has been allied to the medical model for so long that therapists (whether medically trained initially or psychologically trained) not only subscribe to similar hierarchical systems but many still encourage the belief that clients need therapists. Thus clients believe that therapy will be "done to" or "given to" them, and they become dependent upon therapists—if therapists allow them to. There may be concealed here an awesome paradox: we choose to become as disturbed/deluded/crazy as we are because humanity—as a self-organising or living system—invariably fowls up in its interconnectedness and its transactions. Despite our self-awareness as a sentient, prescient species, we are not yet smart enough to know how to live harmoniously. It is almost as if we have not yet adequately learned how to use our remarkable CNS. The paradox lies in our (a) not appreciating that we already are connected (even religion means to rejoin), (b) believing that we are not, anyway, and (c) furthering more complex interconnections (such as huge cities) that are in many ways increasingly dangerous or toxic.[10] There may be, also, a simple explanation concerning our schizophysiology.[11] The neocortex is not well-wired, not well-connected to the older reptilian and mammalian brains that each of us also possesses. That simple explanation, however, may be too simplistic. It may also encourage belief in the objectified notion that we are not at all responsible for being the way we are.

If again complementarity means anything, we are responsible and affected by other systems, the systems in which we are both mobile and embedded. These are groups of people (relationships between those who are our nearest and dearest, work groups, study, recreational, and sociocultural groups, i.e., "the society," "our culture") and other living systems (properties, farms, animals, pets, villages, towns, cities, forests, rivers, ecologies, regions). We are never separate from other, nor from nonperson living systems. The health of any self-organising system is its dynamic balance, its overall integrity as a system, as a whole, to maintain itself. The quality of the transactions that any system has with other systems is a crucial factor in the overall steady state or health of that system. For those of us who do not fully appreciate physics, the steady state of a self-organising system is a state that is far from equilibrium.[12] Each of us is a self-organising system of systems within other systems. When one is not in synchrony with oneself, one cannot be synchronous with others. One's overall health depends on one's own cooperation and integrity and with that quality of interconnectedness with others.

WHAT IS VALUE?

Whether or not the client gets value for the fee paid to a psychotherapist depends largely on the client. This is not to say that the therapist has no responsibility in ensuring that the client gets something that she/he wants. On the contrary: the therapist always has such responsibility. From the above, it can also be inferred that getting what one wants has a great deal to do with one's awareness of both cooperative and integrative tendencies in all of one's transactions within oneself, with others. The therapist, as teacher, must encourage belief in systemic or process-oriented thinking if she/he is to assist the client out of being stuck. Contemporary research and criticism of psychotherapy, psychiatry, psychology, and medicine is such that the therapist will often experience pressures to demonstrate that psychotherapy is of any use at all. What is valued by the client is what she/he already possesses. Presumably, this includes his/her own integrity. As the client already is an integrated whole, she/he needs only to become more aware and accepting of himself/herself: she/he already is whole and is also a part of other systems.

This is not the place to debate the usefulness or efficacy or ultimate value of therapy. The criticisms are bountiful—a healthy sign—and the literature is immense. Therapy derives from a Greek word that means *to tend pain*. To be available to those who want this assistance is the first step in the relatedness that the therapist will encourage with the client. Curiously enough, the word *therapy* is taken to mean treatment, curing, and healing. These notions are reinforced by therapists. Whatever therapy may mean, there are great differences between treatment, curing, and healing, and we can be thankful for the insightful works of writers like Grossinger (1982, p. 369):

> medicine is a desperate act, and all cures are miracles. Healing works against the deep-seated and inevitable fact of disease and decay. But disease embraces life and is its close ally from the beginning when the fertilizing sperm is little more than a virus to which the egg accedes.

While Grossinger's work addresses healing that is apparently physical and biological, his assertions also concern the cultural and the spiritual. These latter concepts are of special interest to us here.

Because most of us in the west have been educated to support and continually reinforce the Cartesian-Newtonian paradigm of reality, we have needlessly encumbered ourselves with limited and partial models of illness and health. Again, a majority in our culture obviously believe that they have little or no responsibility in having "acquired" disease or distress (mechanism, dualism), hence therapy must mean for them that health can be "given to" them. It is thus irresponsible to believe that value can be got from the therapist. That value will flower only when the therapist can find ways to assist the client into his/her own enlightenment. It is thus necessary to teach the client to take responsibility for his/her part in "getting" sick or distressed, otherwise we will continue to subscribe to allopathic, mechanistic medicine, and firmly believe (most of us) that therapy, and indeed health, can be objectively "delivered." Thus we put our faith and belief "outside" ourselves. Such a belief has prompted Ferguson (1980) to ask whether health is delivered to " . . . vein, brain, or acupuncture meridian."

While it is obviously true that therapists have something to do with tending pain, it is equally true, although perhaps less obvious, that they are necessarily teachers. Some therapists appear to trust in themselves as technicians, for most of what they do to a client consists in techniques, and they have not allowed themselves the joy of a good teacher, so that they will themselves always have difficulty in teaching. The therapist as teacher must also have learned the wisdom of not "being a therapist," for the most important thing the therapist will ever have is him/herself.[13] Similarly, says Ram Dass, it is important to have learned that we all have models and that they all have limitations. Some clients will get Freudianised, and others will be gestalted. The therapist is both assistant and educator. The therapist is not a magician who can miraculously make the client well—she/he can, however, teach that the client is his or her own best magician, best expert, and best adviser. Just as the therapist has learned the value of self as person, as therapist, as teacher, so she/he must remind the client of his/her own truths and integrities. Similarly, the therapist must teach that the client has the power (spiritual power) to be healed, and that the client may use the therapist as an assistant. This is why the therapist has a responsibility to the client: to ensure that the client understands where the value is. It has very little to do with the sum of money that changes hands.

To tend pain—whether it may be physical, psychological, fragmentary or holistic—means to attend, to be present. There is an important and often well-hidden message here. It is the client who "has" the pain, although it often appears to those of us who are pain free that it is the pain that has the client. Because it is the client's pain (is systemically part of the client), the therapist can learn by noticing. She/he does this in order to make discoveries that can then be offered to the client as feedback. Whatever else the therapist may be doing at this time, she/he will certainly be theorizing concerning the nature of the client's pain, doing so from his/her particular model and belief system. Pain communicates vital information to the experiment: it notifies the client that something is amiss and advises that the organism is already engaged in self-healing. Pain is a healthy sign. Despite the client being an offhand or casual owner of a most remarkable CNS and mind (all of which is systematically ordered or organised!) she/he will often disregard such elementary communication. The client will instead behave as if the pain is an unfortunate event, an accident or mishap—in fact, anything other than a systemic process which at that moment is central to his or her life. And because clients will generally choose to avoid having created the pain (or of having played their part in its acquisition), they will take no responsibility for experiencing the pain. The pain is "foreign" or "other". Pain here may, of course, also mean *anger, depression, anxiety.* Similarly, clients possibly will learn to take responsibility for owning *excitement, joy,* and *harmony. Value* is similarly self-generated. Thanks largely to the germ theory of disease and to contemporary allopathic medicine, much (if not most) of the client's experience concerning present pain (or disturbance, conflict, or anguish) will be an as if experience: as if the pain had, viruslike, attacked from without.

There is no "without" in a universe which is so elaborately and awesomely interconnected—and changeable. Yet the client will seldom be aware of that simple truth. The therapist has to begin from scratch to teach that we are not alone, that alienation and despair are not essential aspects of a package tour through life. Of course, alienation and despair are real for the client—it needs to be learned and then taught that this *real* is relatively real. So much of what we do to ourselves is based on delusion. In terms, too, of complementarity, alienation is both relatively real and delusional, just as infrared is real if we happen to be tuned to that particular wavelength and delusional if infrared is misperceived as the only waveband.

Value is to be *had* by the client when the client is aware of his/her own powers. There is infinite value in understanding oneself as a self-organising system, for the notion means that we are always attempting to renew ourselves, that we are each capable of self-assertion, self-maintenance, and self-transcendence. Not only are we complex as self-organising systems, but our whole purpose is to become more so. Value cannot be bought.

THERAPISTS AND TECHNICIANS

Psychotherapy, of course, means whatever you or I may wish it to mean. Does anyone really know what proportion of therapists have recognised credentials from "bona fide institutions" ("properly constituted colleges, universities, and institutes")? In California, a person would need to be licensed in order to practice psychotherapy. In New South Wales, Australia, one can practice as a psychotherapist without any kind of license (the most populous state in Australia still does not register, nor license, its psychologists; the Australian Psychological Society (APS) remains powerless and ineffectual in this most important regard). Virtually anyone with or without credentials or training can conduct therapy or describe their work as "psychotherapy" or "counselling" in the State of New South Wales.

The training for a psychotherapist in Australia (who is often assumed to be a bona fide psychologist (i.e., a graduate) consists, generally, in postgraduate work, i.e., more university work. It does not necessarily include any training in an outside institute or training center, unless the graduate seeks this as an extra qualification. By implication — and almost by definition — a psychotherapist is little more than a "university graduate," for despite having completed numerous programmes — including practicum training — most of the training in psychotherapy remains an extension of or an addition to the courses and programmes which typically are presented in a university psychology department. Some departments may be fortunate enough to include a teacher who has been trained in a particular psychotherapy; most do not. Instead, such departments will invariably concentrate on emphasizing how its students can recognize or predict disturbed behavior, and most of these graduates will be clinical psychologists who are expertly familiar with the DSM 111, yet will have no real training in psychotherapy. The people they will work with — clients, patients — will have been depersonalised and pathologised in advance, and they will certainly have been "objectified." While an increasing number of universities and schools are including experiential as well as didactic components in their counselling programmes, this is by no means a widespread phenomenon. There remains an emphasis on abnormal psychology, clinical psychology, and didactic teaching (which translates into book learning and the writing of endless assignments by the students). Consequently, the emerging psychotherapist will have very little practical experience that is of any value. Indeed she/he may have some passing acquaintance of "using behavior modification", or "gestalt techniques" or "communication skills" — but these are not psychotherapy. The training of psychotherapists in Australia produces technicians. The teachers who teach this psychotherapy are often themselves products of the same limiting system of education. Again, those graduates, and those teachers, who have invested themselves in psychotherapy training programmes outside universities will have great advantages over those who do not, or who cannot afford such learning.

Australian psychology is enormously conservative and terribly transparent. Professional psychotherapy needs to be taught by professional psychotherapists who are themselves properly trained — psychotherapy cannot be learned from university teachers who have only their own university training and some undated reading to rely upon. There are obviously degrees and graduations of teachable skills among university teachers, and while they may not all be skilled at teaching skills, many are increasingly going outside the university system to learn such skills. Australian universities have done little, so far, to provide any kind of institute of psychotherapy within psychology departments. Graduates will continue to get their training in the traditional manner, and many of their practicum experiences will be acquired by working with professionals who, again, are also products of the same system. In Australia, for traditional reasons, clinical psychologists are seen as teachers of psychotherapy. This is a curious delusion that is held by many. There is not enough emphasis on graduates experiencing their own change, their own growth. Indeed, some psychology departments in Australian universities will not allow any exploration of groupwork or group psychotherapy.

This *explanation* concerning Australian psychotherapy is personal and biased. It may also be seen as part of the reason for clients or taxpayers getting value for their money." Or of not getting such value, for unless a psychotherapist has the best possible training in whatever it is that she/he purports to do, the client may continue to experience confusions and doubts. Whether or not psychotherapy is of any use or benefit at all must relate to the learning/training of psychotherapists. In Australia, university trained psychotherapists cannot always contribute to the success of psychotherapy, nor to the commonly accepted understanding of what value may mean in psychotherapy.

For the hapless consumer of psychotherapy (at least in NSW) there may be many engagements in which the therapist is a clinician. The clinician may be bursting with knowledge, may have a remarkable understanding of the Rorschach test, and may never have experienced a personal growth group or explored their own disturbances or conflicts. Yet this clinician will be recognised by the APS as *qualified,* and of course, *professional.* Unhappily, the clinician may also believe this to be true. To many Australian psychologists, psychotherapy simply means "learning how to counsel, learning how to use techniques, learning the skills of psychotherapy". There is still little requirement for them to experience their own psychotherapy. For some clinicians, any kind of psychotherapy — or technique — is, by definition, within his or her realm of competence or expertise. Although it is clearly an exaggeration to say so, it is not entirely unlikely that some clients seeking the assistance of a therapist may have had experiences in a growth or therapy growth that the clinician cannot understand — because his/her own experience is self-limited. And although it is also an exaggeration to pose the question, How is a client to go further, to grow, or to learn, for example, of transpersonal approaches to psychotherapy if the therapist is ignorant of experiential learning?

Professional psychology in Australia, i.e., university-based-APS-approved psychology remains unwilling to professionally teach psychotherapy. It will continue on this moribund course until it chooses to evolve professional institutes of psychotherapy within its own system. Clinical psychology or counselling psychology are the best that graduates can hope for. It is the client — who of course does not know what training the therapist has — who is disadvantaged. There are, of course, exceptions. Yet a gestalt therapist, for example, who wishes to offer gestalt therapy must first find a good teacher. As there are no colleges or universities that offer Gestalt therapy programmes (nor psychoanalysis, nor psychosynthesis, nor transpersonal psychotherapy, to name but a few possibilities). The would-be therapist must seek out a gestalt institute or training center where such training is offered.[14]

Thus, what a therapist *is* and what she/he *does* is often bookish and wildly theoretical. A trained therapist, it is suggested, is one who has learned to work from his/her own experience. In other words, the therapist is one who has worked as a client both with a good teacher-trainer-therapist (preferably with two or more) and with his or her peers in training groups. Trained therapists will also almost certainly have good paper credentials from a "real" college or university, i.e., they will have graduate status, they will know something of psychology (essentially, they will have an appreciation of the current system from which psychotherapy can be derived, viz an appreciation of the left-brain bias-halfism in western and Australian psychology), they will have participated in a variety of awareness or growth or therapy groups, they will have sought out at least two reputable trainers, perhaps in two different countries, they will have worked as participants in training groups for 500 to 1,000 hours (of course this is an arbitrary figure, since we necessarily theorise from personal experience!), they will have discovered the absurdity of offering nothing more than techniques (or else they would establish themselves as mere hacks or technicians "objectively" doing something "to" clients), they will have learned, paradoxically, that when they give up trying to be therapists, then they will be therapists, their "professionalism" will mean for them that what they have to offer is themselves as "therapeutic tools," and they will be far beyond "techniques," for techniques are for those who do not have and may not be willing to learn fundamentals of psychology, of experience-based learning, of systems, and of wholeness.[15] They will not be defensive when clients ask what their credentials are, what their training or background might be (clients would be foolish not to seek such information because they are inviting a relationship as well as a therapist-as-teacher). Clients can help to increase the standards of psychotherapy by asking questions of the therapist to be and by asking others in their community what kind of reputation a particular therapist has. There are good and bad therapists; some are trained, some are not.

Clients are entitled to know whether their chosen therapist is a therapist or whether the person is, perhaps, a clinical psychologist or a behaviour modifier. We all work from models. So does the client. She/he had better know what is wanted from a therapist. Some of us work from models that exemplify growth, change, and transformation. I have no difficulty in equating such a model with psychotherapy. I am implying that a model which encourages replacement of undesirable behaviour with "more correct, more appropriate" behaviors is not one that easily integrates with "therapy," "integration," or "healing" (indeed, the modification of behavior is analogous to surgery rather than growth). What matters, it seems to me, is that the client will take responsibility for his/her experience, accept "undesirable" aspects of self, and be excited at adventuring forth into new possibilities, change, and growth. "Going forward into" is an adventure; returning via "ego-supportive strategies" to the awfulness of everyday life is limiting and limited. And what matters (again for me) is that a client discovers or rediscovers the grace and beauty of cheerfully creating possibilities for a healthy life-style. There is no rule which states that we each have to cope with psychopathological immensities; there is every indication that we can go beyond mere coping, venture forth into new realms, and become better organised. Our culture encourages many to put aside personal or individual power when health is a concern. We have come to believe that *health* and *medicine* as well as *peace* and *sanity* can be objectively delivered to us. Psychotherapy can be a way in which all of us remember, relearn, and rediscover the howness of dynamically and continually creating our lives.

Again, clients can get a remarkable return for their money if they will simply learn to be open to their own possibilities. Their renewed growth may be like a rebirth when they take responsibility for their abilities. Otherwise, the assumption is that a therapist is a person who will "do something to" the client to make him/her feel better (and perhaps to enable the client to keep on defeating self). The therapist can only assist. This assistance can also be a form of teaching; it does not mean imposing a particular model on an unsuspecting client. If therapists will not believe that the client is able, responsible, and powerfully creative — beyond or beneath an outward helplessness — then clients cannot truly get any kind of return for their money. They may become, instead, dependent upon a "therapist" who fosters dependency. In terms of complementarity, what the client gets is what the client gets, and that is relative to what the client has already got.

NOTES

1. Readers who are not familiar with the writings of Ken Wilber may find his *spectrum of consciousness* model illuminating (e.g. Wilber, 1979, pp. 8 & 9). He demonstrates that different levels of self-identity, and that there are relevant and appropriate psychotherapeutic models for each of these levels.
2. Capra (1975, 1982), for example, reminds us of the two most important discoveries of contemporary physics: (1) the entire universe (including us) is continually in flux, is continually dynamically changing, and (2) that the universe and everything in it is always interconnected, interrelated, and interdependent. See also, Ferguson (1980); Dossey (1982); Talbot (1980); Zukav (1980).
3. The demise of classical physics began in the late nineteenth century. The "new physics" also reveals the shortcomings of the Cartesian-Newtonian paradigm. Einstein's work — dating from the first decade of the twentieth century — marks the beginning of the new physics.
4. "Transpersonal": "beyond the personal". See Wilber (1979), or Walsh and Vaughan (1980). See also, "The Systems View of Life," in Capra (1982), or the earlier works of Von Bertalanffy.
5. See Diespecker (1982, 1983). I argue that the teaching of psychology in the West and in Australia reflects a left-brain bias and is thus hopelessly conservative and outdated.

6. See Lovelock (1979). Earth, as a superorganism, maintains its integrity as a huge self-organising system. The health, or balance, or steady state of Gaia, is a function of life itself. Since there is mentation or mind at all levels of self organising systems (see Capra, 1982), not only is Earth alive, it is knowingly alive. We are both "wholes" and systemic "parts" of Gaia—and of the universe.
7. See Wilson (1977). He argues that "convictions cause convicts."
8. Psychology and psychiatry are linked by common factors, not the least of which is healing. At the end of the twentieth century (almost), both "sciences" remain stuck in the notion that health—very broadly—means the absence of disease." See also Berliner and Salmon (1979) or Diespecker (1981).
9. Capra (1982), in describing the systems approach to life, reminds us of the differences between the "stratified ordering" of a self-organising (living) system and a "hierarchy". A hierarch is a priest (priestly power which is, of course, patriarchal power). In our culture, patriarchy is now being powerfully influenced by a rising matriarchy.
10. Increased production (manufacturing e.g.) leads to increased entropy because we increasingly turn order into disorder. See Rifkin (1981).
11. See Koestler (1978) and Maclean (1958).
12. Equilibrium, in physics, indicates in a deathly way that nothing is happening. Living systems are, by definition, disequilibrium systems. See Capra (1982) or Prigogine (1976, 1980).
13. See Ram Dass (1975): "If your thing is to do psychiatry, then when you stop trying to do psychiatry you will be the essence of a psychiatrist."
14. There are Gestalt Institutes, Training Centers, or Training Groups in Melbourne, Wollongong, Perth, Brisbane, Townsville, and Newcastle.
15. See Ram Dass (1975).

REFERENCES

Berliner, H. S., and Salmon, J. W. The holistic health movement and scientific medicine: The naked and the dead. *Socialist Review*, 1979, 9(1), 31–52.

Capra, F. *The Tao of Physics*. Boulder, CO: Shambhala, 1975.

Capra, F. *The Turning Point: Science, Society and the Rising Culture*. NY: Simon & Schuster, 1982.

Diespecker, D. *Holistic Health*. Townsville: James Cook University, 1981.

Diespecker, D. The end of 19th century psychology. *The Australian Journal of Transpersonal Psychology*, 1982, 2(2), 127–42.

Diespecker, D. What will we teach in the 80's? *The Australian Journal of Transpersonal Psychology*, 1983, 3(1), 1–23.

Diespecker, D. Applied imagery. In J. Hariman (ed.): *The Therapeutic Efficacy of the Major Psychotherapeutic Techniques*. Springfield, Ill: Thomas, 1983.

Dossey, L. *Space, Time and Medicine*. Boulder, CO: Shambhala, 1982.

Ferguson, M. Crisis of definition: Who delivers health? *Journal of Humanistic Psychology*, 1980, 20(4), 17.

Ferguson, M. *The Acquarian Conspiracy: Personal and Social Transformation in the 1980s.* Los Angeles: Tarcher, 1980.

Grossinger, R. *Planet Medicine: From Stone Age Shamanism to Post-Industrial Healing.* Boulder, CO: Shambhala, 1982.

Koestler, A. *Janus: A Summing Up.* London: Pan, 1979.

Lovelock, J. E. *Gaia: A New Look at Life on Earth.* Oxford: University Press, 1979.

Maclean, P. D. *American Journal of Medicine.* 1958, *25*(4), 611–626.

Naranjo, C. I and thou, here and now: Contributions of gestalt therapy. In F. D. Stephenson (ed.). *Gestalt Therapy Primer.* Springfield, Ill: Thomas 1975.

Prigogine, I. Order through fluctuation: Self-organisation and social systems. In E. Jantsch and C. H. Waddington (eds.): *Evolution and Consciousness: Human Systems in Transition.* Reading, Mass.: Addison-Wesley, 1976.

Prigogine, I. *From Being to Becoming: Time and Complexity in the Physical Sciences.* San Francisco: Freeman, 1980.

Ram Dass. Advise to a psychotherapist. *The Journal of Transpersonal Psychology,* 1975, 7(1), 84–92.

Rifkin, J. *Entropy: A New World View.* New York: Bantam, 1981.

Talbot, M. *Mysticism and the New Physics.* New York: Bantam, 1980.

Von Bertalanffy, L. *Robots, Men and Minds: Psychology in the Modern World.* NY: Braziller, 1967.

Von Bertalanffy, L. *General System Theory: Foundations, Developments and Applications.* NY: Braziller, 1968.

Walsh, R. M., and Vaughan, F. *Beyond Ego: Transpersonal Dimensions in Psychology.* Los Angeles: Tarcher, 1980.

Wilber, K. *No Boundary: Eastern and Western Approaches to Personal Growth.* Los Angeles: Center Publications, 1979.

Wilson, R. A. *Cosmic Trigger: Final Secret of the Illuminati.* Berkeley: And/Or Press, 1977.

Zukay, G. *The Dancing Wu Li Masters: An Overview of the New Physics.* NY: Bantam, 1980.

Chapter 3

MUST MOST PSYCHOTHERAPISTS REMAIN AS INCOMPETENT AS THEY NOW ARE?

ALBERT ELLIS

ABSTRACT: *Although psychotherapy often is effective or helpful for groups of people, it is frequently inefficient and therefore is wasteful for many clients and actually contributes to harming a sizable minority of them. Some of the main aspects of therapeutic inefficiency are discussed in this paper, including: overemphasis on past experience; encouraging dependency and the dire need for love; overemphasis on modeling; the stressing of insight; the use of catharsis and abreaction; the use of cognitive distraction; self-efficacy suggestions; operant conditioning; gradual desensitization; and unselective eclecticism. Specific suggestions for increasing the efficiency of psychotherapy are given.*

Is there substantial evidence that psychotherapists sometimes harm, as well as benefit, their clients? I think that there definitely is and that this has been fairly well documented by several critics, such as Bergin and Garfield (1978), Chapman (1964), Gross (1979), Hadley and Strupp (1976), Lieberman, Yalom and Miles (1973), Maliver (1972), and Rosen (1977). Although the instances cited by these authors are relatively few, it can also be held that therapists often do little good when compared to nontherapeutic controls (Eysenck, 1966) and that certain forms of psychotherapy, such as psychoanalysis, are woefully inefficient and even iatrogenic when compared to more efficient modes of therapy (Ellis, 1968; Gross, 1979; Jurjevich, 1973). Even when therapists significantly help clients, they seem to do so quite inefficiently by using methods that are often distinctly inept and that consequently lead these clients to achieve weak and unlasting results, frequently at the expense of enormous amounts of wasted time and money (Ellis, 1977a, 1980). Since

From Albert Ellis, Must most psychotherapists remain as incompetent as they are now? *Journal of Contemporary Psychotherapy, 13*(1), Spring/Summer 1982, pp. 17–28.

clients are usually in considerable emotional pain when they start therapy, this inefficiency, by a notable sin or omission if not commission, surely adds considerably to therapeutic harm.

This paper will assume, on the basis of some of the evidence just cited, that modern psychotherapy—somewhat like its historical predecessors and like the contemporary shamanistic, magical, and cultist treatment of physical and emotional ills—frequently does harm as well as good. And it will present several hypotheses that try to explain why this kind of inefficiency exists, and (hopefully) what can be done to change it.

Overemphasis on past experiences. Most modern therapists overemphasize their clients' early or past experiences and thereby lead them up the garden path to scores, sometimes hundreds, of wasted sessions. This is useless or iatrogenic for several reasons: (1) All people bring *themselves* and their own innate tendencies to react or overreact to their experiences; and their biosocial predispositions to respond to stimuli cover an enormous range, from incredible vulnerability to equally incredible non-vulnerability, to "traumatic" occurrences in their lives (Garmezy, 1975; Zubin & Spring, 1977). They therefore are as much influenceable as influenced by early experiences and since their influenceability is largely known it is foolish to ignore it—it almost always can be changed—and to focus on their past experiences, which cannot be modified. (2) Even if it were true that past occurrences *caused* clients to become emotionally disturbed—which has never been convincingly shown—there is no evidence that their understanding of what happened to them in bygone days will help them change themselves today. On the contrary there is good reason to believe that their concentrating on their prior history will (a) sidetrack them from working hard to change themselves today; (b) provide them with the cop-out of blaming their parents or their society and thereby refusing to take responsibility for their own feelings; (c) help justify the whining, wailing, and sitting on their asses which is almost always the main core of their past and present disturbances; (d) help them get even more hung up than they naturally are on the so-called horror of what was unfairly done to them and thus to get neurotically obsessed more than ever on the past, the past, the past; (e) encourage them to keep making the major error of wrongly attributing emotional upsets to the events immediately preceding these upsets instead of to their own *view of* and their own *choice of reacting to* such events (Arnold, 1960; Beck, 1976; Ellis, 1962, 1971, 1973; Ellis & Grieger, 1977; Ellis & Whiteley, 1979; Epictetus, 1898; Marcus Aurelius, 1899; Meichenbaum, 1977).

Encouraging dependency and the dire need for love. Most disturbed individuals not only want or prefer approval and love—which seems to be the normal human condition—but devoutly believe that they absolutely *must* have it and that they are worthless or contemptible individuals without it (Ellis, 1957, 1962, 1971, 1973; Maleske, 1980; Peele, 1975; Tenov, 1979). Instead of vigorously combatting this self-defeating philosophy and showing clients how to give it up and be more emotionally independent, many therapists cater to and help intensify this puerile demand by (1) prolonging the therapy for many years; (2) insisting on frequent sessions; (3) forbidding clients to make major decisions on their own during the length of the treatment; (4) deliberately fostering positive therapeutic "transference," (5) advising clients on all kinds of practical problems; (6) providing them with highly gratifying warmth and love or placing them in a therapeutic group which emphasizes physical and emotional endearment. Even when therapists—such as Rogers (1961) and Truax and Carkhuff (1967)—stress unconditional acceptance and empathy rather than love and warmth, they fail to acknowledge the strong tendency of clients to turn this into a concept of conditional acceptance and thereby mainly to accept themselves *because* their therapist does so. Being largely nondirective and nonphilosophic, these therapists fail to show clients how to *un*conditionally accept themselves—whether or not their therapists (or anyone else) loves them.

Overemphasis on modeling. Modeling, as Bandura (1977a) and others have shown, can effectively help people change their behavior. But nondirective, existential, and client-centered therapists often do too much modeling and too little active-directive teaching. Thus, they model trust, honesty, integrity, and leadership and expect clients to pick up the message, "Oh, I can do this, too. So I think I'll try to act as my therapist does and be warmer or more assertive." Left to their own devices, alas, disturbed persons often make just the opposite conclusions, such as: "Oh, my therapist is so good at being warm and assertive, that this shows what a perfect *schmuck* I am! I might as well give up and remain my usual inept and worthless self!" This kind of reaction to the therapist's modeling, naturally, does the clients little good because it omits actively and directively pushing and teaching these clients to *follow* this modeling. Skill training modeling, which is often done in assertion training therapy, is also often ineffective since it neglects to show clients simultaneously how to change their self-sabotaging belief system—e.g., "If I assert myself, people will often disapprove of me, which they *must* not—and that would be terrible!" This kind of nonphilosophic modeling therefore tends to be therapeutically inefficient (Lange & Jakubowski, 1976).

Stressing insight. Systems of therapy like psychoanalysis not only overemphasize past experiences and encourage dependency but also place great emphasis on insight (Freud, 1965). The theory that if clients get insight into the basic causes of their disturbances they will significantly change themselves and become less disturbed is misleading for many reasons, including these: (1) Insight, even when accurate or valid, rarely helps people change unless they also *act* on it or *do* something to make themselves change—as they fairly rarely do. (2) Insight, especially when people are self-blamers, is often quite destructive. Thus, if I come to realize, as a result of therapy, that I really hate my mother instead of, as I wrongly previously thought, that I love her, I may condemn myself thoroughly for this now acknowledged hatred, become very depressed, and even kill myself. Unless my therapy appreciably helps me to change my self-damning attitudes, the insights I receive in the course of it may easily encourage me to be more disturbed. (3) Many therapies give clients insight into unimportant things—e.g., how their parents presumably made them neurotic—instead of more important things—e.g., how to effectively change their dysfunctional feelings and behaviors. (4) Many of the most "brilliant" insights supposedly achieved during therapy are highly exaggerated or false. Thus, almost every male who undergoes classical psychoanalysis finally sees that he has an Oedipus complex and has always wanted to fuck his mother and kill his father— even though he always thought he wanted to kill his puritanical mother and go out fucking with his lascivious father. The percentage of these "brilliant" insights which are actually valid seems to be exceptionally small; and the fact that they are so often accepted as "true" is a huge compliment to creativity and persuasiveness of many analysts (Ellis, 1950, 1968).

Catharsis and abreaction. Many schools of psychotherapy follow the psychoanalytic theory (Freud, 1965) and Reichian theory (Lowen, 1958;

Reich, 1949) which holds that suppressing or bottling up emotion is one of the main causes of emotional disturbance and that letting them out cathartically or abreactively results in cure. This hypothesis probably has little validity; and the use of catharsis and abreaction leads to much therapeutic inefficiency and harm, for several reasons: (1) Literally scores of controlled experiments by clinical, social, and experimental psychologists have shown that when people are encouraged to show their strong feelings, particularly feelings of anger, they tend to become more rather than less hostile and punitive, and to remain so for considerable periods of time (Berkowitz, 1970; Bohart, 1980; Geen, Stonner, & Hope, 1975; Hokanson, 1970; Lieberman, Yalom & Miles, 1973). (2) When clients in therapy are encouraged to vent their suppressed or supposedly repressed negative feelings, they thereby get *in vivo* practice and resensitization (rather than desensitization) of these feelings. Thus, when they express anger toward someone in an individual or group therapy session, they reaffirm and augment their anger-creating beliefs, "He or she absolutely *should not* have acted that way to me and is a thoroughly *rotten person* for doing so." Almost always, their rage toward that individual escalates; and their catharsis prepares them to become equally or more enraged the next time that person acts badly toward them (Ellis, 1977b; Rosen, 1977). (3) The beneficial effects of catharsis that have been pointed out by some commentators (Bohart, 1980; Nichols & Zax, 1978) probably result mainly from acknowledging and facing certain avoided feelings rather than from expressing them. Thus, if you cover up your hostility to a friend and pretend that you don't feel it, you may keep it forever; while if you vent your anger you may face the fact that it is not terrible to feel it and may desensitize yourself to your guilt about it; and you may also be able to think through your relations with your friend and be able to conclude that he or she has not behaved so horribly as you at first thought. This kind of facing covered up feelings and eliminating them by thinking them through can usually be done more effectively, however, by non-abreative methods, such as cognitive restructuring techniques, than by abreactive methods of dealing with hostility (Ellis, 1977b; Novaco, 1975).

Distraction methods. Many common methods of therapy are techniques of cognitive distraction that temporarily divert clients from obsessive thoughts and panicked feelings but that do not really extirpate these symptoms. Thus, Jacobsen's (1958) progressive muscular relaxation and

Benson's (1975) relaxation response teach people to focus so intently on bodily processes that they momentarily haven't the time or energy to make themselves neurotically miserable. And many of the highly evocative role-playing techniques of Moreno (1934) and Perls (1969) get people to concentrate so much on the drama of talking to their dead parents or their internal organs that they lose their self-consciousness for a while and are able to do things (such as become aware of their feelings or perform well before a workshop audience) that they wrongly think that they cannot do. All these methods often divert feelings of anxiety, depression, hostility, and self-pity quite effectively but they rarely change the underlying *musturbatory* philosophies that largely create disturbance; and shortly after they have been "effectively" employed, this disturbance usually returns full blast.

Self-efficacy suggestions. Bernheim (1886) and Coué (1923) showed almost a century ago that if people think they are able to do something well, rather than expect to fail at it, this expectation, even if it is largely false, makes them feel better, leads to increased confidence, and often decreases their emotional ills. Bandura (1977b) has recently systematized this view into a concept of selfefficacy. Showing people, however, that they can do better than they think they can, and teaching them to replace negative with positive thoughts and images, is largely a palliative method that may well boomerang in several pernicious ways: (1) When the positive thinkers or imaginers fail to get the great results they suggest they will get, they tend to become therapeutically disillusioned and depressed and to give up trying to help themselves. (2) Positive autosuggestion is frequently viewed as a form of magical, effortless treatment and stops clients from doing the hard and persistent *work* that is almost always required for basic personality change. (3) Even when positive thinking works it tends to bolster the irrational idea that most disturbed people already hold with a vengeance: namely, that they *have to* (rather than *preferably* had better) perform well and win others' approval, and that they are worthless individuals if they don't. (4) Ripping up self-downing negative philosophies is a more elegant and permanent form of symptom removal, and positive thinking tends to cover up instead of disputing these philosophies, thus encouraging them to soon return.

Operant conditioning. Operant conditioning, especially social reinforcement, has proven to be quite effective in helping people change their neurotic feelings and dysfunctional behavior (Bandura, 1969; Eysenck, 1964; Kazdin, 1978; Skinner, 1971).

For all its clearcut advantages, it also has distinct limitations and hazards. For example: (1) As Maimonides (1980) pointed out, some eight centuries ago, reinforcing or rewarding people for desirable behavior (e.g., reading) frequently tends to get them devoted to the reward (e.g., candy or television) rather than to the intrinsic value and pleasure of the activity itself. (2) Reinforcement may well not change disturbed people's basic philosophy of low frustration tolerance — that is, that they must have, absolutely *need* immediate gratification and will be virtually destroyed without it; and it may well reinforce and help accentuate this kind of childish demanding. (3) One of the chief reinforcers used is that of social reinforcement, or the approval of the therapist or others if clients change their self-defeating emotions and behaviors. But social reinforcement, as noted above, frequently works well to effect symptom removal — but at the grim expense of helping the client become more needy of love, more over-conforming, more suggestible, and less able to do independent, self-interested thinking.

Gradual desensitization. Most behavior therapy methods, such as Wolpe's (1958, 1973) reciprocal inhibition and Skinner's (1971) shaping technique, arrange for gradual desensitization of clients' phobias, compulsions, and other neurotic symptoms. But gradualism, like all behavioral methods, tends to endorse low frustration tolerance, or what I have called discomfort anxiety (Ellis, 1979, 1980b) — a philosophy that states or implies (1) that emotional change has to be brought about slowly, and cannot possibly occur quickly; (2) that it must be practically painless; (3) that it cannot occur through using jarring, painful, flooding methods of therapy. All these assumptions seem to be false, however, and there is considerable evidence that emotional and behavioral change can more effectively occur in a relatively sudden, flooding manner (Ellis & Abrahms, 1978; Ellis & Whitely, 1979; Foa, 1978; Grieger & Boyd, 1980; Marks, 1978; Stampl & Levis, 1967; Walen, DiGiuseppe & Wessler, 1980; Wessler & Wessler, 1980).

Unselective eclecticism. Many behavioral and nonbehavioral therapists use unselective eclectic methods that utilize everything including the kitchen sink. Thus, Shapiro (1979) espouses a combination of behavior therapy and Asian mysticism, and favors clients reaching the Zen Buddhist state of Nirvana. But Nirvana is hardly a condition of joy or effectiveness but one of desirelessness and detachment, not to mention a kind of illusory being at one with the entire universe (Keyes, 1979); and this condition may easily lead to schizophreniclike withdrawal. And bioenergetic and primal techniques, like those endorsed by Palmer (1973), are based on philosophies that espouse extreme forms of abreacting anger and other negative feelings and that may easily lead to considerable individual dependency and social harm.

Some of the soundest researchers and therapists, such as Jerome Frank (1975) and Fuller Torrey (1972) have unfortunately endorsed the view that because some mystical and shamanistic forms of therapy sometimes benefit those who subscribe to them, they are just as legitimate as more scientifically based treatments. A rash view indeed! The craziest and most harmful credos ever promulgated—such as voodoo, satanism, and Naziism—have at least occasionally benefited some of the people some of the time. But before we endorse such "therapies," we had better investigate their woeful inefficiency and iatrogenicity—and evaluate them accordingly. At present, many therapists avidly vouch for some highly dubious forms of treatment. For example, a reputable behavior therapist, Palmer (1973), endorses bioenergetics (Lowen, 1958) and primal therapy (Janov, 1970), both of which almost certainly considerably sidetrack and harm, as well as occasionally help, therapy clients. These kind of therapies, instead of being eclectically endorsed, had better be investigated and criticized with scientific rigor (Ellis, 1975; Hook, 1975).

I could, as some of you might well imagine, go on indefinitely with more major disbenefits and inefficiencies of most of the systems of psychotherapy that are presently popular; but since this is only a summary article rather than a book, I shall stop right here. Let me now get on to answering the rhetorical question that serves as a title to this paper: "Must most psychotherapists remain as incompetent as they now are?" As you might well expect, my answer is a resounding NO. After practicing psychotherapy for almost forty years and after spending much of this time trying to develop a system of psychological treatment, rational-emotive therapy (RET), I naturally believe that psychotherapists *can* become competent, and can desist from their iatrogenic and inefficient practices. How? Let me suggest some possible ways:

1. Therapists can distinctly focus on being efficient as well as effective: that is, on developing theories and techniques that not only

significantly help clients ameliorate their symptoms but do so in a relatively brief (and economically inexpensive) period of time. Not that all clients can be helped with brief therapy; but many clearly can be—and often just as well, or even better, than in longterm treatment (Ellis & Abrahms, 1978; Small, 1979).

2. Efficiency in therapy includes depth-centeredness—not in the sense of clients' psychoanalytically knowing everything about themselves, including their presumably deep-seated repressed feelings, but in the sense of their making a profound philosophic change. They had better not revel in their past histories but understand their fundamental neurosis-creating philosophies and how these can be substantially changed. Symptom removal is a fine therapeutic goal; but unless clients truly see how they keep upsetting themselves and how they can refuse to do so in the present and in the future, they will mainly get symptomatic relief and will not prevent themselves from making themselves redisturbed.

3. Efficient therapy had better be pervasive—that is, help clients deal with many of their problems, and in a sense their whole lives, rather than merely concentrating on one or two presenting symptoms and helping to alleviate them. It will show clients not only how to deal with their present disturbances but how they can easily keep creating new and different symptoms with the same basic attitudes and beliefs; and how to stop doing this.

4. Efficient therapy is extensive, in that it helps clients to actualize and enjoy themselves, as well as understand and minimize their self-defeating tendencies. It encourages them to experiment with their own sensations, pleasures, and creativeness to discover more of what they want to do in their present and future existence; and it includes skill training that may help them in this respect.

5. Efficient therapy is thoroughgoing and multifaceted. It utilizes a number of cognitive, emotive, and behavioral methods; and it selectively employs several pathways of possibly helping clients and tests these pathways to see which of them work best and which had better be used minimally or abandoned (Ellis, 1969a, 1969b, 1973, 1980c; Ellis & Grieger, 1977; Ellis & Whiteley, 1979; Lazarus, 1971, 1976).

6. Efficient therapy strives not only for immediate gain but for

continued and long-maintained therapeutic progress. No matter how pleased clients may feel about their so-called cures, it does not accept these as real emotional health until and unless there is some evidence that they will (1) be maintained for quite a period of time; and, preferably, (2) lead to augmented therapeutic results after formal psychotherapy has ended (Ellis & Whiteley, 1979).

7. Efficient therapy remains keenly aware of potential harm and waste in psychotherapy. It recognizes that all therapeutic techniques have philosophic as well as emotional and behavioral effects and implications and it actively looks for the pernicious, as well as the beneficial, effects of these implications (Ellis, 1980b). It tries to parcel out the basic ingredients of basic personality change and to abet these in an active-directive manner (Ellis & Abrahms, 1978; Ellis & Whiteley, 1979). But it recognizes the potential harm of all therapy methods, even the best of them, and it tries to minimize this harm.

8. Like the scientific method itself, efficient therapy remains flexible, curious, empirically-oriented, critical of poor theories and results, and devoted to effective change. It is not one-sided or dogmatic. It is ready to give up the most time-honored and revered methods if new evidence contradicts them. It constantly grows and develops; and it sacredizes no theory and no methodology.

If the concept of efficiency is included in psychotherapy, and if an elegant and profound solution to the problem of emotional disturbance is sought rather than the less elegant solution of symptom removal, then present-day waste and iatrogenicity in therapy may well be diminished. In that event, most psychotherapists will refuse to remain as incompetent as they now are, and their clients, and the public in general, will hopefully receive considerably more benefit and less harm than now seems to be the case.

REFERENCES

Arnold, M. *Emotions and personality.* (2 volumes). New York: Columbia University Press, 1960.

Bandura, A. *Principles of behavior modification.* New York: Holt, Rinehart & Winston, 1969.

Bandura, A. *Social learning theory.* Palo Alto: Stanford University, 1977. (a)

Bandura, A. Self-efficacy: Toward a unifying theory of behavioral change. *Psychological Review,* 1977, *84,* 191-2-5. (b)

Beck, A. T. *Cognitive Therapy and the Emotional Disorders.* New York: International Universities Press, 1976.

Benson, H. *The relaxation response.* New York: Morrow, 1975.

Bergin, A. E., & Garfield, S. L. (Eds.) *Handbook of Psychotherapy and behavior change.* 2nd ed. New York: Wiley, 1978.

Berkowitz, L. Experimental investigations of hostility catharsis. *Journal of Consulting and Clinical Psychology,* 1970, *16,* 710–717.

Bernheim, H. *Suggestive therapeutics: A treatise on the nature of hypnosis.* New York: London Book Company, 1886, 1947.

Bohart, A. C. Toward a cognitive theory of catharsis, *Psychotherapy,* 1980, *17,* 192–201.

Chapman, A. H. Iatrogenic problems in psychotherapy. *Psychiatry Digest,* Sept. 1964, 23–29.

Coue, E. *My method.* New York: Double Page, 1923.

Ellis, A. *An Introduction to the scientific principles of psychoanalysis.* Provincetown, Mass.: Journal Press, 1950.

Ellis, A. *How to live with a "neurotic."* New York: Crown, 1957. Rev. ed. New York: Crown, 1975.

Ellis, A. *Reason and emotion in psychotherapy.* Secaucus, N.J.: Lyle Stuart and Citadel Press, 1962.

Ellis, A. Is psychoanalysis harmful? *Psychiatric Opinion,* 1968, *5*(1), 126–24. Reprinted: New York: Institute for Rational Living, 1968.

Ellis, A. A weekend of rational encounter. In A. Burton (Ed.), *Encounter.* San Francisco: Jossey-Bass, 1969. (a)

Ellis, A. A cognitive approach to behavior therapy. *International Journal of Psychiatry,* 1969, *8,* 896–900. (b)

Ellis, A. *Growth through reason.* Palo Alto: Science and Behavior Books and Hollywood: Wilshire Books, 1971

Ellis, A. *Humanistic psychotherapy: The rational-emotive approach.* New York: Crown Publishers and McGraw-Hill Paperbacks, 1973.

Ellis, A. Critique of Frank's "The limits of humanism." *Humanist,* 1975, *35*(6), 33–34.

Ellis, A. How to be efficient though humanistic. *Dawnpoint,* 1977, *1*(1), 38–47. (a)

Ellis, A. *How to live with — and without — anger.* New York: Reader's Digest Press, 1977, (b)

Ellis, A. *Discomfort anxiety.* Cassette recording. New York: Association for the Advancement of Behavior Therapy and BMA Audio Cassettes, 1979.

Ellis, A. The value of efficiency in psychotherapy. *Psychotherapy: Theory, Practice and Research,* 1980. (a)

Ellis, A. The philosophic implications and dangers of some popular behavior therapy techniques. In C. Frank M. Rosenbaum (Eds.), *Proceedings of the World Congress on Behavior Therapy.* New York: Academic Press, 1980. (b)

Ellis, A. Discomfort anxiety. Part II. *Rational Living,* 1980, *15* (1), 25–30.

Ellis, A., & Abrahms, E. *Brief psychotherapy in Medical and health practice.* New York: Springer, 1978.

Ellis, A., & Grieger, R. *Handbook of rational-emotive therapy.* New York: Springer, 1977.

Ellis, A., & Whiteley, J. *Theoretical and empirical foundations of rational-emotive therapy.* Monterey, Calif.: Brooks/Cole, 1979.

Epictetus. *The works of Epictetus.* Boston: Little, Brown, 1898.

Eysenck, H. J. (Ed.). *Experiments in behavior therapy.* New York: Macmillan, 1964.

Eysenck, H. J. *The effects of psychotherapy.* New York: Science House, 1966.

Foa, E. B. Failure in treating obsessive compulsives. *Behavior Research and Therapy,* 1979, *17,* 169–176.

Frank, J. The limits of humanism. *Humanist,* 1975, *35*(5), 50–52.

Freud, S. *Standard edition of the complete psychological works of Sigmund Freud.* (James Starchey, ed.: translator.) London: Hogarth, 1965.

Garmezy, N. *Vulnerable and invulnerable children: Theory, research and intervention.* Washington: American Psychological Association, 1975.

Geen, R. S., Stonner, D., & Hope, G. L. The facilitation of aggression. *Journal of Personality and Social Psychology,* 1975, *31,* 721–726.

Grieger, R., & Boyd, J. *Rational emotive therapy: A skills based approach.* New York: Van Nostrand Reinhold, 1980.

Gross, M. L. *The psychological society.* New York: Simon and Schuster, 1979.

Hadley, S. W., & Strupp, H. H. Contemporary view of negative effects in psychotherapy.

Hokanson, J. E. Physiological evaluation of the catharsis hypothesis. In E. I. Megargie & J. E. Hokanson (Eds.), *The Dynamics of Aggression.* New York: Harper & Row, 1970.

Hook, S. Critique of Frank's "The limits of humanism." *Humanist,* 1975, *Archives of General Psychiatry,* 1976, *33,* 1291–1302. *35*(6), 34–35.

Jacobsen, E. *You must relax.* New York: Pocket Books, 1958.

Janov, A. *The primal scream.* New York: Delta, 1971.

Jurjevich, R. M. *Direct psychotherapy.* Miami: University of Miami Press, 1973.

Kazdin, A. E. *History of behavior modification.* Baltimore: University Park Press, 1978.

Keys, K. *Handbook to higher consciousness.* Berkeley, Calif.: Living Love Center, 1979.

Kiernan, T. *Shrinks, etc.* New York: Dial, 1974.

Lange, A., & Jakubowski, P. *Responsible assertive behavior.* Champaign, Il.: Research Press, 1976.

Lazarus, A. A. *Behavior therapy and beyond.* New York: McGraw-Hill, 1971.

Lazarus, A. A. *Multimodal therapy.* New York: Springer, 1976.

Lieberman, M. A., Yalom, I. D., & Miles, M. B. *Encounter groups: First facts.* New York: Basic Books, 1973.

Lowen, A. *The language of the body.* New York: Collier, 1958.

Maimonides, M. A thought from Moses Maimonides (1135–1204). *Newsletter Israeli Association for Behavior Therapy,* Summer 1980, No. 2, 2.

Maleske, H. *You really don't have to.* Irvine, Calif.: Natural Therapy Foundation Press, 1980.

Maliver, B. L. *The encounter game.* New York: Stein and Day, 1972.

Marcus Aurelius. *Meditations.* Boston: Little, Brown, 1899.

Marks, I. M. *Living with fear.* New York: McGraw Hill, 1978.

Meichenbaum, D. *Cognitive behavior modification.* New York: Plenum, 1977.

Nichols, M., & Zax, M. *Catharsis in psychotherapy.* New York: Wiley, 1978.

Moreno, J. L. *Who shall survive?* Washington: Nervous and Mental Diseases Publishing Company, 1934.

Novaco, R. *Anger Control.* Lexington, Mass.: Lexington Books, 1975.

Palmer, R. D. Desensitization of the fear of expressing one's own inhibited aggression: Bioenergetic assertive techniques for behavior therapists. *Advances in Behavior Therapy,* 1973, *4,* 241–253.

Peele, S. *Love and addiction.* New York: Taplinger, 1975.

Perls, F. S. *Gestalt therapy verbatim.* Lafayette, Calif.: Real People Press, 1969.

Reich, W. *Character analysis.* New York: Orgone Institute Press, 1949.

Rogers, C. R. *On becoming a person.* Boston: Houghton-Mifflin, 1961.

Rosen, R. D. *Psychobabble.* New York: Atheneum, 1977.

Shapiro, D. *Precision nirvana.* Englewood Cliffs, N.J.: Prentice-Hall, 1979.

Skinner, B. F. *Beyond freedom and dignity.* New York: Knopf, 1971.

Small, L. *The briefer psychotherapies.* New York: Brunner-Mazel, 1979.

Stampl, T. F., & Levis, D. J. Phobic patients: Treatment with the learning approach of implosive therapy. *Voices,* 1967, *3,* 23–27.

Tenov, D. *Love and limerence.* New York: Stein and Day, 1979.

Torrey, E. F. *The mind game: Witchdoctors and psychiatrists.* New York: Emerson, 1972.

Truax, C. B., & Carkhuff, R. R. *Toward effective counseling and psychotherapy: Training and practice.* Chicago: Aldine, 1967.

Walen, S. R., DiGiuseppe, R., & Wessler, R. L. *A practitioner's guide to rational-emotive therapy.* New York: Oxford, 1980.

Wessler, R., & Wessler, R. L. *Rational-emotive therapy: A cognitive-behavioral approach.* San Francisco: Jossey-Bass, 1980.

Wolpe, J. *Psychotherapy by reciprocal inhibition.* Stanford, Calif.: Stanford University Press, 1958.

Wolpe, J. *The practice of behavior therapy.* New York: Pergamon, 1973.

Zubin, J. & Spring, B. Vulnerability—a new view of schizophrenia. *Journal of Abnormal Psychology,* 1977, *86, 103–126.*

Chapter 4

IS PSYCHOTHERAPY
MORE EFFECTIVE THAN A PLACEBO?

EDWARD ERWIN

Controversy about the possible benefits of psychotherapy has not ended. Some commentators argue that the benefits have been shown to be quite substantial (Smith et al., 1980), but skeptics argue that psychotherapy has not been shown to be more effective than a placebo (Prioleau et al., 1983). I argue, first, that the skeptic's conclusion is sufficiently plausible that it is worth asking about its implications. I then argue that it does not imply a lack of evidence of effectiveness, but it does have serious adverse implications for the psychotherapy enterprise.

META-ANALYSIS AND PSYCHOTHERAPEUTIC EFFECTIVENESS

In recent years, the case for the general effectiveness of psychotherapy has rested primarily on the meta-analysis of Smith et al. (1980). They claim that the evidence they analyze overwhelmingly supports the efficacy of psychotherapy, that the past rationalizations of academic critics of the psychotherapy outcome literature have nearly been exhausted, and that such critics can scarcely advance new excuses without feeling embarrassed or without raising suspicions about their motives (p. 182). If Smith et al. are right, then the outcome issue has now been settled and, therefore, there is little point in asking if psychotherapy is more effective than a placebo. A brief look at their argument, then, is in order.

In an important paper (Smith & Glass, 1977) and book (Smith et al., 1980), Smith and her colleagues make several contributions to the debates about psychotherapy. First, they reject the findings of earlier reviews (Eysenck, 1952, 1966; Rachman, 1971), which had been essentially skeptical about the effectiveness of nonbehavioral psychotherapy.

They even argue that the methods of earlier reviewers are hopelessly inadequate for integrating and making sense of the complex data bearing on psychotherapeutic effectiveness. Second, they introduce a new method of research integration called *meta-analysis*. An *effect size* is calculated for each study by subtracting the average score for the outcome measure for the control group from the average score for the treatment group and dividing the result by the within-control-group standard deviation. Smith et al. (1980) found 475 controlled studies of psychotherapy and calculated for these studies approximately 1,760 effect sizes. Third, on the basis of their meta-analyses, Smith et al. argue for four major conclusions. The two that are of most interest here are the following:

(1) Psychotherapy is beneficial, consistently so and in many different ways. Its benefits are on a par with other expensive and beneficial interventions such as schooling and medicine.
(2) Different types of psychotherapy (verbal or behavioral, psycho-dynamic, client-centered, or systematic desensitization) do not produce different types of or degrees of benefit. (Smith et al., 1980, pp. 183–184).

The merits and liabilities of meta-analysis are still being debated, but one conclusion is now beyond doubt: Its use has not ended controversy about the effectiveness of psychotherapy. In a recent symposium, more than twenty leading scholars debated the subject (Prioleau et al., 1983), with some defending the argument of Smith et al. and others rejecting it; as Garfield (1983) points out, the use of meta-analysis instead of ending debate has appeared to raise the level of controversy to new heights. One could agree with this assessment and still argue that there is solid and convincing evidence of psychotherapeutic effectiveness; perhaps the critics are demonstrably wrong and, as Smith et al. contend, should be embarrassed by their continued recalcitrance. I do not think, however, that this is a tenable position. Several recent articles (Rachman & Wilson, 1980; Wilson & Rachman 1983; Eysenck, 1983a, 1983b) have exposed serious defects in the arguments of Smith et al. One of the major problems is their grouping together and weighting equally evidence from relatively good and bad studies. Smith et al. justify their treatment of the evidence primarily by arguing that the results of good and bad studies are roughly the same. However, this argument, in turn, rests on a dubious assumption concerning what counts as a *good* study.

Erwin (1984) argues that their criteria for evaluating studies are inadequate and that their entire argument for treating all studies alike is a failure. Once that is shown, then the criticism of Rachman and Wilson (1980) becomes decisive; they show in detail how the treatment of the evidence by Smith et al. seriously weakens their overall argument.

Even if the above criticism is set aside, another problem remains. Most critics of psychotherapy do not deny that some forms of behavior therapy and cognitive therapy are effective for treating certain clinical problems; they question, rather, whether so-called "insight" or "verbal" therapies have been shown to be effective in treating neurotic patients. In the summary of their results (Smith et al., 1980, p. 89) most of the verbal psychotherapies have an effect size that is only marginally greater than the effect size for what they call a "placebo treatment." This suggests the following question: What would the results be if a meta-analysis were restricted to studies comparing verbal psychotherapy to a placebo control? An answer to this question can be found in the review by Prioleau et al. (1983). They found a mean effect size of .42, but some of the studies they analyzed did not deal with neurotic outpatients; others used rational emotive therapy or group social learning therapy, which are more akin to the behavior therapies than to traditional verbal psychotherapy (Erwin, 1978). For outpatient neurotics, Prioleau et al. found that there was a close to zero difference between the effect size of the verbal psychotherapy and placebo therapy.

One could argue for the effectiveness of psychotherapy without relying on meta-analysis, but the remaining evidence also has serious weaknesses, as shown by Rachman and Wilson (1980). One persistent problem has been the failure to rule out a placebo explanation of any beneficial therapeutic results. Even the Sloane et al. (1975) study, which in many respects is exemplary, used a wait-list group rather than a placebo control. There are, of course, ethical and practical difficulties in using placebo controls, but if neither a placebo control nor an adequate substitute is used, the epistemological problem remains: How can one know that any beneficial effects have been caused by psychotherapy rather than placebo factors? Prioleau et al. (1980) contend that there is not a single convincing demonstration anywhere that the benefits of (nonbehavioral) psychotherapy exceed those of a placebo for real patients. On the basis of this fact, plus the findings of several reasonably designed studies in which the psychotherapy benefits were not greater than the placebo benefits (Brill et al., 1964; Gillian and Rachman, 1974; McLean and Hakstian, 1979), they speculate that the benefits are approximately equivalent. I do not think that this speculation has been established, but I think their work supports a weaker conclusion, i.e., that there is no firm evidence so far that the benefits of (nonbehavioral) psychotherapy for real patients exceed that of a placebo. This conclusion is also controversial, but it is sufficiently plausible that one may reasonably inquire about its implications. I turn next to this subject.

PSYCHOTHERAPY AND PLACEBOS

Some writers conclude that a therapy worth no more than a placebo is ineffective, but others disagree. For example, Frank (1983) reports that in his own research he has found symptom relief with a placebo to be, on the average, identical with four months of psychotherapy, but he does not infer that psychotherapy is ineffective. The placebo, he suggests, *is* psychotherapy.

Along the same lines, Cordray and Bootzin (1983) argue that a placebo control condition is appropriate for answering questions about theoretical mechanisms but not for demonstrating effectiveness. A therapy may be no more effective than a placebo, they claim, and still be effective. Brody (1983) disagrees, as does Eysenck (1983 c).

Some of the disagreement about the implications of equating psychotherapeutic and placebo effects may arise because the term *placebo* is not always used in the same sense. As Grünbaum (1981) has shown, there has been much confusion caused by the use of this term in clinical psychology. To illustrate, suppose that we take a sugar pill as a paradigm case of a *placebo* and then define the concept so that it applies to anything that is like a sugar pill, in that it is physiologically inert, with respect to a certain disorder, but is potentially efficacious for psychological reasons. If we then apply the concept to psychological procedures, *all* (or most) potentially effective therapies qualify as placebos. To avoid this result, some writers define *placebo* in terms of lack of specific effects or activity. For example, a placebo, when used as a control in experimental studies, is a substance or procedure that is without specific activity for the condition being studied (Shapiro & Morris, 1978). The problem then becomes to say what counts as *specific* activity. If we use a medical definition and classify a procedure as lacking specific activity if and only if it is physiologically inert, then the first problem reappears. All (or almost all) psychological therapies would be without specific activity and so would be placebos. Another suggestion is that *specific activity* is the therapeutic influence attributable solely to the contents or processes of the therapies rendered (Shapiro & Morris, 1978). But what does this mean? Suppose that a procedure is efficacious, but only through the intervening activity of certain thought processes. For example, we use a procedure in treating a phobic response, and the treatment causes a change in belief about the phobic object, and that change in turn eliminates the phobic response. Is this a case where the therapeutic effect is *not* attributable *solely* to the contents of the therapy? After all, the change in belief also played a causal role. If the answer is "yes," then, again, our definition is too wide. Any effective therapy that works partly by changing a client's belief or expectations will be a placebo. If we say "no," then our definitions is too narrow. Even the procedure of providing a sugar pill would no longer be a placebo. By giving the pill to a client, we may change his/her beliefs or expectations; this psychological change may be due solely to our pill procedure and may, in turn, have a therapeutic effect. The problem here is that what are commonly called placebos in psychotherapy research often have quite specific therapeutic effects. Speaking of lack of specific effects or activity, then, does not distinguish placebos from effective nonplacebos.

It may be that the use of the term *placebo* in psychotherapy research is likely to cause continued confusion, and perhaps the term should be abandoned, as some writers have suggested (O'Leary & Borkovec, 1978). If it is to be used, its use should be explicated precisely. Grünbaum (1981) has recently provided such an explication, one that does not use the notion of "specific activity." His key suggestion is that the concept of a placebo be relativized not only to a particular disorder but also to a clinical theory. A given procedure, then, may be a placebo for a certain disorder, but not others, and may be a placebo with respect to a particular theory, but not others. By a *therapeutic theory,* Grünbaum means a theory that specifies characteristics of a therapy that singly or in combination are remedial for a certain disorder. Thus, a cognitivist and behaviorist may have the same therapeutic theory concerning systematic desensitization, even though one gives a cognitive and the other a counter-conditioning explanation of how the therapy works. They have the same therapeutic theory if they agree, for example, that completion of an imagery hierarchy is the remedial characteristic of systematic desensitization in treating phobias.

Suppose, then, that a certain therapeutic theory specifies that factors F_1, F_2, and F_3 of treatment T are remedial for disorder D. Relative to that theory, T is a placebo for D if and only if none of the F factors is remedial for D. A more complicated definition is required to distinguish intended from inadvertent placebos, but this distinction need not concern us here (see Grünbaum, 1981, p. 159).

If we use the term placebo in the above defined sense, what follows from the supposition that all psychotherapy procedures, again excluding behavior therapy, are no more effective than placebos? In particular, does it follow that no such procedure is effective? It does not. Some procedures may be placebos with respect to a certain theory, Q, and disorder, D, and yet be effective for D; the theory may have simply failed to specify correctly the characteristics that are remedial. If a given form of psychotherapy is as effective for D as such a placebo, then it too will be effective for the same disorder.

If the equivalence of psychotherapy to a placebo does not imply ineffectiveness, neither does it imply effectiveness. The placebo might be effective but then again it might not. We need to look at the particular placebo before inferences can be reasonably drawn about the psychotherapy to which it is compared. Consider some examples.

In the Brill et al. (1964) study of 299 predominantly neurotic patients, the treatment consisted of psychotherapy, drugs, or a placebo. The placebo was a chemically inert pill. At the end of one year, each of the treatment groups did better than a wait-list control, but the improvement for each treatment group was approximately the same. Prioleau et al. (1983) cite this finding as evidence that the effects of psychotherapy are equivalent to those of a relatively minimal placebo.

In contrast to the minimal placebo in the Brill study, much more elaborate placebos have been used in studies of systematic desensitization. For example, in a study by Lick (1975), subjects in two placebo control conditions were told that they would be viewing pictures of phobic stimuli flashed too rapidly for the conscious mind to perceive. They were also told that these pictures would register in the unconscious, that any responses elicited would be recorded on a multichannel polygraph, and that the polygraph was hooked up to a shock generator that would deliver a mild electric shock to their fingers when unconscious responses of a certain amplitude were detected. The subjects, all of whom were either spider or snake phobics, were also given a comprehensive rationale for the treatment, emphasizing the unconscious nature of phobias, the ability of an unpleasant stimulus to suppress behavior, and the principle of *subliminal perception*. One of the placebo groups was also given feedback concerning the therapeutic experience; the other group was not. The two placebo groups and the systematic desensitization group showed approximately the same rate of improvement, and all three were superior to a no treatment group. It might be concluded that this study provides evidence for the effectiveness of flashing pictures of phobic stimuli too rapidly for the conscious mind to perceive and, perhaps, for the theory that the unconscious mind plays a major causal role in the development of phobias. The conclusion would be mistaken. In fact, the pictures the subjects viewed were blank, and the shocks were prearranged and not contingent on unconscious responses. The entire elaborate procedure was devised merely to make the placebo treatment as credible as the systematic desensitization.

The placebo in the Lick study was much more complex than the inert pill of the Brill et al. study, but both were intended to possess one important property: credibility. In other studies, too, placebos that have been used to control for expectancy effects, no matter how different they are, have been designed to be *believable* therapies. The idea, of course, is that by being believable they will generate in the subject expectations of favorable therapeutic change. Such expectations may not be created, or may not be maintained through the course of the therapy; some placebos are simply not sufficiently credible (Kazdin & Wilcoxin, 1976). Furthermore, even where the placebo is credible and the placebo group does better than a no treatment control, we may still lack grounds for thinking the placebo effective. The improvement might have been due to the initial intake interview or to something else besides expectancy factors. Frank (1983) points out that in his placebo studies, many patients experienced a marked drop in symptomatic distress following the extensive initial work-up and *before* they received the placebo (a pill). In a case where all improvement is caused prior to the administration of the placebo, then clearly the placebo was not therapeutic. What about cases, however, where the placebo is credible and does create favorable expectations that cause therapeutic change? Is the placebo effective in such cases? There are two views of this phenomenon.

According to the first, the placebo is not effective; what brings about therapeutic change is the expectations of the client. On the second view, the placebo is effective.

The standard argument for the first view is something like the following. If none of the specific ingredients that constitute a therapy contributes to therapeutic change, then it is not the therapy that is efficacious. But if a client's expectations cause the change, then no specific ingredient in the therapy is responsible, so the therapy is ineffective. The opposing view, which now seems to me to be plausible, denies the second premise of the above argument. In the sort of case being discussed here, the specific ingredients of the therapy, at least some of them, do make a contribution; they do so by generating favorable expectations that, in turn, have causal efficacy. It might even be true that most effective psychological therapies work by generating a certain kind of expectation (Bandura, 1977), but whether that is so or not, a therapy is not ineffective merely because it affects a client's beliefs and expectations, which in turn affect his behavior. Suppose someone believes that he/she cannot engage in public speaking without suffering extreme panic and anxiety. If I change his/her belief through rational argument and, as a consequence, he/she is able to engage in public speaking, my arguing made a contribution to his/her improvement. What is the difference, then, between arguing and giving the client a sugar pill that he/she believes will end the panic attacks? In both cases, the procedure is effective, but each works by changing the client's beliefs and expectations.

I am not suggesting that we do not need either a placebo control or an adequate substitute before we can infer clinical effectiveness. If we use merely a wait-list control, it may be impossible to rule out the possibility that the therapist's attention, or the initial interview, or something else accounted for all clinical improvement. I am suggesting, rather, that where a placebo treatment is credible and produces favorable expectations in the client, and, as a consequence, the client improves, then the placebo is effective. If some form of psychotherapy is equally effective, then it too is effective.

Those who take the position that psychotherapy is ineffective if its benefits are equivalent to a placebo, and who also believe in that equivalence, tend to have doubts about the psychotherapy enterprise. I now want to argue that their doubts are justified even if equivalence does *not* imply ineffectiveness. In one important respect, then, it does not matter which position is adopted; if the therapeutic value of psycho-therapy is no greater than a placebo (of the kind typically used in studies of psychotherapy), then the doubts about the psychotherapy enterprise are warranted *whether or not psychotherapy is effective*. It is possible for a procedure with powerful therapeutic effects to be used as a placebo control, but, as far as we know, that has not been a common practice of psychotherapy researchers. Procedures are generally selected to be place-bos because they are believed (sometimes falsely) to be credible and to work, if at all, only by creating favorable expectations in a client. Let us call placebos that work in this fashion "weakly effective." This terminology, I concede, could be misleading if it suggests that such a placebo could not possibly have strong therapeutic effects. However, I intend no such implication. The point of classifying a procedure as being only "weakly effective" in this technical sense is to indicate that it is replaceable by any other procedure that is equally credible and has the capacity to create the same favorable expectations of improvement. Any form of psychotherapy, then, that is capable of producing therapeutic benefits, but none greater than that of a weakly effective placebo, is only weakly effective.

A complication arises, however, because of Bandura's self-efficacy theory (Bandura, 1977). On this theory, effective psychological therapies work by generating or strengthening "self-efficacy" expectations, i.e., expectations that one will be able to execute a certain task successfully. If this account is right, are we then forced to say that all effective therapies are only weakly effective? No. I am not classifying a therapy as weakly effective merely because it works by generating expectations; it is also necessary that all of its therapeutic benefits be due to its credibility. An effective therapy, if Bandura is right, is not only credible (and thus generates in the client the expectation that he/she will improve as the result of the treatment) but also creates or strengthens a different kind of expectation, i.e., one of self-efficacy. Suppose, for example, that an agoraphobic has read a good deal of Freudian psychology and believes that orthodox psychoanalysis is an effective treatment for all phobias. The client may begin Freudian treatment and be confident that it will work. Because of this confidence, the client's morale may improve (Frank, 1983) and he/she may show some improvement; he/she may at least feel better about his/her future. His/her confidence in the therapy may even be sustained for a very long time in the face of much counter evidence. He/she may continue, then, to expect to be helped, but never develop the confidence that he/she can leave his/her house without undergoing a severe panic attack. The therapy, in brief, may be credible without generating any expectation of self-efficacy. Suppose, however, that a particular client's expectation of being helped was instilled by the therapy and generated a strong self-efficacy expectation sufficient to resolve the clinical problem. In that case, I would still classify the therapy as being weakly effective if all of its beneficial effects stem from its credibility, even if it occasionally brought about powerful changes. As I have already indicated, a placebo, or any standard therapy, may be weakly effective and yet may sometimes bring about strong changes. The point, once again, of calling it weakly effective is not to rule out the possibility of its having strong effects, but to make clear that it is *replaceable* by any other treatment that is equally credible. I should add, however, that there is little warrant for thinking that the weakly effective treatments generally used as placebos in psychotherapy research (sugar pills and the like) are powerful treatments for serious clinical problems. So, finding that a form of psychotherapy does as well, but no better, than one of these placebos is not likely to provide evidence that the psychotherapy is a powerfully effective treatment.

DOUBTS ABOUT THE PSYCHOTHERAPY ENTERPRISE

There are many different types of psychotherapy, perhaps more than a hundred (Karasu, 1977). Research that is now being done might show that some of the *nonbehavioral* verbal psychotherapies are generally superior to a placebo, but it is doubtful that this superiority has been demonstrated so far for even one, let alone most, of these therapies. This lack of evidence supports certain doubts about therapists' training, psychotherapeutic theories, and the satisfaction of the needs of consumers.

Therapists' Training

If, on current evidence, psychotherapy is at best weakly effective, then why do we need psychotherapy institutes or extended periods of training for psychotherapists? It does take time to train people to use psychoanalysis and other such techniques, but it would seem simpler and more cost-effective to train people how to administer a placebo. What is the clinical advantage in providing the more elaborate kind of training? One possible answer is that trainees in psychotherapy institutes learn a good deal more than how to administer specific techniques. They acquire, for example, a special expertise that is necessary for dealing effectively with mental health problems. This claim, however, raises the same sort of issue as that concerning the effectiveness of psychotherapy. What evidence is there that the special expertise acquired in typical psychotherapy training programs contributes to clinical effectiveness? In one study bearing on this issue, psychotherapists who were both trained and highly experienced treated fifteen patients suffering from neurotic depression or anxiety (Strupp & Hadley, 1979). A comparable patient group was treated by college professors who had neither training nor experience in psychotherapy, but who were chosen for their ability to form understanding relationships. Patients treated by the professors showed, on the average, as much improvement as patients treated by the professional therapists. It would be rash to infer from this one study that neither psychotherapeutic training nor experience ever contributes significantly to a therapeutic outcome. However, the Strupp and Hadley study and the findings of Smith et al. (1980) of no significant correlation between therapist experience and therapeutic outcome, when combined with the *tentative* finding that psychotherapy tends to be no more effective than a placebo, does raise serious questions about current training procedures.

Psychotherapeutic Theories

Trainees in psychotherapy are often taught certain theories about how therapy works and about the etiology of mental disorders. *If* most forms of psychotherapy are no more effective than a placebo, this creates a serious embarrassment for many of these theories. For example, if Freud's account of the origin and maintenance of neurosis is correct, then it seems reasonable to predict that a placebo will be less effective than properly administered psychoanalysis. A placebo, on Freudian theory, would not be effective in rooting out repressions or in strengthening the ego sufficiently to deal with assaults from the id or superego. A psychoanalyst could try to supplement Freudian theory to explain why psychoanalysis is no more effective than a placebo, but Freudian theory as it stands does not predict this finding.

CONSUMER SATISFACTION

Even if one agrees that psychotherapy is at best weakly effective, one could defend its use on the following grounds. People who go to psychotherapists, it might be argued, tend to be satisfied with their treatment. For example, Babbie & Stone (1977) examined data originally collected by Ornstein et al. (1975) concerning EST (Erhard Seminar Training), a therapy that is very popular in the United States. When asked about the effects of their training, more than half of the EST graduates surveyed rated them "very favorably;" only 6 percent rated the effects of their training unfavorably. Other studies of other types of psychotherapy have also found widespread consumer satisfaction with psychotherapy (Lebow, 1982). It might be argued, then, that the worth of psychotherapy to the consumer (the patient) does not depend on its being superior to a placebo. Whether it is or is not superior is a theoretical question of interest to theoreticians; in judging the practical worth of psychotherapy, what matters is consumer satisfaction. Judged by this latter criterion, psychotherapy is indeed worthwhile.

The above defense provides a partial justification for doing psychotherapy. Some people might value psychoanalysis or EST, or even voodoo or faith healing, even if they agreed that the treatment was worth no more than a credible placebo. They might not change their attitude even if they concluded that there was no causal connection at all between the treatment and beneficial outcome. One reason for this attitude is that some clients enter therapy partly for reasons unrelated to clinical outcome. For example, some clients want someone to listen to their problems, and they find it inconvenient to talk at length with friends, bartenders, or taxi drivers; others want to enter into a therapeutic relationship with a warm, caring person.

A therapy, then, may be of some value even if it is worth no more than a placebo. However, it is also potentially misleading to judge a therapy primarily in terms of consumer satisfaction. First, it is likely that many consumers approve of their therapy mainly because they believe that it produced in them beneficial changes. If they found out that there was no warrant for this belief, or even that the same benefits could have been produced by a sugar pill, then their rating of the therapy might change dramatically. Second, in cases where psychotherapy can be replaced without loss of benefit to the client by a sugar pill or some other inexpensive, credible placebo, then why do psychotherapy at all? Why not use the more cost-effective procedure?

It might be replied that, for most psychological problems, clients are not likely to believe that a pill will resolve their difficulty. They need a therapy that they can have faith in. However, in well-controlled comparisons of behavior therapy or psychotherapy and a placebo, the clients have had confidence in the placebo procedure (any study in which the placebo was significantly less credible than the treatment was not well controlled). So, we do have grounds for believing that placebos, even of a minimal kind, such as a pill placebo, are often credible (Brill et al., 1964). Still, what clients find credible depends on several factors, including their theoretical beliefs about traditional psychotherapy. Some, for example, who have been taught to believe in the superiority of psychoanalysis may have faith in no other therapy. Some of these clients *may* be better off undergoing psychoanalysis if undergoing even a weakly effective therapy is worth the cost. For many other clients, however, use of a less expensive placebo would be feasible and preferable; or, better yet, they might benefit from some form of behavior therapy or cognitive therapy that is more effective than a weakly effective placebo (Kazdin & Wilson, 1978; Erwin, 1978; Rachman & Wilson, 1980).

REFERENCES

Bandura, A. Self-efficacy: Toward a unifying theory of behavioral change. *Psychological Review*, 1977, 84, 191–215.

Babbie, E., and Stone, D. An evaluation of the EST experience by a national sample of graduates. *Brosci. Commun.*, 1977, 3, 123–140.

Brill, N., Koegler, R., Epstein, L., and Fogey, E. Controlled study of psychiatric outpatient treatment. *Archives of General Psychiatry*, 1964, 10, 581–595.

Brody, N. W. Where are the emperor's clothes? *The Behavioral & Brain Sciences*, 1983, 6, 303–308.

Cordray, D., and Bootzin, R. Placebo control conditions: Test of theory or of effectiveness? *The Behavioral & Brain Sciences*, 1983, 6, 286.

Erwin, E. *Behavior Therapy: Scientific, Philosophical and Moral Foundations.* New York: Cambridge University Press, 1978.

Erwin, E. Establishing causal connections: Meta-analysis and psychotherapy. *Midwest Studies in Philosophy*, 1984, in press.

Eysenck, H. J. The effects of psychotherapy: An evaluation. *Journal of Consulting Psychology*, 1952, 16, 319–324.

Eysenck, H. J. *The Effects of Psychotherapy.* New York: Inter-Science Press, 1966.

Eysenck, H. J. Meta-analysis: An abuse of research integration. Unpublished manuscript, 1983 a.

Eysenck, H. J. Special review. *Behavior Research & Therapy,* 1983 b, 21, 315–320.

Eysenck, H. J. The effectiveness of psychotherapy: The specter at the feast. *The Behavioral & Brain Sciences,* 1983 c, 6, 290.

Frank, J. The placebo is psychotherapy. *The Behavioral & Brain Sciences,* 1983, 6, 291–292.

Garfield, S. Does psychotherapy work? Yes, no, maybe. *The Behavioral & Brain Sciences,* 1983, 6, 292–293.

Gillian, P., and Rachman, S. An experimental investigation of desensitization and phobic patients. *British Journal of Psychology,* 1974, 124, 392–401.

Grunbaum, A. The placebo concept. *Behavior Research & Therapy,* 1981, 19, 157–167.

Karasu, T. Psychotherapies: An overview. *American Journal of Psychiatry,* 1977, 134, 851–863.

Kazdin, A., and Wilcoxin, C. Systematic desensitization & nonspecific treatment effects: A methodological evaluation. *Psychological Bulletin,* 1976, 83, 729–758.

Kazdin, A., and Wilson, G. T. *Evaluation of Behavior Therapy: Issues, Evidence & Research Strategies.* Cambridge, Mass.: Ballinger, 1978.

Lebow, J. Consumer satisfaction with mental health treatment. *Psychological Bulletin,* 1982, 91, 244–259.

Lick, J. R. Expectancy, false galvanic skin response feedback & systematic desensitization in the modification of phobic behavior. *Journal of Consulting & Clinical Psychology,* 1975, 43, 557–567.

McLean, P., and Hakstian, A. Clinical depression: Comparative efficacy of outpatient treatments. *Journal of Consulting & Clinical Psychology,* 1979, 47, 818–836.

O'Leary, K. D., and Borkovec, T. D. Conceptual, methodological & ethical problems of placebo groups in psychotherapy research. *American Psychologist,* 1978, 33, 821–830.

Ornstein, R., Swencionis, C., Deikman, A., and Morris, R. *A Self-report Survey: Preliminary Study of Participants in Erhard Seminars Training.* San Francisco: EST Foundation, 1975.

Prioleau, L., Murdock, M., and Brody, N. An analysis of psychotherapy versus placebo studies. *The Behavioral & Brain Sciences,* 1983, 6, 275–285.

Rachman, S. *The effects of psychotherapy.* Oxford: Pergamon Press, 1971.

Rachman, S., and Wilson, G. T. *The Effects of Psychological Therapy.* Oxford: Pergamon Press, 1980.

Shapiro, A. K., and Morris, L. A. The placebo effect in medical & psychological therapies. In *Handbook of Psychotherapy & Behavior Change,* 2nd edition, Garfield, S. & Bergin, A. (eds.). New York: Wiley, 1978.

Sloane, R., Staples, F., Cristol, A., Yorkston, N., and Whipple, K., *Psychotherapy Versus Behavior Therapy.* Cambridge, Mass.: Harvard University Press, 1975.

Smith, M., and Glass, G. Meta-analysis of psychotherapy outcome studies. *American Psychologist,* 1977, 32, 752–760.

Smith, M. Glass, G., and Miller, T. *The Benefits of Psychotherapy.* Baltimore, Md.: Johns Hopkins Press, 1980.

Strupp, H., and Hadley, S. Specific vs. nonspecific factors in psychotherapy. *Archives of General Psychiatry,* 1979, 36, 1125–1136

Wilson, G. T., and Rachman, S. Meta-analysis & the evaluation of psychotherapy outcome: Limitations and liabilities. *Journal of Consulting & Clinical Psychology,* 1983, 51, 54–64.

Chapter 5

THE BATTLE OVER PSYCHOTHERAPEUTIC EFFECTIVENESS.

H. J. EYSENCK

In 1952, I published an article on "The Effects of Psychotherapy" (Eysenck, 1952), in which I examined several outcome studies that primarily evaluated treatment of neurotic patients, and compared the results with estimates of improvement of patients that occurred in the absence of therapy ("spontaneous remission"). My main conclusion was that there was no good evidence to suggest that psychotherapeutic or psychanalytic treatment of any kind improved the chances of neurotic patients to recover or be cured, when compared with no treatment. These conclusions were borne out by later studies, summarised in further publications (Eysenck, 1960, 1965). My conclusion has frequently been criticized on the grounds that the data did not *prove* psychotherapy to be ineffective, but of course I never claimed that. Absence of proof of effectiveness is not the same as proof of ineffectiveness, an important point saliently brought out recently by Erwin (1978).

Similar conclusions were reached around this time by many other psychologists, e.g. Denker (1946); Landis (1937); Wilder (1945); Zubin (1953); all dealt with pretty much the same evidence, and the debate resulting from it has been well summarised by Kazdin (1978). Hundreds of studies have since been done, technically superior to this early work; is it necessary to revise my early conclusion in the light of the later evidence?

It is interesting to note that different authors, summarising all the evidence to date, give different answers. Rachman and Wilson (1980) conclude what to my mind is the best available survey by saying that, "Our review of the evidence that has accumulated during the past 25 years does not put us in a position to revise Eysenck's original estimate". (P. 259) They do argue that there is a strong case for refining my estimate of the occurrence of spontaneous remission for each of a different group of neurotic disorders, as the early assumption of uniformity of spontaneous remission rates among different disorders is increasing difficult to defend. They go on to say, given the widespread occurrence of spontaneous remissions, that the claims made for the specific value of particular forms of psychotherapy begin to look exaggerated. "It comes as a surprise to find how meagre is the evidence to support the wide-ranging claims made or implied by psychoanalytic therapists . . . We are unaware of any methodological study . . . which has taken adequate account of spontaneous changes or, more importantly, of the contribution of non-specific therapeutic influences such as placebo effects, expectancy, and so on." (P. 259) Altogether, the conclusion is that with the exception of behaviour therapy, the traditional psychotherapeutic and psychoanalytic methods of treatment have not shown themselves to be superior to no treatment at all. Kazdin and Wilson (1978), Zilbergeld (1983), and many others have come to the same conclusion.

In marked contrast are the conclusions of Bergin (1971), Bergin and Lambert (1978), Luborsky et al. (1975), and particularly Smith et al. (1980), who introduced their method of "meta-analysis" to survey a larger portion of the literature than anyone had previously done. They concluded that, "Psychotherapy is beneficial, consistently so and in many different ways. It's benefits are on a par with other expensive and ambitious interventions, such as schooling and medicine. The benefits of psychotherapy are not permanent, but then little is." (P. 183) They go on to say that, "Psychotherapy benefits people of all ages as reliably as schooling educates them, medicine cures them, or business turns a profit. It sometimes seeks the same goals sought by education and medicine; when it does, psychotherapy performs commendably well — so well, in fact, that it begins to threaten the artificial barriers that tradition has erected between the institutions of amelioration and cure. We are suggesting no less than that psychotherapists have a legitimate, though not exclusive, claim, substantiated by controlled research, on those roles in society, whether privately or publically endowed, whose responsibility is to restore to health the sick, the suffering, the alienated, and the disaffected." (P. 184) They go on to praise, in this somewhat lyrical way, the benefits of psychotherapy, and their book has been extremely influential because of the apparent thoroughness of their analyses. How can we reconcile two such quite different estimates of the effectiveness of psychotherapy? As far as the Bergin and Luborsky studies are concerned, an adequate criticism is presented by Rachman and Wilson (1980). It is apparent from their review of these summaries that the authors have been highly selective in their choice of studies to be included, have omitted important studies going counter to their preconceived opinions, and have on the other hand included studies completely irrelevant to the question of effectiveness of psychotherapy and completely misinterpreted by the authors. These criticisms are fully justified, as any independent reading of the original sources, and the Rachman and Wilson critique, will demonstrate. How about the meta-analyses performed by Smith et al.? Meta-analysis is presented as a technique that obviates certain pitfalls of integrating divergent research findings, giving a greater degree of objectivity than is forthcoming in the usual type of research summary. We are told that the objective of the review of research is to analyse and present the separate studies in such a way that an overall conclusion can be reached about the nature of the process studied. How is this normally done? Smith et al. (1980) state that, "Data in the form of findings from research studies are aggregated or accumulated almost in the same way as measurements on individuals are accumulated in primary research to form conclusions about the variables studied." (P. 7) The major problem in the way of coming to a conclusion, as they point out, arises when the findings of the individual studies do not agree, or the characteristics or contexts of the studies are different. The solution is usually sought through selection of good as opposed to bad studies, through critique of results obtained by means of inappropriate methodology or statistical analysis, and generally through what Smith et al. condemn as subjective appraisals of a qualitative kind.

Smith et al. have devised a method of meta-analysis to satisfy three basic requirements. (1) Studies should not be excluded from consideration on arbitrary and a priori grounds, the major premise being that some boundaries must be drawn around fields, but it is better to draw them wide than narrow. (2) Study findings should be transformed to commensurable expressions of magnitude of experimental effect of correlational relationships. (3) Features of studies that might mediate their findings to be defined and measured, and their covariation with findings should be studied.

Meta-analysis thus uses all available studies, good, bad, and indifferent; it attempts to measure the effectiveness of a given technique by comparing the amount of change induced with the amount of change obtained in control groups not subjected to the treatment in question. This is done by using a simple statistical technique expressing all changes in standard terms. Where there are parameter differences between studies, these may be summed separately in order to throw some light on the relevance of the parameter to the final conclusion; thus we may separate out different forms of psychotherapy and analyse them separately and compare them with each other. We may also look at variables like duration of treatment, length of training of the therapist, etc, and assess their influence. A general criticism of meta-analysis has been made by the writer (Eysenck, in press), and this would not be the place to go into it in any detail. Let us merely consider whether the conclusions arrived at by Smith et al. in undertaking these meta-analyses really justify the conclusions just quoted.

They accept, as a definition of psychotherapy, a quotation from Meltzoff and Kornreich (1970): "Psychotherapy is taken to mean the informed and planful application of techniques derived from established psychological principles, by persons qualified through training and expe-rience to understand these principles and to apply these techniques with the intention of assisting individuals to modify such personal characteris-tics as feelings, values, attitudes, and behaviours which are judged by the therapist to be maladaptive and maladjustive." (p. 6) Although Smith et al. do not say so explicitly, certain implications are obvious in this definition, in the sense that psychotherapists whose views are encapsu-lated in it would insist on the inclusion of these points. One would be that the training and experience of the therapist would be an important variable; if it were not, then it would be meaningless to include a sentence about "persons qualified through training and experience." Another point would be the inclusion of the temporal element; by and large the longer the involvement of the therapist with the patient, the more successful (within limits) the outcome should be. This is a transla-tion of the simple dose-effect relationship familiar to researchers in psychopharmacology.

We are now in a position to look at the overall effects of different types of psychotherapy as presented in the form of a table on page 89 of their book; this lists 18 types of therapy, compared with no-treatment control groups. The effects are listed in terms of average effect size (ES), i.e., listed in standard terms. The average effect over the 18 different types of treatment is .85, which, as the authors argue, is certainly not negligible; it amounts to something like four-fifths of the standard deviation. One also notices, however, that one of the 18 "types of therapy" is placebo treatment! Now this is a curious inclusion. Placebo treatment can hardly be identified as meaning "the informed and planful application of techniques derived from established psychological principles, with the intention of assisting individuals to modify such personal characteristics as feelings, attitudes, and behaviours which are judged by the therapist to be maladaptive or maladjustive." The intention of placebo treatment is simply to provide a semblance of treatment, which, according to psychological principles, would have no effect in assisting individuals to modify their characteristics and behaviours! Indeed, placebo treatment is a proper *control* that should be used in making comparisons with different types of therapy. It is difficult to see how it came to be listed as a "type of therapy," and it may be interesting to consider for a moment the effect of using placebo treatment as a control, as, of course, it is usually taken to be. Placebo treatment has an average effect size of .56; psychodynamic therapy has an average effect size of .69; substracting the latter from the former gives an average effect size of psychodynamic therapy of .13, an effect that is so small as to be completely negligible, even though we are comparing 200 placebo treatment effects with 108 psychodynamic therapies, a number of instances large enough to indicate an appropriate degree of effectiveness, if such existed.

Thus, using placebo treatment as a proper control (which it undoubtedly is), we find that the alleged effectiveness of psychodynamic therapy vanishes almost completely. The positive outcome reported by Smith et al. (1980) is merely a consequence of their sleight of hand in using placebo treatment, not as a control, but as a type of therapy. They do not even defend this completely inadmissible intrusion; they simply assume that the reader will not be watchful enough to discover it. Eysenck (in press) goes on to consider the make-up of the "no-treatment" control groups, and makes severe criticisms of the method of choice used by Smith et al.; I will not go into this point here, other than to say that placebo control groups are obviously more appropriate than no-treatment control groups, the latter having been used in my original work simply because no control groups of the former kind were available.

Let us consider some further results of the meta-analyses performed by Smith et al. As pointed out above, the definition of psychotherapy accepted by them would require, among other things, that the duration of therapy would be related to its effectiveness. Averaging over 1,735 ES measures, the authors find a correlation with duration of therapy of −.05! Thus, effectively there is no relationship between duration of therapy and effectiveness of therapy. When it is realized that the duration of therapy ranged from one hour to over 300 hours, the fact that the "effect of therapy bore no simple or consistent relationship to its duration" (p. 115) is truly astounding. Smith et al. argue that "the lower effect sizes in the therapies of extremely long duration should be viewed in the light of the diagnosis and severity of the problems their clients of long-term therapies probably present" (p. 116). This can, of course, be argued, but it seems to represent exactly the type of subjectivity that Smith et al. try to eradicate from the discussion of summaries of results. Indeed, my own interpretation would be exactly the opposite. Longest from the point of view of duration are usually psychodynamic and psychoanalytic investigations, and in these, clients are very carefully selected in such a way that the most serious cases are excluded, and the most hopeful ones (showing intelligence, education, and high socioeconomic status) are included. Thus, one would have expected precisely the long-continued cases to be suffering from less serious illnesses, and to do correspondingly better.

A therapist's experience would clearly be considered a very important variable by practically all therapists, regardless of their persuasion or general theory. In the Smith et al. study, the correlation over 1,637 ES measures is exactly zero! The authors have little to say about this truly astounding finding, which renders absurd their whole claim to have demonstrated the "effectiveness of psychotherapy." Psychotherapy of any kind applies techniques that are based on certain theories, and these theories demand not only that there should be correlation between success and length of treatment, but also that the training and experience of the therapist should be extremely important. To find that neither of these corollaries is in fact borne out must be an absolute death blow to any claims to have demonstrated the effectiveness of psychotherapy. Smith et al. may have demonstrated something, but that something must be entirely different from what is usually conceived to be psychotherapy of any kind, and is much closer to the nonspecific effects of placebo treatment.

In assessing the effectiveness of the different kinds of therapy, and of therapy as a whole, Smith et al. pay little attention to the very marked decline of effectiveness over time, when therapy is completed. Their mode of argument, in fact, grossly underestimates the actual decline, because it omits the well-known spontaneous remission effects, which would go in the opposite direction (Eysenck, in press). Thus, what we should conclude from the data presented by Smith et al. themselves is that there is a relatively slight effect of psychotherapy, as compared with placebo controls, rapidly vanishing over time. This tiny and evanescent effect, which is irrespective of duration of treatment or training and experience of the therapist, is surely far removed from claims made by the authors that meta-analysis enables them to show strong and large-scale effects of psychotherapy.

Eysenck concludes his examination of the claims of Smith et al. by saying that, "On the basis of these fallacious and badly calculated data, showing very small and evanescent effects which contradict in detail all the assumptions and predictions of practising psychotherapists, the authors advance grandiose claims which find no support whatsoever in their own work." It will be clear that we do not consider Smith et al. to have succeeded in contradicting the conclusions reached by Rachman and Wilson as regards the failure of modern research to have demonstrated any effectiveness of psychotherapy, as compared with placebo treatment. This is an important conclusion regarding the question of cost-effectiveness, which is the major theme in this volume; if placebo treatment, conducted over a very short period of time by poor practitioners is as good as psychoanalysis, conducted over years by highly trained and experienced practitioners, then surely we should advise patients to make use of the former, rather than of the latter.

· Behaviour therapy, as compared to verbal therapy, is significantly superior even in the Smith et al. comparisons; as they admit: "Behavioural therapists reveal larger average effects for measures of global adjustment." (P. 99) The superiority of behavioural over verbal methods was apparent with different types of patients, ranging from the neurotic and true phobic to the psychotic and depressive. True to form, the authors tried to argue themselves out of what is clearly, for them, an inconvenient admission by using a highly subjective and quite inadmissible argument, which is discussed in detail by Eysenck (in press); it is curious that what is supposed to be a method to overcome and eliminate subjectivity in interpretation relies more than any other summary on precisely such subjective judgments!

We thus arrive at the two clear-cut conclusions that follow, from published work on the effectiveness of spontaneous remission, placebo treatment, psychotherapy, psychoanalysis, and behaviour therapy; namely that, as compared with spontaneous remission, there is no good evidence to suggest that psychotherapy and psychoanalysis have effects that are in any way superior, but that behaviour therapy is significantly better than psychotherapy and psychoanalysis in its effect on neurotic patients. When it is also realised that behaviour therapy is much shorter than psychotherapy or psychoanalysis, and that training for behaviour therapy, which does not involve a medical degree, is shorter and much cheaper than training for psychoanalysis and psychotherapy, which usually, though not always, requires a medical degree, then it is obvious that the cost-effectiveness of behaviour therapy is vastly superior to that of psychoanalysis and psychotherapy. This conclusion would be true even if the greater effectiveness of behaviour therapy had not been demonstrated; given such a demonstration, the taxpayer's dollar is obviously better spent on behaviour therapy than on any alternative method of treatment available for neurotic disorders of various kinds.

Monetary considerations are not everything; we must also look at the ethical implications of any decision that might be made. I have always felt that it is completely unethical to subject neurotic patients to a treatment the efficacy of which has not been proven, and indeed, the efficacy of which is very much in doubt—so much so that there is no good evidence for it, in spite of many hundreds of studies devoted to the question. Patients are asked to spend money and time they can ill afford, and subject themselves to a gruelling experience, to no good purpose at all; this surely cannot be right. At least there should be a statutory warning to the effect that the treatment that they are proposing to enter has never been shown to be effective, is very lengthy and costly, and may indeed do harm to the patient (Strupp et al., 1977). In addition, patients should be given rational alternatives, such as behaviour therapy; they might not wish to choose this alternative, but it should be available, and they should be furnished with some knowledge about the relative advantages and disadvantages of the different therapies.

Nor does it seem ethical or meaningful to demand lengthy training, usually including a medical degree of psychoanalysts and psychotherapists, when the evidence even of Smith et al. indicates clearly that the amount of training plays no part in the effectiveness of the treatment (if any); the large amounts of money paid by the State and the student for such training are clearly wasted. It is difficult to see any logical justification for the current state of affairs, which is roundly condemned both on ethical and cost-effective grounds. That such a conclusion is not popular today any more than it was in 1952 is obvious; psychiatrists and clinical psychologists who earn a living by exercising a nonexistent skill are naturally reluctant to admit the applicability of the null hypothesis to their endeavours. In due course, no doubt, the truth will become apparent even to them, but in the meantime, large amounts of money will have been wasted and many suffering patients will have their hopes and expectations destroyed and disappointed. It does not seem to me that there is a logical answer to the points here made, and it also seems to me that scientific psychology has a bounden duty to take sides in this dispute, and require better evidence than is available at the moment before any positive claims are made by practitioners for the efficacy of psychotherapy and psychoanalysis.

REFERENCES

Bergin, A. E. The evaluation of therapeutic outcomes. In A. E. Bergin, and S. L. Garfield (Eds.), *Handbook of Psychotherapy and Behavior Change.* New York: Wiley, 1971.

Bergin, A. E., and Lambert, M. J. An evaluation of therapeutic outcomes. In S. Garfield, and A. E. Bergin (Eds.), *Handbook of Psychotherapy and Behavior Change.* New York: Wiley, 1978.

Denker, P. G. Results of treatment of psychoneuroses by the general practitioner. *New York State Journal of Medicine,* 1946, 36, 2164–2166.

Erwin, E. *Behavior Therapy.* Cambridge: Cambridge University Press, 1978.

Eysenck, H. J. The effects of psychotherapy: An evaluation. *Journal of Consulting Psychology,* 1952, 16, 319–324.

Eysenck, H. J. The effects of psychotherapy. In H. J. Eysenck (Ed.), *Handbook of Abnormal Psychology: An Experimental Approach.* London: Pitman, 1960.

Eysenck, H. J. The effects of psychotherapy. *International Journal of Psychiatry,* 1965, 1, 99–144.

Eysenck, H. J. Meta-analysis: An abuse of research integration. *The Journal of Special Education,* in press.

Kazdin, A. E. *History of Behavior Modification.* Baltimore: University Park Press, 1978.

Kazdin, A. E., and Wilson, G. T. *Evaluation of Behaviour Therapy: Issues, Evidence and Research Strategies.* Cambridge: Ballinger, 1978.

Landis, C. A. A statistical evaluation of psychotherapeutic methods. In L. E. Hinsie

(Ed.), *Concepts and Problems of Psychotherapy.* New York: Columbia University Press, 1937.

Luborsky, L., Singer, B., and Luborsky, L. Comparative studies of psychotherapies. *Archives of General Psychiatry,* 1975, 32, 995–1008.

Meltzoff, J., and Korureich, M. *Research in Psychotherapy.* Chicago: Aldine, 1970.

Rachman, S., and Wilson, G. T. *The Effects of Psychotherapy.* New York: Pergamon, 1980.

Smith, M. L., Glass, G. V., and Miller, T. I. *The Benefits of Psychotherapy.* Baltimore: Johns Hopkins University Press, 1980.

Strupp, H. H., Hadley, S. W., and Gomez-Schwartz, B. *Psychotherapy for Better or Worse.* New York: Jason Aronson, 1977.

Wilder, J. Facts and figures on psychotherapy. *Journal of Clinical Psychopathology,* 1945, 7, 311–347.

Zilbergeld, B. *The Shrinking of America.* Boston: Little, Brown, and Co., 1983.

Zubin, J. Evaluation of therapeutic outcome in mental disorders. *Journal of Nervous and Mental Disease,* 1953, 117, 95–111.

Chapter 6

PROFESSIONAL DISCLOSURE: THEORY, RESEARCH, AND APPLICATION

STANLEY J. GROSS

ABSTRACT: *Professional disclosure is a structured procedure for sharing information about practitioners and their services in order to enhance consumer decision making. Increased consumer sophistication brings the need to the attention of professionals. The procedure was stimulated by Sidney Jourard's work on therapist self-disclosure and the experience with product disclosure in industry-consumer relationships. Research suggests highly complex interactions are involved that defy the common wisdom on the effect of confirming client expectations for therapy and the effect of therapist self-disclosure on client productivity and satisfaction variables, suggesting instead the need to control relevant variables and to test the effect of unique therapist information. Regulating professional disclosure hypothesizes three functions: demystifying relationships, protecting clients, and recognizing professions. Preparing professional disclosure statements requires professionals to allow increased vulnerability, clarify professional identity, acknowledge unintended effects of practice, and realistically describe purposes and philosophy.*

Several circumstances have coalesced to increase interest in professional disclosure—a means of sharing information about provider services so that potential consumers will have the knowledge to make informed decisions about the use of such services. Mass education and instant communication are generating an increasing sophistication about health and helping services among an evergrowing proportion of the American population. Many persons have the information and the inclination now to demand to play a part and have their needs met in compatible relationships with competent providers. The self-help, self-care, and consumer movements are all indications of growing trends in

Presented at the meeting of the American Psychological Association, August 23, 1982 in Washington, D.C.

62

American society to call an end to traditional professional dominance in client-provider relationships. The public is increasingly critical of what is seen as provider distance and arrogance given the exceedingly costly and questioningly effective system of health and helping services. The growing organization and militancy of "new" health and helping professions that are less committed to authority-based models also have stimulated questions about the nature and adequacy of the credentials used to verify competence.

Professional disclosure is an alternative to traditional credentialing arrangements. Providers who want to enhance informed consent by clients; professional organizations who want to encourage informed consent by clients and greater mutuality in client-provider relationships; consumers who want more reliable and valid information from their service providers; and state governments who want to regulate the flow of information about services—all will find professional disclosure to be a means to suit their purposes. The potential of disclosure, however, is limited presently by the extent of public dependency and mystification, which causes a large portion to desire protection and avoid responsibility. The following discussion assumes there is a need to educate the public to desire greater responsibility and to develop the skills to achieve it, to train providers in how to disclose, and to regulate disclosure to limit misuse.

THE NATURE OF DISCLOSURE

Self-disclosure is not understood to mean that providers share highly personal material. Johnson's (1972) definition of self-disclosure emphasizes relevance of information to the transaction between therapist and client rather than, "intimate details of your past life" (p. 10). He also indicated that self-disclosure involved specific information shared in order to improve a relationship.

Professional disclosure was probably stimulated in part by Sidney Jourard's (1968) work on therapist self-disclosure. Jourard pointed out that when clients "came to know" counselors, several things happened. First, mystification was avoided and trust, rather than defensiveness, was encouraged. Second, counselor disclosure begat client disclosure, the so-called dyadic effect. Finally, mutual openness enhanced the quality and depth of the relationship between the two. The attempts, however, to relate therapist self-disclosure to process and outcome variables have not had consistent results (Cozby, 1973; Curtis, 1981b). Attempts to relate the confirmation or disconfirmation of client expectations to process and outcome variables have shown similarly inconsistent results in reviews of research (Duckro, Bean, & George, 1979; Tinsley, Workman, & Kass, 1980). The explanations for such inconsistency provides an introduction to the complexities involved in the attempt to create more mutual client-therapist relationships.

Commonsense logic indicates that pretherapy information should promote more realistic expectations for therapy by clients. These more realistic expectations should, in turn, impact upon measures of client productivity and satisfaction. The fact that this has not been clearly substantiated has been explained, not by rejecting the logic, but by assuming that the research has not adequately attended to the complexities of the relationships involved. Curtis (1981b) points to the need for researchers to control for experimenter bias and for halo effects (separating self-disclosure per se from other aspects of interpersonal communication). Cozby (1973) cites the inadequacy of paper and pencil measures of disclosure and argues for behavioral measures.

Research related to demand characteristics reveals that the type of disclosure requested from clients makes a difference in their response (Berger, 1978). Duckro et al. (1979) found mild support for role induction as a strategy to modify pretherapy expectations toward more congruence with actual therapist style. Davidshofer and Richardson (1981) showed that the amount of information possessed by clients can be increased through a precounseling training program. Interesting as these studies are, none of them actually used self-disclosure or professional disclosure as the independent variable, substituting, instead, information about therapy. Gill and Taylor (1982) similarly use information about counseling, but in the form of a professional disclosure statement approved in advance by all counselors involved in the study. They found that clients had clearer expectations regarding their behavior and potential outcomes, but that this did not generalize to their actual behavior in counseling or their satisfaction with it. Their explanation was, "Although there was initial approval of the content of the statement by all counselors, they may not have behaved in a manner consistent with this description during each session" (p. 6). These studies suggest indirectly that what has not been tested in the research to date is valid and unique information about the therapists and their particular styles and services, the necessary content of a professional disclosure statement, which is what Jourard (1968) seemed to have in mind in the first place.

The impact of selective factors on invalidity for studies relating self-disclosure to counseling variables offers some clues to how expectancy influences therapy and support for the importance of unique information. Tinsley et al. (1980) found that clients vary in their expectations for counseling on four dimensions (in decreasing order of importance): degree of client commitment necessary, need for facilitative conditions, importance of counselor expertise, and desire for nurturance. Duckro et al. (1979) indicated that client expectancies may differ on the basis of whether a characteristic is predicted or whether it is desired. Curtis (1981a) shifts to the characteristics of the theoretical approach as influencing the efficacy of self-disclosure by therapists. He suggests that self-disclosure is appropriate for humanistic, existential, and behavioristic approaches for four reasons: The modeling effect increases client disclosure, therapist vulnerability reduces client anxiety, reciprocity and the feeling of equity increase trust; and self-disclosure promotes a strong therapeutic alliance. However, for the psychodynamic orientation, self-disclosure contaminates transference, erodes the placebo effect, contributes to patient resistance, restricts patient behavior; reduces patient motivation, and acts as a poor precedent for future sessions.

Shifting to research in medical sociology, Haug and Lavin (1981) propose a model focused on the interaction between patient orientation and physician orientation. Patients are characterized as "consumerist"—those who have been socialized to question authority—or "dependent"—those who have been socialized to accept physician authority and good will. Physicians are characterized as "take charge" types—those who are not willing to persuade or accommodate to patients—and those who are. Four types of interactions of patient-physician orientation are hypothesized. Category I interaction is between take charge physicians and consumerist patients. The result is conflict between the two. Category II interaction is between accommodating physicians and consumerist patients. In this case bargaining between the two orientations would occur. Category III puts take charge physicians together with dependent patients. A congruence of orientations occurs here. Finally, Category IV contrasts the accommodating physician with the dependent patient. The result is "an uncomfortable disjuncture (which) may decay into (the) doctor being in charge or patient may try to find a more 'take charge' doctor" (p.223). Of the four situations only one, condition II, is the situation structured so that the parties involved would be open to either self-disclosure or professional disclosure. Such information would not be of any interest to either party in condition III. In conditions I and IV professional disclosure may confuse the parties. The lack of disclosure in I and disclosure in IV would warn the patients that they would not likely find what they want in the physician.

Research and theory related to selective factors suggest that the efficacy of unique disclosure should vary according to: (a) the content of client expectations (commitment, conditions, expertise, nurturance), (b) whether these client expectations deal with predicted or preferred characteristics, (c) the therapist's orientation to treatment, and (d) the interaction between the two sets of expectations on the authority/ responsibility issue. Research needs to be done that controls for the factors cited in order to determine the selective impact of disclosure: When does disclosure fit the needs of the parties and their social context? To what extent may disclosure change the context and the needs?

In the meantime, Duckro et al. (1979) suggest that caution is the wisest course.

> Clearly, the conclusion that it is important to meet client role expectations in psychotherapy does not deserve the sustained support that it has received. It must be removed from its status as *demonstrated* in the common wisdom of psychology. (p. 269)

Nor is it appropriate to assume that disclosure in the hands of all therapists will necessarily enhance relationships, increase client responsibility, demystification, or self-protection, clarify or make expectations more realistic, or change the approach of therapists. Presently, disclosure is merely a means by which therapists can increase the amount and quality of information they share with potential clients. Other impacts are not consistently demonstrated, may be selective in their power to influence, and depend on the intent of the therapist.

PROFESSIONAL DISCLOSURE AND REGULATION

The use of professional disclosure in health and helping services was also probably stimulated in part by information disclosure about products that emerged as an expression of the consumer movement. Aaker and Day (1978) indicate that product information disclosure requirements have proliferated at a great rate since 1970 as a result of efforts to enhance consumers' "right to know." Consumer-movement proponents see that information improves product quality and competition, because it encourages consumers to compare products and better match them to their needs. Businessmen see it as a way of reducing complaints that result from product misuse, from improper maintenance, and from purchase of the wrong product for the buyer's purpose. Providing consumer information also has had policy implications such as promoting interest in nutrition and energy conservation. Regulation of consumer information has been seen to be necessitated by self-serving industrial promotion efforts that leave consumers to find the search for information to be complex and the cost of their searching for information to be high when compared to their yield of useful information. The result, according to Aaker and Day (1978), is a small amount of consumer search even in complex and risky product categories.

Research on product-oriented information disclosure indicates a primary benefit to middle-class consumers, who can opt to act on the information, but little evidence of effect on buyer search or choice behavior. Information does enhance confidence in choice by reassuring the buyer about the product adequacy, appropriateness, and price (Day, 1976). Product information disclosure requirements change the marketing environment for businessmen who must adjust their procedures to minimize adverse effects and exploit opportunities. Day (1976) suggests trade association leadership to voluntarily provide needed information as the best way to avoid highly restrictive disclosure regulation.

Professional disclosure statements have been suggested (Gross, 1977, 1981) as one part of a system of state regulation that would replace the more restrictive practice and title acts now used to license professionals and is also included in proposed licensing legislation for counselors (Gill, 1982). Professional disclosure emerges as one alternative to licensure from the search to find ways to counter the tendency for the professions to use state licensure to advance their own self-interest by monopolizing service markets. The conclusion that licensing serves the professions rather than the public is commonplace in the scholarly literatures of sociology and economics. Such respected researchers as

George Stigler (1971), Lee Benham (1980), and Eliot Freidson (1970) have found licensing to be primarily in the interest of the professions. Licensing grants a monopoly of a service area which, in turn, results in increased income, prestige, and career insurance for providers. State licensing is the key to the monopoly, since it is not just knowledge but the *control* of knowledge that provides the professions with an exclusive mandate to limit information dissemination in a designated area (Freidson, 1973; Krause, 1977).

The self-serving nature of this arrangement would not be questioned if licensing fulfilled its purposes of protecting the public against quacks and incompetents. It is clear, however, that self-regulation by the professions themselves does not serve the public interest (Daniels, 1973; Mechanic, 1976), nor does the state operated licensing authority, which primarily serves the interests of professional groups, according to recent reports by state legislative study commissions (Ayadi, 1977, in Michigan; Haberfield et al., 1978 and Summerfield, 1978, in California; Payne, 1977, in the State of Washington; and Whitesel, 1977, in Wisconsin). These conclusions are substantiated by the finding that neither competency nor quality are defined operationally in terms that provide clear benefit to the public and that traditional credentials, at best, only presume competence (Koocher, 1979; McClelland, 1973; National, 1982). Further, Cohen and Miike (1974) indicate that licensing boards fail to fulfill the necessary functions of providing public protection. Assessment of initial competency generally relies on invalid criteria, emphasizing the amount of knowledge rather than its application (Koocher, 1979; Mechanic, 1979). Monitoring continued competence has not progressed beyond mandating continuing education, a questionably effective activity, at best (Shimberg, 1977). Licensing creates rather than ameliorates the problems of distribution of professionals and utilization of paraprofessionals (Roemer, 1970). Licensing boards have been indifferent to their disciplinary role of dealing with the incompetency of professionals and mostly directing their activities toward prosecuting unlicensed practitioners (Krause, 1977).

The criticism of licensing as a consumer protection device and the rhetoric of professionals supporting licensing out of a concern for public welfare is certainly at odds and raises questions about the credibility of professionals. Though the public is generally apathetic, the criticism of the professions has been increasing. The complex system of licensure is entrenched, but it is vulnerable. Mechanic (1976) indicates that sophisticated consumers have been straining the conventional "doctor-patient" relationship. The self-help, self-care, and consumer movements are indicators of a developing trend to change the relationship between consumers and professionals so that effective service and information are available inexpensively. There is no "going back," as these changes have been generated by mass education and instant communication. Further changes in information utilization may be expected as computer technology impacts on consumer knowledge and ways of serving the public. Professions will need to change to accommodate to increased consumer sophistication. Licensing is an antiquated and rigid structure that will change as professionals adapt to roles that emphasize advisory and educational functions as opposed to decision and, in the case of psychology and the major health professions, treatment functions. Concern will become foremost about the quality of information rather than the control of information by professionals. Thus, it is in the long term interest of professionals to explore alternative ways of achieving credibility.

Less restrictive regulation (acts restricting the use of the title "psychologist" rather than restricting the practice of psychology) is a likely outcome of these changes in the client-provider relationship. Fewer restrictions would stimulate competition among the professions that would, in turn, cause them to increase the information they share with the public about the nature of their services. The hope is that this would direct more and higher quality information to the public and afford consumers the opportunity to become more responsible for their own choosing, and thus be more genuinely self-protecting. The problem remains, though, that even when providers compete with one another, the very imbalance of information between them and consumers encourages consumer mystification and dependency. It is also true that many consumers do not want to be bothered or confused, so they are not open to receiving information. The potential for provider deception in such a circumstance would still require some regulation of information presented to the public. A professional disclosure statute is one way of regulating the quality of information disseminated to the public.

The assumption underlying professional disclosure statements is that the public would be in a better position to evaluate the competence of practitioners if it had high quality information about the services offered. The opportunity to accept responsibility would be permitted by actual disclosure of quality information where presently it is made difficult by monopoly and information control. The choice to be self-protecting would be more likely than at Present, with licensing acts that assume a public protection attitude. Schutz (1981) articulately espouses a more appropriate role for government.

> The government is not in a good position to decide on technical competence. It *is* in a good position to make certain that people tell the truth. The holistic education approach to licensing would expect truth from therapists and self-responsibility from clients. This may be accomplished through requiring therapists to post publicly, and to make available to prospective clients, full disclosure of all their qualifications—education, experience, and so forth. It is then the responsibility of the client to select a therapist. The government's role is to assure that the therapist's statements are true and to punish lying. (p. 384)

Schutz's goal would be implemented by a professional disclosure statute that would require (under penalty of revoking permission to practice and invoking suitable fines) conspicuous posting of statements, sharing statements with potential clients before services are received, and filing statements in a state office charged with investigating irregularities in statements, fraudulent or misleading statements, and complaints from consumers about services and statements.

The function of introducing accurate information about provider qualifications and services into the relationship between providers and consumers is to decrease the mystification of the consumers. Regulating the accuracy of the disclosure permits a second function of increasing protection of the public. Attaching disclosure to a registration act offers a third function giving professions an opportunity for public recognition.

Demystification

The result of the monopolization of knowledge by the licensed professions has been an inequality in the amount of information held by clients and professionals and in their influence over one another. In order to maintain power, professionals establish a social distance, where there is also inequality in personal informational disclosure, with the result that a climate of mutual mistrust develops. Lopata (1976) reports

> Particularly in "personal" service occupations, the client is expected to supply information about the self in order for the expert to convert generalized

knowledge into relevant case application. The expert does not traditionally reveal any personal information about herself or himself. (p. 440)

To do so weakens the authority of the professional. The authority rests on the sense of mystification created by the unequal information. If clients knew the professional's background and purposes, and if clients believed that they could know what professionals know, much of the structure responsible for dependency and for much of the mystery underlying the placebo effect would evaporate, resulting in the equalization of authority. However, the essential role of the professional—the organization and dissemination of knowledge—would remain. Reiff (1974) is convinced that

If the institution of professionalism—its educational systems and organizations— were compelled to share their power with society, it would inevitably result in the democratization of knowledge and a new social contract between the professions and the society that supports them and the clients they serve. (p. 459)

Gone too would be the strong supports for "the indifferent, dehumanized, self-perpetuating, entrepreneurial enterprise characteristic of professionalism today" (p. 461). What would be gained would be the fuller participation of clients in their own problem solving, in the prevention of their problems, and in a maximizing of their potentials.

To change the authority balance so it is more nearly equal, it is essential to help more than merely a small, already knowledgable and assertive minority to become self-determining and self-responsible. Expecting consumers to protect themselves implies an informed, or at least informable, public. In this regard, Rogers (1973) quotes Richard Farson, who believes, "The population which has the problem possesses the best resources for dealing with it" (p. 383). Consumers have the capacity and the responsibility to protect themselves. They have experience with the service and its consequences and the potential energy to do something about it. What they need is sufficient information to make sense of their experience and to overcome their mystifying dependence. It is clear that it is not knowledge itself but its control that is at the base of the inequality of authority. It follows, as Reiff (1974) has said, that "If every professional were required to educate his clients and the public about what he is doing and why, the power of professionalism would be substantially weakened" (p. 460).

Protection

If competition between service givers were to become a reality, it would be most likely that more information in the form of advertising would be directed toward the public. According to a Federal Trade Commission report (1979)

an increase in the number of sellers in a market not only increases the number of potential sources of information; it also reduces the likelihood that sellers will be able to agree (either tacitly or through explicit collusion) to cut back on information dissemination. (p. 191)

The converse is also true—increased information sources in most cases encourage competition by aiding the entry of new sellers into the market. This was the basis of FTC activity that was directed at loosening self-imposed advertising restrictions in the professions. The FTC targeted physicians, dentists, accountants, veterinarians, and funeral directors. A Supreme Court decision (*Bates v. State Bar of Arizona*, 1977) and the voluntary removal of advertising prohibitions by private associations ultimately made FTC action unnecessary. The benefits noted by the FTC include reduced cost of consumer searching, increased competition, lower prices, increased access for new entrants, service to previously underserved groups in society, and an increase in alternative service providers. Specific drawbacks included a failure to affect other advertising-inhibiting restraints, an unsubstantiated concern that quality of services might be affected, and the need to police deceptive advertising.

Advertising is a fact of life in our highly mobile lives and in our anonymous communities. In effect, advertising replaces word-of-mouth communication and personal experience with products and services that existed in earlier times and in communities where change was not a constant and communication actually reached most decision makers. This began to change during the nineteenth century, which is identified as the height of the caveat emptor era in America. During this time, "sellers apparently did not distinguish between giving consumers objective information and motivating them to buy. They seemed to recognize only two choices—provide truthful information or provide false information" (FTC, 1979, p. 148). In markets characterized by an oversupply of products or services, false and deceptive information became viable alternatives to the truth as sellers attempted to distinguish themselves from one another. False information increasingly became a target for regulation, but deceptive information (including such subjective claims as puffery, social-psychological claims, and nonverbal images) proved more difficult to control. The question of how to tailor restrictions on deceptive or unfair advertising so as not to stifle "truthful commercial speech" (FTC, 1979, p. 180) remains hard to answer.

The FTC has used "affirmative" disclosure of information as the "backbone of . . . [its] initiatives to enhance the quality and quantity of information available to consumers" (p. 276). Disclosure has been a remedy "for deception by omission or by misleading implications . . . [and] to correct unfairness generated by the imbalance in information availability between buyer and seller" (p. 276).

Recognition

The logic supporting the attempt by new professions to gain state licensing is that legal recognition makes professions legitimate in the public eye. Legal recognition is thought to be an attribute of a mature profession, granting prestige synonymous with that of established professions to a new profession. This gives practitioners credibility that they would not have if the statutory authority of the state were not enlisted. Increasingly, as third parties, such as insurance companies and the federal government, pay an ever larger share of health providers' charges, state licensing is requested to identify which providers should be reimbursed for their fees. Unlicensed professions lose out in the competition, even in nonmonopoly service markets, because their services are not eligible for third-party payments. Thus, the logic finds licensing to be essential to the recognition and eligibility necessary to compete with other provider professions. Professional disclosure is not seen by some to provide for these functions (Witmer, 1978). However, if professional disclosure were to be part of a registration statute, the registration act itself would provide legal recognition similar to licensing acts. Thus, recognition for new professions would be forthcoming without supporting monopolistic practices or encouraging the public to falsely believe a license offers them protection against quacks and incompetents. By offering accurate information to consumers in an environment of information and service oversight, professional disclosure offers a greater degree of protection and stimulates the public to be informed and encouraged to protect itself.

The question of finding a competency test to meet the needs of third-party payers to replace the competency inferred from the licensing process is beyond the purposes of this paper. This function, however, can be fulfilled by the provider professions themselves (e.g. American Board of Professional Psychology), as long as they are supervised by an accrediting agency that ensures they meet appropriate standards. This is now being done by the National Commission for Health Certifying Agencies.

THE PROFESSIONAL DISCLOSURE STATUTE

Regulating professional disclosure is a remedy for the inequality of authority, a means to restrain advertisers from false and deceptive claims, and an alternate way to recognize the status of professions. The following example is drawn from specific experience with a professional disclosure statute for counselors, though it is generalizable to other professions. It was first described by Gross (1977).

The professional disclosure statute has the purpose of increasing consumer access to information relative to the type and quality of service available. It assumes that accurate information about the service offered by a practitioner is the consumer's best chance for getting what he or she wants and needs and the best protection against harm and exploitation. It would give consumers information to aid in their evaluation of the competency of counselors, and in their mutual compatibility it would restrict counselors to doing what they say in their statement they will do.

The statute would provide a system of honest professional disclosure to prospective clients by those who designate themselves as counselors and would require the registration of this disclosure. It would not regulate who can or cannot do counseling. The disclosure would include name, business address and telephone number, philosophy of counseling, specifics of formal education, particulars of informal education and association memberships, and fee schedule.

The method by which the statute would be implemented includes these provisions: (a) Disclosure would be made to prospective clients before any counseling for which a fee may be charged. Disclosure would be legible, on a printed form, and posted conspicuously. (b) The fact that disclosure would be required would be disclosed, including information about the particular department of state government that oversees the procedure, so that a complainant would know to whom a complaint is to be made. (c) A notarized form would be filed annually or whenever a change in the statement would be made. (d) Additional disclosure forms would be necessary for supervisors and employers. (e) Complaints would be made to the department of state government that has responsibility for investigation and public hearings. (f) Provision would be made for privilege of counselor records during processing of complaints. (g) Judicial review of decisions would be possible. (h) The offense covered by the statute would be the willful filing of false or incomplete information. (i) Punishment would include the judgment of "misdemeanor" and the prohibition from practice.

There has been some interest in the counseling field for professional disclosure, though to date no law requiring professional disclosure has been implemented. Winborn (1977) uses the concept of "honest labeling," but describes a similar system of disclosure. Witmer (1978) does not think professional disclosure should stand alone but instead should be a part of a counselor licensing statute. Swanson (1979) shows how the disclosure concept could be used as an alternative to or complement of a statement provided by a counselor in a community directory of counseling services. Gill (1982) offers some aid to counselors attempting to write such statements and gives some examples of statements appropriate for different settings. The California Board of Medical Quality Assurance Proposal (1982) suggests professional disclosure as an alternative to licensure and ties it to a system of registration. The proposal includes the following:

1. Unlicensed practitioners would be required to register, file copies of disclosure statements, and document any claimed training.
   a. A registration fee would be collected to cover an aggressive enforcement program.
   b. Parameters would be specified for use of titles, degrees, etc.
2. Registered practitioners would be required to give each patient full disclosure of
   a. Training and education,
   b. Experience,
   c. The procedures the practitioner intends to offer or use,
   d. A disclaimer indicating the state does not evaluate credentials,

test competence, or in any way certify as to the practitioner's knowledge, competence, efficacy, or safety.

3. Stiff fines or other penalties would be specified for
   a. Unregistered practice
   b. Failure to observe disclosure requirements,
   c. False or misleading advertising.

ISSUES IN PREPARING
PROFESSIONAL DISCLOSURE STATEMENTS

Preparing a professional disclosure statement poses some problems for traditional socialized professionals. The statement is to be written to serve the interests of the consumer rather than to protect the interests of the provider or the profession. The effects intended are to increase the body of usable information held by the consumer, positively affect consumer self-responsibility and decision making, and reduce the social distance between professional and consumer. Four issues emerge in the preparation of statements to suit such purposes.

Vulnerability

The first issue to be confronted by the preparer is the resistance to disclosure. The emotional basis of such resistance is revealed by feelings of vulnerability by the provider, which are associated with the increase in the power of the consumer in a mutual relationship. Giving information away as the professional disclosure statement does, in a professional milieu that values information control for its power and economic advantages, will cause the well-socialized professional to feel more exposed. Because they will receive little support from their professional organization, providers need to have a strong belief that consumers deserve accurate and understandable information. Even the relatively strong statement in the 1981 *Ethical Standards* of the American Personnel and Guidance Association is not very specific as to the procedure. Section B, item 7 says

> The member must inform the client of the purposes, goals, techniques, rules of procedure and limitations that may affect the relationship at or before the time that the counseling relationship is entered. (p. 3)

Psychologists are enjoined by the 1981 *Ethical Principles of Psychologists* to represent their professional qualifications, affiliations, and functions both accurately and objectively. Principle 4 sets guidelines and gives examples to aid psychologists. The purposes of these public statements is to aid the public in making informed judgments and choices, but there is no indication that psychologists *should* do so. The 1977 *Standards for Providers of Psychological Services,* adopted by the American Psychological Association, indicates only that "users" should have information about the composition and organization of a psychological services unit. None of this has the specificity to constitute much support. The effect of the lack of organizational support is to enhance resistance to disclosure efforts and leave potential disclosers isolated and vulnerable.

Professional Identity

The ability to prepare an effective professional disclosure statement is related to the clarity of the provider's professional identity and belief in the activities of his/her practice. Gill (1982) describes the benefit of clarifying professional identity in terms of the practitioner's professional development. The practitioner must define his or her competencies and must examine "Personal beliefs, values, strengths and weaknesses, and goals regarding the client relationship" (p. 444). Effective professional disclosure states the qualifications and intentions of the provider in language free of jargon. In preparing the statement the provider must develop a point of view both well-substantiated by theory and professional practice norms and at the same time not hide behind jargon or ignore the questions the profession has not settled.

Unintended Effects

Though it is the function of science to note and catalogue the unintended side-effects and abuses of professional strategies and procedures, individual practitioners may be loath to acknowledge that *their* interventions may have negative effects. Professional norms tend to work against providers acknowledging their contribution to unintended effects. The focus upon process rather than upon outcome measures of performance, and the inhibition of feedback from consumers and colleagues are two ways professional norms assist providers to ignore the consequences of their acts. Providers who do not know the unintended effects of their procedures will have to study their clients and gain feedback from them. Those who do know about such effects will need to examine their procedures and find a way to describe such effects so that their potential clients, who both need and want the service the provider offers, will have an accurate basis for decision making.

Accurate Expectations

Given the clarity of professional identification, the desire to inform consumers accurately, and the willingness to describe unintended effects, there remains the issue of carefully expressing purposes and philosophy. The goal is to have consumers understand what the provider intends in positive terms without promising more than can be realistically delivered. Providers need to make decisions about what expectations are legitimate and useful and what is important about their work and structure this concisely and clearly into their statements.

There is a tendency for professionals to be concerned with protecting their own interests and those of their professions. Professional organizations support measures that do no more than pay lip service to an ideal of concern for consumer interests (ethical codes are widely recognized as not serving to actually protect the public). Instead, professional organizations support practices, professional socialization strategies, and an identity protective of the interests of professionals. It is no wonder that interest in professional disclosure by providers is relatively low at this time. When there is greater attention given to the questions of consumers, or when a reduction in monopoly protection occurs, more interest might be expected. Nonetheless, professional disclosure is revealed to be a potentially powerful, if essentially untested, tool for expanding consumer knowledge.

REFERENCES

Aaker, D. A., and Day, G. S. (Editors). *Consumerism: Search for the Consumer Interest* (Third Edition). New York: Free Press, 1978.

American Personnel and Guidance Association. *Ethical Standards.* Falls Church, VA: Author, 1981.

American Psychological Association. *Ethical Principles of Psychologists* (Rev. Ed.). Washington, D.C.: Author, 1981.

American Psychological Association. *Standards for Providers of Psychological Services* (Rev. Ed.). Washington, D.C.: Author, 1977.

Ayadi, N. (Comp. and Ed.), *Report of the Special Committee to Investigate the Department of Licensing and Registration.* Lansing, Michigan: House of Representatives, 1977.

Benham, L. The demand for occupational licensure. In S. Rottenberg (Ed.) *Occupational Licensure and Regulation.* Washington, D.C.: American Enterprise Institute, 1980.

Berger, S. N. The effects of different sets of disclosure instructions on subject productivity and rated satisfaction. *Journal of Counseling Psychology,* 1978, *25,* 506–513.

Board of Medical Quality Assurance. *2052 Study: The legal definition of the practice of medicine.* Sacramento, CA: State of California Department of Consumer Affairs, 1982.

Cohen, H. S., and Miike, L. H. Toward a more responsive system of professional licensure. *International Journal of Health Services,* 1974, *4*(2), 265–272.

Cozby, P. C. Self-disclosure: A literature review. *Psychological Bulletin,* 1973, *79,* 73–91.

Curtis, J. M. Indications and contraindications in the use of therapist's self-disclosure. *Psychological Reports,* 1981, *49,* 499–507. (a)

Curtis, J. M. Effects of therapist's self-disclosure on patient's impressions of empathy, competence, and trust in an analogue of a psychotherapeutic interaction. *Psychological Reports,* 1981, *48,* 127–136. (b)

Daniels, A. K. How free should professions be? In E. Freidson (Ed.), *The Professions and Their Prospects.* Beverly Hills: Sage Publications, 1973.

Davidshofer, C. O., and Richardson, G. G. Effects of precounseling training. *Journal of College Student Personnel,* 1981, *22,* 522–527.

Day, G. S. Assessing the effects of information disclosure requirements. *Journal of Marketing,* 1976, *40,* 42–52.

Duckro, P., Bean, D., and George, C. Research on the effects of disconfirmed client rate expectations in psychotherapy: A critical review. *Psychological Bulletin,* 1979, *86,* 260–275.

Federal Trade Commission. *Consumer information remedies: Policy session.* Washington, D.C.: U.S. Government Printing Office, 1979.

Freidson, E. *Professional Dominance.* New York: Atherton, 1970.

Freidson, E. (Ed.). *The Professions and Their Prospects.* Beverly Hills: Sage Publications, 1973.

Gill, S. J. Professional disclosure and consumer protection in counseling. *Personnel and Guidance Journal,* 1982, *60,* 443–446.

Gill, S. J., and Taylor, S. H. *The effects of a counselor professional disclosure statement on client expectations, behavior, and satisfaction.* Paper presented at the American Psychological Association Convention, Washington, DC, 1982.

Gross, S. J. Professional disclosure: An alternative to licensing. *Personnel and Guidance Journal,* 1977, *55,* 586–588.

Gross, S. J. The myth of professional licensing. *American Psychologist,* 1978, *33,* 1009–1016.

Gross, S. J. Public policy implications for studies on licensing and competency. *Rutgers Professional Psychology Review,* 1980, *2,* 5–14.

Gross, S. J. Holistic perspective on professional licensure. *Journal of Holistic Medicine,* 1981, *3,* 38–45.

Haberfield, S., Saxby, D., and Schletter, D. The problem of occupational licensure in perspective. In *Professional Licensing in California.* California Department of Consumer Affairs, 1978.

Haug, M., and Lavin, B. Practitioner or patient: Who's in charge? *Journal of Health and Social Behavior,* 1981, *22,* 212–229.

Johnson, D. W. *Reaching Out.* Englewood Cliffs, N.J.: Prentice-Hall, 1972.

Jourard, S. M. *Disclosing Man to Himself.* Princeton, NJ: D. Van Nostrand Co., 1968.

Koocher, G. P. Credentialing in psychology: Close encounters with competence. *American Psychologist,* 1979, *34,* 696–702.

Krause, E. A. *Power and Illness.* New York: Elsevier, 1977.

Lopata, H. Z. Expertization of everyone and the revolt of the client. *The Sociological Quarterly,* 1976, *17,* 435–447.

McClelland, D. C. Testing for competence rather than "intelligence." *American Psychologist,* 1973, *28,* 1–14.

Mechanic, D. *The Growth of Bureaucratic Medicine.* New York: Wiley, 1976.

Mechanic, D. *Future Issues in Health Care.* New York: The Free Press, 1979.

National Academies of Practice formed. *Professional Regulation News,* 1982, *1*(10), 2–3.

Payne, P. E. *Licensure: Professions and Occupations.* Report to the House of Representatives Commerce Committee, State of Washington, Olympia, Washington, 1977.

Reiff, R. The control of knowledge: The power of the helping professions. *The Journal of Applied Behavioral Science,* 1974, *10,* 451–461.

Roemer, M. Controlling and promoting quality in medical care. *Law and Contemporary Problems,* 1970, *35*(2), 284–304.

Rogers, C. R. Some new challenges. *American Psychologist,* 1973, *28,* 379–387.

Schutz, W. Holistic education. In R. J. Corsini (Ed.), *Handbook of Innovative Psychotherapies.* New York: John Wiley and Sons, 1981.

Shimberg, B. S. Continuing education and licensing. In D. W. Vermilye (Ed.) *Relating Work and Education.* San Francisco: Jossey-Bass, 1977.

Stigler, G. J. The theory of economic regulation. *The Bell Journal of Economics and Management Science,* 1971, *2*(1), 3–21.

Summerfield, H. L. *Review of Psychology Examining Committee and State Board of Behavioral Science Examiners: A Report of the Regulatory Review Task Force.* California Department of Consumer Affairs, 1978.

Swanson, J. L. Counseling directory and consumer guide: Implementing professional disclosure and consumer protection. *Personnel and Guidance Journal,* 1979, *58,* 190–193.

Tinsley, H. E. A., Workman, K. R., and Kass, R. A. Factor analyses of the domain of client expectancies about counseling. *Journal of Counseling Psychology,* 1980, *27,* 561–570.

Whitesel, R. *Regulation and licensing: An overview.* Legislative Council Staff Research Bulletin 76–7, State Capitol, Madison, Wisconsin, 1977.

Winborn, B. B. Honest labeling and other procedures for the protection of consumers of counseling. *Personnel and Guidance Journal,* 1977, *56,* 206–209.

Witmer, J. M. Professional disclosure in licensure. *Counselor Education and Supervision,* 1978, *18,* 71–73.

Chapter 7

ARE PSYCHIATRISTS, SOCIAL WORKERS, AND CLINICAL PSYCHOLOGISTS REALLY DOING THEIR JOBS?

Richard P. Halgin and Dana D. Weaver

During the past thirty years there have been revolutionary changes in the field of mental health. Resulting from an increased concern with psychological well-being, there has been dramatic growth in those professions which respond to the emotional needs of people. Three specific professions have evolved and prospered in this revolution: psychiatry, clinical psychology, and psychiatric social work. Never before have there been more professionals devoting their energies to the advancement of intrapsychic and interpersonal harmony. Unquestionably, society has benefitted from the professionalization of these three mental health professions; however, in recent years a significant problem has arisen that could easily threaten the future of the mental health field. Simply stated, the problem is that each of these professions has moved substantially away from its original purpose; psychiatrists no longer want to practice medicine, social workers no longer want to do case work, and clinical psychologists no longer want to do research. What does everyone want to do? Psychotherapy.

The practice of psychotherapy is very attractive for so many reasons, both psychological and financial in nature. Individuals are attracted to such work out of a humanitarian concern to better the world through providing assistance to those in need. In addition to such an admirable rationale, there are other attractions which may not always be realized consciously or discussed objectively. For example, many individuals aspire to be psychotherapists because the work seems exciting and challenging; fantasies abound in which one can daily rescue the less fortunate from their psychological pain. Narcissistic strivings can be

82

gratified by the thought that as a psychotherapist one can easily become a central figure in the lives of so many people. The pulls of subtle voyeurism, curiosity, or just plain nosiness may attract one to a line of work that gives legitimized cause for inquiring into the lives and secrets of others. Add to this complex of needs and motives one powerful component in the process of choosing a career: the promise of a modicum of financial security, and possibly even considerable wealth. All these factors add up to making the profession of the psychotherapist a very appealing one indeed. Yet there is one problem: no such profession yet exists. *Psychotherapy* per se has not been sanctioned as an independent profession; nevertheless, it has been attained by many individuals through a variety of legitimized routes. Most commonly, these routes have included medical training followed by psychiatric specialization, social work graduate school, or clinical psychology doctoral training. Thousands of individuals appear to have "suffered" through these standard academic training procedures with the exclusive determination to discard most of their training and become psychotherapists who are licensed in the professional categories of psychiatrist, psychologist, or social worker.

Interesting "scripts" have evolved for aspiring psychotherapists who are applying for admission to programs in medicine, social work, or clinical psychology. It has become fairly well known that applicants should say certain things to enhance their likelihood of acceptance, and should definitely *not* say certain other things. The medical school applicant is supposed to espouse a pledge to community medicine; the social work applicant is supposed to swear a commitment to the underprivileged; and the clinical psychology applicant is supposed to express an overwhelming yearning to become immersed in research. Though each of these applicants is permitted to express mild interest in the acquisition of psychotherapeutic skills, s/he should not indicate that becoming a psychotherapist is a primary aim; under no circumstances should the applicant admit to anyone that becoming a private practitioner is the real goal. Those applicants with the most convincing scripts are the ones who are admitted, and a good number of them willingly endure the designated (though irrelevant) training program in order to become psychotherapists.

The purpose of this chapter is to examine this professional travesty that has plagued the field of mental health. It will be suggested that the members of each of these three professions go back home, back to the work for which they were trained and commissioned—back to medicine, back to case work, and back to research. This return home need not necessitate abandonment of their psychotherapeutic endeavors, but it is recommended that psychotherapy be done within the context of the specialized mission of each of these professions. Psychiatrists should reestablish familiarity with medical practice, becoming once again able to deal comfortably with physical and medical concerns that affect emotional functioning. Social workers should once again immerse themselves in tasks that address the well-being of clients in the social context. Psychologists should return to the scientific base of knowledge and model of inquiry, so that new clinical areas can be investigated and new findings evaluated. The field of mental health, and ultimately those in need of psychological help, will certainly benefit from each of these professionals carrying out well the work for which s/he is prepared. An additional proposal will be proffered that recommends the establishment and legitimization of a field of *Psychotherapy,* which most logically might take up its existence within the structure of the professional schools of psychology.

What follows is a discussion of some of the problems that exist in the current systems of training and professional functioning in the three major fields in mental health. Some of the absurdities found in each of these fields will be pointed out, and recommendations will be made that the fields of psychiatry, social work, and clinical psychology should train practitioners to work within their unique specialties.

PSYCHIATRY

Historically, psychiatrists have enjoyed the status and prestige of leadership within the mental health field, and have also received the highest salaries (Sundberg, Taplin, & Tyler, 1983). They have benefitted from the general respect that is accorded to all physicians, and within mental health they have accrued particular power from the medical model of mental illness and treatment that has been the rule for the past century. Ironically, the medical knowledge and expertise that led to psychiatrists achieving such prominence has diminished alarmingly during the past few decades.

Many individuals who wish to become professional psychotherapists recognize that there are quicker and easier routes to such a goal, such as social work schools or professional schools of psychology. Still, psychiatrists enjoy far greater professional autonomy and financial security than any of the alternative professions; so, for many, the grueling undertaking of medical training seems worth it all in the end. What is distressing is the degree to which this base of medical knowledge is subsequently abandoned by so many psychiatrists, who go on to become professional psychotherapists rather than physicians specializing in *comprehensive* psychodiagnosis and psychotherapy.

Psychiatrists have an advantage of being able to carry out truly comprehensive diagnostic evaluations and treatment programs. They should be able to evaluate not only the roles of intrapsychic and interpersonal factors in emotional disorder, but also the roles of genetic, neurological, and other biological factors. Where appropriate, they should be able to provide treatment programs that incorporate medical interventions.

When psychoanalysis began to evolve within the field of psychiatry, especially during the 1940s and 1950s, no one predicted that the result would be a decline in medical knowledge and practice by psychiatrists. However, few psychiatrists do comprehensive physical evaluations or medical history taking when initiating treatment with patients. Many of the patients who could benefit from such evaluations and treatments are being seen by nonmedical professionals such as psychologists, social workers, or nonmedically oriented psychiatrists. Psychologists and social workers who confront a patient with an emotional disorder of possible physical etiology are unlikely to consult with a psychiatrist, because the psychiatrist very often is no more knowledgeable about the physical problem than they are. This should not be the case. The psychiatrist should be the medical specialist in the realm of mental health who is comfortable and familiar with the gamut of disorders affecting emotional functioning, from neurological disorders to dietary problems and somatopsychological disorders.

During the 1970s there were rapid advancements in neurochemistry and psychopharmacology, resulting in speculation that psychiatry was renewing old alliances with medicine (Karasu, Stein, & Charles, 1975). However, surveys found that psychiatric residents continued to move away from an identification with medicine and increasingly toward analytically oriented psychotherapy. Greden and Casariego (1975) found that if a distinction between psychotherapeutic and somatic orientations were employed, 95 percent of the psychiatric respondents would be classified as psychotherapeutic. Langsley and Hollender (1982) surveyed 483 psychiatric practitioners and educators in an attempt to qualify the definition of a psychiatrist. The highest ranked single skill deemed necessary for a psychiatrist was perceived to be the ability to develop and implement a treatment program of any type. Importantly, the ability to provide supportive psychotherapy was the next ranked skill and was considered more important than the ability to prescribe psychoactive medication or treat neurological problems. For a period during the 1970s, a medical student going into a psychiatric residency was not even required to have a medical internship. Fortunately, the American Psychiatric Association recognized the detrimental consequences of such an omission in the training sequence and reinstituted a medical internship as a training requirement. If other changes in both the training and practice of psychiatry could be brought about so that medical expertise would return to the field, there would very likely be an increase in the number of medical students opting for this specialty. Sierles (1982) reported a ten year decline in the number of medical school graduates entering psychiatric residencies; Weintraub, Balis, and Donner (1980) specifically found that the rate of medical graduates choosing psychiatry as a career dropped from 10 percent to 4 percent since World War II. Many psychiatric residency slots currently go unfilled.

Not only have psychiatrists lost interdisciplinary credibility because of their deficient practice of medicine, but even within the medical field they are held in low regard by their colleagues. Yager, Lamotte, Nielsen, and Eaton (1982) discovered that within the medical school community, psychiatry is viewed as a specialty with low prestige and little scientific precision. A dramatic turnaround in this trend could be effected if psychiatry were willing to return to its medical roots and serve a function that is desperately needed in the field of mental health. One very promising response to this crisis in psychiatry has been formulated at West Virginia University and the University of Virginia medical schools (Shemo, Ballinger, Yazel, & Spradlin, 1982). These universities have developed a teaching and clinical program that leads to partial integration of their departments of psychiatry and internal medicine; this collaborative approach consists of conjoint programs in internal medicine and behavioral medicine, which lead to Board eligibility in both specialties. Indeed, this is good news that reflects the growing alarm in the field of medicine about the lack of medical knowledge possessed by most psychiatrists. It is time for psychiatrists to once again be physicians.

SOCIAL WORK

Social work as a profession has historically concerned itself with tasks of social advocacy, community work, the establishment of appropriate resource systems for the needy, and a number of other functions, all dedicated to the facilitation of social harmony and the emotional well-being of designated clients. In recent years, social workers have been attracted to more clinical aspects of their field, and have become increasingly involved in providing traditional psychotherapy (Johnson & Rubin, 1983). The consequence of this redefinition of the professional role is that social workers often no longer wish to do that for which they were trained and commissioned, and the field of social work has become the most expedient route to becoming a licensed independent practitioner of psychotherapy. In many social work schools, the students are tolerating that part of their education deemed irrelevant to their career goals, just as the clinical psychology students tolerate statistics courses and aspiring psychiatrists tolerate anatomy courses. But who will take on the tasks to which social workers formerly responded? A second, more difficult question is whether the limited psychotherapy training that most social workers presently receive is sufficient to qualify them as psychotherapists.

Wallace (1982) asserts that social workers are becoming more attracted to private practice because employment within an agency allows little room for professional advancement, and the status, salary, and working conditions are inappropriate. Also, many of those who choose private practice discover that they have an advantage over psychiatrists in that clients report less experience of stigma than they would associate with seeing a "shrink." Many social workers who once aspired to a career as agency caseworkers felt driven out of the agency system upon discovering that rather than doing case work, they were expected to carry out a myriad of administrative functions such as supervision, program evaluation, and administrative planning. (Schodek, 1981).

Though the social work establishment engaged in vigorous debate in the 1950s about whether social workers should engage in exclusive clinical practice, that debate has since subsided. As Wallace (1982) notes, the field has formally sanctioned clinical practice for social workers and has established certification procedures for such individuals through the Academy of Certified Social Workers, the *National Register of Clinical Social Workers* (National Academy of Social Workers, 1976), and the *Registry of Health Care Providers in Clinical Social Work* (National Registry of Health Care Providers in Clinical Social Work, 1981). In addition to these credentials, social workers in some states are not only legally registered and licensed, but have vendorship status as well.

The rapid growth and interdisciplinary accreditation of social work during the last two decades has had both positive and negative consequences. One of the major benefits of this transition is that social workers have moved from being "interveners" to "preventers" (Germain, 1980). Germain asserts that, "knowledge and skill in preventive efforts at the level of the individual, family, institutions, and community are developing" (p. 485). Though Germain sees this as a positive progression for clinical social work, she asserts that social work as a discipline has not been traditionally prepared for the clinical environment, and thus the practitioner encounters confusion when entering the mental health field. In the struggle for professional autonomy, s/he may seek to identify with the role of the psychiatrist or clinical psychologist and become a diagnostician and treater of mental disorders. In such circumstances Germain admits, "Clients are deprived of the uniqueness of a social work service, and the clinical social worker has only a limited opportunity to develop a sense of social work identity, competence, and autonomy" (p. 486). Germain does note that significant changes have been undertaken in the educational system for social workers with the intent to meet the needs of the oppressed more effectively. However, she does not provide evidence that the academic programs are becoming more attentive to preparing social workers for exclusive clinical practice.

Borenzweig (1981) conducted an exploratory study of both agency and private practitioners in Los Angeles and uncovered some interesting characteristics about the private practitioners in his sample. He attributes their low level of postgraduate education to complacency regarding their acquired education, and surprisingly to their feeling "that their training compares favorably with the training received by psychiatrists and psychologists" (p. 240). Those in private practice were more likely than their agency counterparts to identify themselves with nonsocial work titles such as "psychotherapist." The private practitioners provided predominantly psychodynamic psychotherapy services to "middle-class and upper-class neurotic individuals," while workers in agencies saw "the poor, the psychotic, children, young adults, and the aged..." (p. 243). The depiction in this study of the private social worker is that of an individual opting for a career as a psychotherapist, leaving the the poor to public agencies.

We are not suggesting that social workers should steadfastly avoid the acquisition of any psychotherapeutic skills in either training or practice. What we are recommending is that such skills be enmeshed within the context of broader social work responsibilities. For example, the chronically mentally ill have a continuing need for psychotherapeutic care. Just as important, however, is their need for support in making a transition from institution to community, and becoming engaged with programs and systems designed to meet their needs. The social worker is typically the best equipped professional to attend to these varied needs. Effecting a balance between therapeutic intervention and resource provision is difficult. Often the agencies and systems within which social workers function add to the confusion by giving social workers responsibilities outside their areas of training and experience, and quite often this is for the economic reason that social workers command less salary than psychologists or psychiatrists. The result is an insidious trap in which social workers find themselves gratified by the more prestigious role of being psychotherapists and become quite reluctant to be involved ever again with the more mundane tasks of casework.

It is imperative that some profession take responsibility for the social needs of the public. Social workers have traditionally done this job admirably and should continue to function in the tradition of service that they have established during this century. Psychotherapeutic functions should be contained within the professional role of case manager, not as autonomous enterprises that are undertaken either in agencies or private practice. Let those aspiring to a career of a psychotherapist train to become just that, and function as legitimized psychotherapists per se.

CLINICAL PSYCHOLOGY

Of the three professions considered in this chapter, clinical psychology seems to have given the most extensive attention to the formulation of professional definition and training. The initial formal consideration of professional identity took place at the Boulder Conference (see Raimy, 1950). This landmark conference was a response to a request to the American Psychological Association from the Veterans Administration and the United States Public Health Service to standardize a program of university training that would lead up to an agreed upon definition of skills and responsibilities for clinical psychologists. The model that was established was that of the "scientist/professional," an individual with a doctorate who would not only provide clinical services, but would also devote a comparable amount of energy to research endeavors. Research skill and active research participation were considered essential to the work of the clinical psychologist, who was seen as a professional who would contribute to a scientific body of knowledge and also have the skills to evaluate the development of new clinical techniques.

In 1955 the Stanford Conference (Strother, 1957) and in 1958 the Miami Conference (Roe, Gustad, Moore, Ross, & Skodak, 1959) reaffirmed the Boulder Conference's emphasis on integrating scientific work with clinical endeavors in the training and functioning of clinical psychologists. In 1965, the Chicago Conference (Hack, Ross, & Winder, 1966) broadened the scientist/professional model with its recommendation for programs to become more innovative. This trend was reinforced at the Vail Conference in 1973 (Korman, 1976), but a dramatic shift occurred in the provision of the professional/scientist model of training and practice as an acceptable alternative. It is unlikely that the Vail Conference intended to de-emphasize the role of research in the work of the clinical psychologist, but many construed that to be the case. By the late 1970s there was a surprising proliferation of programs which defined themselves as "professional programs or schools," and students were flocking to such programs by the hundreds. A concern about the varying quality of such programs led to the convening of the Conference on Education in Professional Psychology at Virginia Beach in 1978 (Watson, Caddy, Johnson, & Rimm, 1981). Although this conference affirmed that professional programs must abide by the Standards for Providers of Psychological Services (American Psychological Association, 1977), there was the disturbing acknowledgement that "only a small percentage of the (professional) programs emphasize or even include, evaluative research in their curricula" (p. 518).

The substantial redefinition of the training and professional roles of psychologists has stirred considerable debate in the field (see Polonsky, Fox, Wiens, Dixon, Freedman, & Shapiro, 1979). Traditionalists feel that this new breed of psychologist is completely out of synchrony with the historical definition of what a clinical psychologist should be. There seems to be no question on either side of the issue that the professional schools' primary intent is to produce practitioners or psychotherapists. If such students pick up some research knowledge along the way, that is regarded as good but not completely necessary. Individuals applying to the professional schools know what such programs offer, and typically state quite openly their preference to acquire only those skills needed to make them legitimized psychotherapists. One might therefore conclude that those individuals who wish to become scientist/professionals are the only ones who apply to the Boulder model clinical programs. Ironically, this is not the case. Probably the majority of applicants to the Boulder model programs primarily want to become practitioners, but they are willing to "tolerate" the scientific training in such programs because presently, graduates of such programs still enjoy a degree of prestige that may not as yet have been reached by their professional school peers. This increased prestige probably is due to the respected quality of the academically based Boulder model programs, which causes admission to such programs to be unbelievably competitive. The irony is that many of the Boulder model program applicants would have been happier in the professional schools, and also may have found more appropriate training there. Such individuals do not want to be psychologists; they want to be psychotherapists, and they go on to become just that.

It should come as no surprise that annual employment surveys of psychologists show that psychologists specialize in psychotherapy more than in any other work in the field, and that most clinical psychologists are surprisingly underinvolved in research endeavors. A major function of which education prepared them is characteristically ignored so that psychotherapy can become the exclusive focus of professional energies. Only a small number of clinical psychologists are left to do the scientific inquiry so necessary for the advancement of knowledge in the field. Just as with psychiatry and social work, there seems to be a substantial waste of educational effort in training clinical psychologists to do work which from the onset most of them do not wish to pursue.

One other area in which psychologists have traditionally played an important role was psychodiagnosis. Most programs in clinical psychology have required students to become familiar with formal assessment as well as psychometric concepts and procedures. Though psychological testing and test construction are taught in graduate school, a very small amount of the work of clinical psychologists is devoted to testing, and the percentage continues to decrease. In 1960, a national sample of clinical psychologists reported spending 44 percent of their professional time in testing, but by 1969 the proportion was reduced to 28 percent (Lubin & Lubin, 1972). A survey of its listees done by the administrators of the *National Register of Health Service Providers in Psychology* (Wellner, 1983) found that 54 percent of the respondents in the sample designated "individual therapy" as their first ranked service, whereas only 8 percent ranked "diagnosis" first. Fewer clinical psychologists are doing formal assessments, and fewer maintain familiarity with developments in psychological testing. The traditional image of the psychologist being a resource person in this area for other professionals is no longer accurate.

The unfortunate consequence for the clinical psychologist who becomes ignorant and uninterested about research or psychometrics is a forfeiture of a very valuable component of professional identity. As Hartman (1981) very succinctly stated, "It would be naive to assert that all clinical psychologists must be researchers. But unless our applied interventions (with patients, in schools, prisons, organizations, or industry) are guided by a sophisticated methodological rigor, then the very foundation of applied psychology as an empirically oriented endeavor is spurious at best" (p. 439). Clinical psychologists should return to that base of knowledge which gives them such an important niche in the mental health field; otherwise, why bother with the extensive education in empiricism that is given them? Hebb (1974) summed up the issue quite emphatically when he asked, "When the clinical psychologist forgets that he is a psychologist too, what does he become? If he's real good, he becomes a second rate psychiatrist since he lacks medical competence" (p. 71).

THE SOLUTION

The field of psychology may have inadvertently provided the solution to the problem faced by each of these professions when it moved toward the establishment of professional schools. Though the creation of professional schools brought significant confusion to clinical psychology, it also provided an appropriate option for all of those aspiring psychotherapists who previously had sought admission under false pretenses to psychiatry, social work, and traditional clinical psychology programs. Professional schools have provided such individuals with a more direct route to their goal of becoming psychotherapists. Our major complaint with such programs is that they may be maintaining a facade somewhat parallel to that presented by so many of those abovementioned applicants to the traditional programs. It seems that many of these programs really want to be schools of psychotherapy, but they feel a need to be affiliated with psychology so as to be legitimized, for the profession of psychotherapy in and of itself has never been legally sanctioned. Individuals are licensed as physicians, as social workers, or as psychologists, and often the particular licensing criteria of each of these professions may have little to do with the practice of psychotherapy. For example, in psychology, almost all states require a person to pass an examination prepared by the Professional Examination Service; the examination assesses knowledge about general psychology rather than psychotherapeutic or psychodiagnostic competency (Cartsen, 1978).

Licensing and certification procedures should serve a very important function for the public, but at the present time they probably serve to create more confusion than clarification. We recommend that appropriate professionals be licensed as *psychotherapists*. But even more importantly, we recommend the formalization of legally sanctioned training programs in psychotherapy. It seems most logical that such programs be placed in the professional schools of psychology, and that such schools correctly identify themselves for what they are. Optimally, these schools of psychotherapy would be multidisciplinary and would derive their curriculum from the most relevant aspects of the educational systems in psychiatry, social work, and psychology. These programs would be appropriate for those individuals working to become psychotherapists who presently pursue that goal via psychiatry, social work, and clinical psychology. These programs would also be appropriate for those individuals currently pursuing a psychotherapy career via the increasingly popular routes provided by psychiatric nursing, pastoral counseling, and educational guidance.

Obviously the thousands of already practicing psychotherapists who currently function under the names of various professions would want and deserve protection and would derive their license or certification through a "grandparent clause." But the end result could be a more accurate designation of the functions of both professional psychotherapists and the programs that educate them.

Perhaps some might worry that this would dramatically alter the academic programs in psychiatry, social work, and clinical psychology. Assuredly it would, but what a terrific opportunity to return to those skills and tasks so desperately needed today! Let the psychiatrist once again be a physician who knows medicine and somatic treatment. Let the social worker once again be trained and willing to work with social systems, caring for those persons most desperately in need. Let the clinical psychologist once again do scientific inquiry and evaluation. And let the *psychotherapist* do psychotherapy!

REFERENCES

American Psychological Association (1977). *Standards for the providers of psychological services* (Ref. ed.). Washington, DC: Author.

Borenzweig, H. (1981). Agency vs. private practice: Similarities and differences. *Social Work, 26,* 239–244.

Carsten, A. (1978). A public perspective on scoring the licensing exam. *Professional Psychology, 9,* 531–532.

Germain, C. B. (1980). Social context of clinical social work. *Social Work, 25,* 483–488.

Greden, J. F., and Casariego, J. L. (1975). Controversies in psychiatric education: A survey of residents' attitudes. *American Journal of Psychiatry, 132,* 270–274.

Hartman, L. M. (1981) Clinical psychology: Emergent trends and future applications. *Journal of Clinical Psychology, 37,* 439–445.

Hebb, D. O. (1974). What is psychology about. *American Psychologist, 29,* 71–79.

Hoch, E. L., Ross, A. O., and Winder, C. L. (Eds.) (1966) *Professional preparation of clinical psychologists: Proceedings of the Conference on the Professional Preparation of Clinical Psychologists meeting at the Center for Continuing Education, Chicago, Illinois, August 27–September 1, 1965.* Washington, DC: American Psychological Association.

Johnson, P. J., and Rubin, A. (1983). Case management in mental health: A social work domain? *Social Work, 28*, 49–55.

Karasu, T. B., Stein, S. P., and Charles, E. S. (1975). Attitudes of psychiatric residents toward the necessity of internship. *American Journal of Psychiatry, 132*, 274–277.

Korman, M. (Ed.) (1976). *Levels and patterns of professional training in psychology: Conference Proceedings*, Vail, Colorado, July 25–30, 1973. Washington, DC: American Psychological Association, 1976.

Langsley, D. G., and Hollender, M. H. (1982). The definition of a psychiatrist. *American Journal of Psychiatry, 139*, 81–85.

Lubin, B., and Lubin, A. W. (1972). Patterns of psychological services in the U.S.: 1959–1969. *Professional Psychology, 3*, 63–65.

NASW Register of Clinical Social Workers (1976). 1st ed. Washington, DC: National Association of Social Workers.

Polonsky, I., Fox, R. E., Wiens, A. N., Dixon, T. R., Freedman, M. B., and Shapiro, D. H. (1979). Models, modes, and standards for professional training. *American Psychologist, 34*, 339–349.

Raimy, V. (Ed.) (1950). *Training in Clinical Psychology (by the Staff of the Conference on Graduate Education in Clinical Psychology held at Boulder, Colorado in August of 1949)*. New York: Prentice-Hall.

Registry of Health Care Providers in Clinical Social Work. (1981). Lexington, KY: National Registry of Health Care Providers in Clinical Social Work.

Roe, A., Gustad, J. W., Moore, B. V., Ross, S., and Skodak, M. (Eds.) (1959). *Graduate Education in Psychology: Report of the Conference on Graduate Education in Psychology (Sponsored by the Education and Training Board of the APA and held at Miami Beach, Florida, November 29 to December 7, 1958)*. Washington, DC: American Psychological Association.

Schodek, K. (1981). Adjuncts to social casework in the 1980's. *Social Casework, 62*, 195–200.

Shemo, J. P., Ballenger, J. C., Yazel, J. J., and Spradlin, W. W. (1982). A conjoint psychiatry-internal medicine program: Development of a teaching and clinical model. *American Journal of Psychiatry, 139*, 1437–1442.

Sierles, F. (1982). Medical school factors and career choice of psychiatry. *American Journal of Psychiatry, 139*, 1040–1042.

Strothers, C. R. (Ed.). (1957). *Psychology and Mental Health. A Report of the Institute of Education and Training for Psychological Contributions to Mental Health, held at Stanford University in August, 1955*. Washington, DC: American Psychological Association.

Sundberg, N. D., Taplin, J. R., and Tyler, L. E. (1983). *Introduction to Clinical Psychology: Perspectives, Issues, and Contributions to Human Service*. Englewood Cliffs, NJ: Prentice-Hall.

Wallace, M. E. (1982). Private practice: A nationwide study. *Social Work, 27*, 262–267.

Watson, N., Caddy, G. R., Johnson, J. H., and Rimm, D. C. (1981). Standards in the education of professional psychologists: The resolutions of the conference at Virginia Beach. *American Psychologist, 36*, 514–519.

Weintraub, W., Balis, G. V., and Donner, L. (1982). Teaching: An answer to psychiatry's recruitment problem? *American Journal of Psychiatry, 139*, 1036–1039.

Wellner, A. M. (Ed.) (1983). Characteristics of services—preliminary overview. *Register Report, 18,* 3.

Yager, J., Lamotte, K., Nielson, A., and Eaton, J. S. (1982). Medical students' evaluation of psychiatry: A cross-country comparison. *American Journal of Psychiatry,* 139, 1003–1009.

Chapter 8

"BAREFOOT" PSYCHOTHERAPISTS: THE RELATIVE EFFECTIVENESS OF PARAPROFESSIONALS IN MENTAL HEALTH SERVICES

JOHN A. HATTIE, CHRISTOPHER F. SHARPLEY, AND H. JANE ROGERS

Although there are strict guidelines set down for accreditation by a range of professional organizations, the issue of the paraprofessional in psychotherapy remains unresolved. As recently as 1981, there has been debate in the literature regarding the relative effectiveness of professional versus paraprofessional counsellors, with some evidence for each side (e.g., Durlak, 1979, 1981; Nietzel & Fisher, 1981). Certainly it cannot be denied that paraprofessionals *are* being used (quite effectively, if one is to judge from clients' reports), and that the possession of postgraduate academic qualifications is no sure indicator of therapeutic effectiveness. On the contrary, personal experience as therapists and counsellor-educators has led us to conclude that it is the attributes of the person rather than the academic degree that contributes most to counsellor effectiveness.

The present paper examines the previous literature regarding experimental comparisons between professional and paraprofessional counsellors by means of a method not hitherto used to answer the question of relative effectiveness—meta-analysis (Glass, 1976, 1978; Glass & Smith, 1979; Glass, McGaw, & Smith, 1981). This method is being used increasingly in areas where the body of literature is large and a narrative description (such as a literature review) is no longer adequate for the purpose of integrating the knowledge accumulated. Meta-analysis integrates the findings of previous research in such a way that those features of the studies which may mediate the outcomes (e.g., design quality, sample size) can be incorporated in the evaluation and their influence determined.

Meta-analysis transforms the experimental findings into numerical values. This numerical value is termed an "effect size," and in the present review was calculated by the following procedure:

$$\text{effect size} = \frac{\underline{X}\,(\text{paraprofessional}) - \underline{X}\,(\text{professional})}{\text{s.d.}\,(\text{professional})}$$

This statistic is biased (Hedges, 1983) and has therefore been modified by use of a gamma function that includes the number of degrees of freedom used to estimate the standard deviation.

THE EXPERIMENTAL STUDIES REVIEWED

The articles that are the basis of this report are exactly those reviewed by Durlak (1979, 1981) and Nietzel and Fisher (1981). These authors could reach no agreement as to the comparative effectiveness of professional and nonprofessional counsellors. Altogether, 39 studies were able to be coded, and these studies yielded a total of 154 separate effect sizes. The overall effect size was .34 (standard error = .10), indicating that there was a difference of .34 standard deviations between the mean effects for paraprofessionals and professionals. This result may be seen more clearly in Figure 8-I, which shows that the average client who consulted a paraprofessional was more likely to achieve problem-resolution than 63 percent of the clients who consulted a professional. This finding may be viewed from two perspectives. First, while this rather dramatic figure certainly needs to be tempered by such cautions as the relative complexity of problems presented by the sort of client who consults professionals versus paraprofessionals, overlap of problem-type did occur in the studies reviewed, and therefore meaningful comparisons are possible at this level. Second, 63 percent represents a large proportion of clients who most probably were either paying for treatment or were institutionalized while receiving that treatment. The implications for health rebate schemes and government funding are obvious.

Meta-analysis, however, goes further than this bald statement of the relative effectiveness of professional versus paraprofessional counsellors. There were significant differences between studies on the basis of design quality. Those studies which were most rigorous experimentally favoured the paraprofessional counsellors, suggesting that the finding

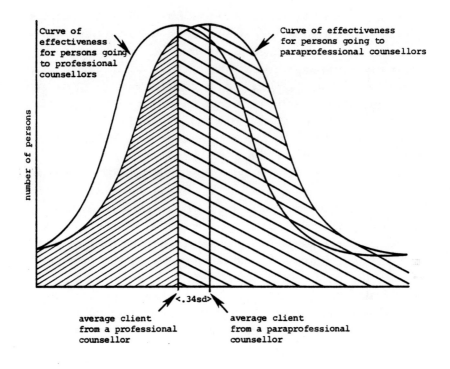

Figure 8-I. Relative effectiveness of professional and paraprofessional counsellors.

discussed above is even more dramatic than first thought.

The issue of exactly what constitutes a paraprofessional counsellor has been addressed in some degree by Durlak (1979), who suggested that

> individuals who have received post-baccalaureat formal clinical training, professional programs of psychology, psychiatry, social work, and psychiatric nursing were considered to be professionals. Those who have not received this training are paraprofessionals. (p.80)

This position has been questioned by Nietzel and Fisher (1981) who were dubious as to whether faculty members, graduate students, an experimental psychologist with little clinical experience, or an intern undertaking residency training in psychiatry were really "professionals". In an effort to utilize the data from these studies rather than discard it in the face of ongoing debate, these various categories of therapist were coded into subcategories and then analysed using the meta-analysis procedures to test for relationships with the effect size.

Two subsets of paraprofessionals were formed. First, those who had some sort of clinical experience (e.g., medical students, speech pathologists, public health workers), and second, those who were inexperienced (e.g., volunteer adults, college students). While the latter were still effective, those who had had some experience were significantly more effective (F = 6.20, df = 1,152, p <.01).

Professionals were likewise categorized into graduate students and supervisory personnel (e.g., college faculty) in one subset and more traditionally-defined professionals in the other subset (e.g., psychologists, counsellors, psychiatrists, behaviour therapists). The mean difference between the paraprofessional and graduate students was −.23, supervisors −.33, and professionals −.55, indicating that those who were training therapists and the trainee therapists were markedly less effective than paraprofessionals. The comparison of paraprofessionals with professionals (.55) and with supervisors (−.33) suggests that training procedures need to be drastically improved, perhaps by greater use of those professionals already in the field. Perhaps as a consolation, persons with recent advanced-level training were the most effective professionals, and experienced paraprofessionals scored higher on effectiveness than inexperienced paraprofessionals, with three categories of time (brief, up to 15 hours, 15 plus hours) showing that the longer training period was directly correlated with effectiveness.

Duration of therapy was correlated with effect (r = .48, df = 117, p <.01), as was the actual number of sessions (r = .39, df = 42, p <.01) and the total hours of the sessions (r = .45, df = 51, p <.01), indicating that longer interventions were more effective.

In terms of outcome measures, paraprofessionals were most favoured by client ratings and academic outcomes such as achievement changes. There was no difference between professionals and paraprofessionals when specific client behaviour change was used as the outcome measure. It seems that not only do clients prefer to consult paraprofessionals, but that on the relatively independent measure of behaviour change, the *preferred* paraprofessional counsellor is equally if not more effective than the professional.

CONCLUSIONS

Even at the most conservative estimate, these data indicate that paraprofessionals are *at least* as effective as professionals, in spite of a massive difference in training. With a little more than fifteen hours training, hitherto inexperienced persons with no formal academic training in counselling have been shown to be both preferred by clients and more therapeutically effective than persons with lengthy tertiary training in the formal disciplines of psychology, psychiatry, etc. Implications for training, health services funding, and health rebates are powerful. The present authors do not wish to suggest that there is no need for rigorous public legislation and professional organisational guidelines to protect the public in the mental health field. Rather, we maintain the opposite, taking the point of view that empirical investigation of the effectiveness of training procedures should be paramount over accreditation based upon traditional academic qualifications. Society, as well as individual clients, has the right to ask which (if any) psychotherapeutic procedures are effective, and then to sanction those for public access.

REFERENCES

Durlak, B. J. Comparative effectiveness of paraprofessional and professional helpers. *Psychological Bulletin,* 1979, *86,* 80–92.

Durlak, J. A. Evaluating comparative studies of paraprofessional and professional helpers: A reply to Nietzel and Fisher. *Psychological Bulletin,* 1981, *89,* 566–569.

Glass, G. V. Primary, secondary, and meta-analysis of research. *Educational Researcher,* 1976, *5,* 3–8.

Glass, G. V. Integrating findings: The meta-analysis of research. In L. S. Shulman (ed.), *Review of Research in Education,* Vol. 5, Itasca, Ill.: Peacock, 1978.

Glass, G. V., McGaw, B., and Smith, M. C. *Meta-analysis in social research.* Sage: Beverly Hills; 1981.

Glass, G. V., and Smith, M. L. Meta-analysis of research on the relationship of class-size and achievement. *Educational and Policy Analysis,* 1979, *1,* 2–16.

Hedges, L. V. Combining independent estimators in research synthesis. *British Journal of Mathematical and Statistical Psychology,* 1983, *36,* 123–131.

Nietzel, M. T., and Fisher, S. G. Effectiveness of professional and paraprofessional helpers: A comment on Durlak. *Psychological Bulletin,* 1981, *89,* 555–565.

Chapter 9

NO LAUGHING MATTER:
THE LACK OF HUMOR
IN CURRENT PSYCHOTHERAPISTS

VICTOR N. HIRSCH AND WALTER E. O'CONNELL

AVOIDANCE OF HUMOR

The age of scientific research has been with us for many years, and countless amounts of monies have been spent looking for the truths of humankind. Research has been developed in many areas, and a large amount of money has been spent in the area of mental health. Most of this money has come from the taxpayer's pocket book. What have we gleaned from this vast amount of research in the area of mental health, and from the psychotherapist particularly? We believe that the taxpayers have received very little in return from psychotherapists because of the widespread professional avoidance of humor in our everyday lives. What the future of humankind really needs is a *crash* program on humor and a war on witless worry.

Nothing is more vital and necessary in life than an enlivening sense of humor and the ability to play and be loving. Humor represents finding alternative ways toward unconditional worth and belonging when failure appears. All of these human qualities are lacking in those we choose to call the *mentally ill*. It is not that these unfortunates are helpless victims of a disease that strips them of the skills to be happy encouraging achievers, but rather the inability to be learners and to find appropriately human teachers that renders bright-eyed, eager children into humorless, deadly serious, loveless peripheral discards of society. For hundreds of years we have taught our young to follow fearfully institutional authority instead of responding to the paradoxes of life and teaching them a sense of humor. Numerous articles are beginning to appear in newspapers and magazines as to the benefit of humor and laughter in our lives. Humor can be an important coping device and is a healthy release for the anxiety, tension, and depression that springs up in everyday life, strangling our creativity and natural good feelings. The humorous attitude is a wonderful way toward accepting and actualizing the human spirit. In spite of its expansive and socially-responsive effects, the sense of humor is the most misunderstood and maligned of all human movements.

You may already have been curious as to why all the professional avoidance of a humorous attitude. This is a valid question, and is one that has not been answered or even asked by most professionals. To pursue it is to discover why the taxpayers have not gotten their money's worth. Mental health sciences are preoccupied with symptomatic-pathological entities and easily quantified external events instead of with greatly-needed joy, happiness, creativity, courage, and humor. Following the Charcot-Freud model of man, proper and reputable science still clings to its faith in man as *homo pathologicus*. Traditionally, psychotherapists have been trained in the medical model that examines the pathology at the intracellular level. With this view has come the widespread search to find the cause of the disease (abnormal) and a heavy dependence on medication rather than on the pursuit of a healthy, well-functioning organism. In examining the body internally, about the closest anyone has come to looking at humor has been in the anatomy of the eye (aqueous humor). Behavioral scientists have analyzed animal behavior in mazes, looking for controls and patterns of observable behavior. It is of little wonder that these researchers have abandoned the sense of humor for lack of evidence. Have you ever heard a rat displaying a sense of humor or tell a joke?

In its early stages, American psychiatry reflected a belief in living the democratic ideal. The cure rates of hospitals prior to the advent of tranquilizers and professionalizers would put "scientific" psychiatry to shame (Bockoven, 1963; Sterling, 1980). Humorless institutions focus upon the ego-needs of doctors to be only doctors, hence the urge for documentation at the expense of the patient, staff (growth), and the taxpayer. However, arousal states, not attitudes of discouragement, are affected by pills. Pills produce an artificial state where humor is either inappropriate or nonexistent.

The humorist is often viewed as a threat to society in general and professions in particular simply because our addictive egos are too weak to tolerate more than a handful of humorists at any one time. So much the worse for our society and its taxpayers. The humorist is "individuated," to use Carl Jung's term, but society is not.

The influential religions should also take some blame for our lack of humor. In Christian societies, the churches have traditionally focused on the imperfection of man (sin) and have preoccupied themselves with death. Perhaps if Jesus had made several humorous remarks while on the cross we wouldn't take life or death so seriously. Although the writers of the gospels failed to record anything humorous about the situation, we believe that Jesus must have had a sense of humor because of his likeness with God. We know God has a sense of humor; just look at the world he created.

What about the status of psychologists, our modern priests and shamans? Psychotherapists have exerted a certain amount of influence on our society, but most of it hasn't been positive or growth seeking, and does not allow the individual to function in an everchanging paradoxical world. So why have these behavioral scientists not been enthralled by the study of humor? The simple reason for that avoidance is that institutional science follows in the footsteps of institutional society. Science has its mavericks, akin to the humorist whose watered down ideas, but not elevated spirits, have been honored. As George Bernard Shaw well illustrated in his play, *Saint Joan* (1924), we worship saints (as well as humorists and maverick scientists) after their deaths, but would be racked with unwanted arousal states if they were addressing us now with their humanistic expectation.

FREUDIAN HUMOR

Sigmund Freud, the so-called father of modern psychiatry, did write on the sense of humor (O'Connell, 1975). We must give him credit for that. But his disciples confused wit with humor, a mistake that Freud himself did not commit. With modern behavioral science's commitment to the pathological and strong faith in easily quantified external rewards or punishments, wit has become popular, since it is an ego weapon (at times) in service of competition. Wit invariably is seen as a form of "indirect hostility" instead of also being regarded as a voice to communicate an important message about mistaken motives and actions of others. There seems to be plenty of wit in our society, of which the taxpayers are getting more than they desire, for true wit can be a weapon, just as water can be used to drown in. Wit must be used with all delicacy. If it is perceived by the weak (e.g., discouraged) as proof of worthlessness, wit is a deadly weapon. There is a point in the interaction between people where wit directed against useless diseased attitudes and actions becomes similar to humor. Both wit and humor use indirect communication (sudden switches exposing hidden meanings) to get a message into awareness, but humor is used more often to deflate our own ego-controlling addictions (guilt, perfection, separation, and control), whereas wit may be used to deflate the egos of others.

Freud saw the humorous attitude as the hallmark of maturity when used to buoy one up against inescapable facts, like the gallows. Some theorists (Bateson, 1960; Watzlawick, Helmick, and Jackson, 1967) view schizophrenics as having made the choice toward insanity when comforted with inescapable fates and choices. Freud regarded humor as the only defense mechanism that did not require the presence of others. He believed that humor was a mature attitude, carried out within the individual person. Wit, on the other hand, was an interpersonal mechanism, hostile in intent.

Freud, however, got horribly confused about humor and dropped the topic (he, too, took it too seriously.) The masterful mind, which could grasp the multiple meaning of wit and humor, could not conceive of the many meanings of "reality." Reality was the reality of the psychiatrist, and any denial of what he called reality was sick. In descriptive psychiatry, denial of time, place, and person is a sign of *disease*. Yet there is the reality of the physicist in which solid states of disease are a delusion: reality is both a flux of particles and wave motion, another humorous resolution of opposites.

Modern psychologists have often subscribed to the notion that *consciousness* is not a basic reality but a paradoxical flow of apparent solidity. To many, persons have no solid essence, but are flowing resolutions of opposites: man-God, male-female, past-future, living-dying, conscious-unconscious. Over concern with one pole of a dynamic pair such as *living* calls forth, in the sudden switch of humor, the paired opposite (*dying*). In other words, living contains both living and dying, not exclusive concern with either extreme. If sixty years ago Freud could have been less addicted to a belief of the "solidity" of reality, therapists might now be merry teachers of humor, and never dull, discouraged diagnostic labelers.

NATURAL HIGH: AN ALTERNATIVE

What humankind needs is a program to initiate and guide humor into the theories and practices of psychotherapists, thus giving taxpayers better return for their monies. Any method that increases the patient's self-esteem, social interest, and enjoyment of existential paradoxes is teaching the individual at least the rudiments of the humorous attitude. Natural High (NH) Therapy (O'Connell, 1981) is just such a theory and is an optimistic, action-oriented approach to living in the here-and-now that stresses the response-ability of each person for the creation of one's own state of self-actualization. Natural High theory and therapy focuses upon the sense of humor (or lack of it) as the essential criterion of the actualization process. A sense of humor comes from self-training for the expansion of one's sense of worth and feelings of universal belonging, as well as the development of an appreciation for the basic paradoxes of the human condition. Directive or action techniques (O'Connell, 1969d) readily highlight the "patient's" paradox. O'Connell has researched humor more than anyone else (1981b), and as a result sees the wasted monies and times spent on traditional pathologies as no laughing matter. Why is humor so valuable? O'Connell (1981b) summarized his major findings in the area and concluded that an appreciation of humor is a stable personality trait associated with maturity, and that humor, in contrast to wit, did not appear to be affected by situational stressors. Community leaders were the highest in humor appreciation, while hospitalized schizophrenics were very low. In general, low-humor response was related to repressive life-styles. Appreciation for humor is negatively associated with anxiety about death, especially the fear of one's own physical dissolution.

Through his research on humor, O'Connell has developed NH and advocates the use of humor throughout our lives. Humor combines the attitude of actualization with an awful affinity for the timeless mysteries of life with humor. The smiles of the humorist herald at least temporary resolution of our fixed and seemingly solid perceptions. Through NH using humor, life becomes a flow of loving, authentic energies: the "many" parts reconcile with the "one" whole. We cease existing in a jungle, within enemy territory. A potential friend-enemy is the weak ego (ours and all others), which terrorizes us with guilt, demands, and negative nonsense. But ego also calls our attention very dramatically to our constant need to let go of solid arbitrary boundaries. Humor helps us get out of the ego-monkey-trap of grasping and hanging to external frames of reference for proof of power and worth. NH assists us to drop our negative autohypnosis and smile at our ego delusions of desertion and death. At times, when we are touching the timeless energies of deep self and feeling our unique interactions with the universe, all ego noise becomes "child's play" and "terrors for children."

Those quotes reflect the attitude of Thomas More, who gave up the life he loved without reactive hostility, paranoia, and depression, but with brilliant flashes of humor. As he approached the scaffold in a physically-enfeebled state, he implored his executioner, "Please sir, help me up the stairs. Coming down, I'll fend for myself." Freud wrote of the prisoner being hanged on Monday who happily went to the gallows quipping, "This is a fine way to start the week." Zen masters told the tale of the person trapped on a grass rope, tigers above and below him. As mice gnawed away at the rope, the dangling figure reached out and picked a strawberry. "How delicious!" he exclaimed. In a similar way, we are all under a death sentence. Only the hour and the means are a mystery. The humorist knows this fact. However, he or she is also aware that whether hanging from a rope or dropping the body in an efficient sterile hospital room, there is always complete control of one's inner worth and belongingness. NH theory and therapy teaches that esteem and belonging are the only two acts in life completely in our control. However, most people have learned to see life entirely reversed. With that mistaken certainty, feelings of significance and social interest are the only two goals completely beyond their self-training skills. But these misguided people are not to blame, for they invested their tax monies into a system that was supposed to produce efficient, competent theories to be used by psychotherapists. Instead what they received was a theory and system that not only guided them away from humor, but taught them to be unhappy and discouraged, a rigid perfectionist displaying guilt if goals are not obtained. And so it goes. The humorous attitude continues to be unpopular in societal institutions aimed at external conformity to delusions that material goods and services are the one and only holy grail.

A CRASH PROGRAM IS NEEDED

Before more money is spent by taxpayers in search of the holy grail, what we need is a *crash* program on humor. And it may all start with you, gentle reader. NH helps by being the only personality theory built upon solid research on the "sense" (or rather the self-trained) attitude of humor (O'Connell, 1975, 1981a–d). No other approach takes humor seriously. NH will give you the tools to be a perpetually-practicing-pupil in the growth-fullfilling game-of-games. The game-of-games of humor seeks to overcome one's rigid ego-identity, which is constantly rein- forced by society's discouraged demands for "doing" and "having." The NH way is to become an ultimate athlete of the self, beyond the concepts of space and time. The humorist denies death (of the eternal self), but speaks loudly of the death of both the addictive ego and the decaying body.

So how does one get humor and learn NH, and better yet, how can we teach the mental health field to incorporate humor into the education of the psychotherapist, thus giving taxpayers better return for their monies? First we must shift away from the negativity and discouragement in our society and institutions that reflect the attitude of "homo-pathology". Our current culture, which worships weak-ego ploys (guilt, control, perfection, and separation) and youthful bodies would be regarded as psychopathological in a NH diagnostic system that sees grudgeless and playful humor as a goal in life. We are born with conflict, being god-humans who are never taught by institutional forces of home, church, and state how to convert polarities into assets for actualization. Today's institutions simply repeat on a larger scale the workings of our strivings for perfection, control, separation, time-addiction (remorse for the past or concern for the future), and guilt.

This sad state must be changed, and it needs to come from the institutions themselves. Society must start revering its live humorists instead of its dead ones. In using humor, we must defuse the "mystifying" dehumanizing forces of society. Institutions need to teach inner and outer movements of how to optimize feelings (or convictions) of uncon- ditional worth and belonging. We will never develop authentic social interest (SI) unless we can become aware and accepting of constrictions of all people without guilt (self and/or other directed). Thus institutions need to be encouraging rather than discouraging. Perfection can never be achieved, so we need to stress and reinforce humor in all phases of life to combat the paradoxical situations we encounter (encounter of the humorous kind).

Instrumental religions that teach with clarity how to love self, neighbor, and God need to teach and stress a humorous side of life to the imperfections of man. We need to see persons as worthy creatures of God even though we are imperfect in our actions.

Our monies need to be spent in the areas of humor research. We need to find the most efficient way to teach humor, have it last, and have it generalize to our daily lives. We need to bring more humor courses and workshops into our schools and institutions. Research on humor can be utilized in the field of health psychology. Health psychology is growing rapidly, and humor could greatly effect the recent discoveries of the body's own opiate-like substances (endorphines, etc.) to combat pain stress and depression.

ROLE OF THE PSYCHOLOGIST

The psychotherapist must be taught to play a role in expanding humor and battling constrictive egos, because therapists can change much easier than institutions. No psychotherapist can claim to be a tutor in humor until he or she has experienced the tragic-comic paradox in his/her own life. Thousands of therapists have just been eliminated! Therapists who need to see patients as always sick and themselves as always well (who never can smile at the foibles of doctors, patients, and the world at large for fear of hostile regressions and fragile egos) are a solid barrier to the potential and development of the humorist.

In brief, a psychotherapist tutors in humor by teaching, modeling, and reinforcing from the strength of being a significant other. The NH humorist is a teacher helping fellow therapists and patients learn the movements of growth, even outside the doctors office. The NH therapist models humor in his or her own life, especially face-to-face with the patient. The therapist has sufficiently developed self-reflexivity (Oliver and Landfield, 1962) to be able to explain his mistakes in his own theory. The humorist must be skilled at a sudden distancing from overinvolvement. The humorist-therapist can make sudden changes in how he perceives the patient, but never blames or punishes the person. This kind of therapist can, by understanding and reflecting the patient's felt misery, establish a significant relationship. At other times he distances himself to note the patients' creative arrangement and his selection of proof to be miserable. He never carries the cross for others, yet does not reject them either. In truth, one must have a touch of the humorist to thrive as a therapist.

Natural high is an alternative to the *homo pathological* view of mankind that focuses on the sense of humor and provides the tax payer with an imperfect plan for his investment. NH theory is a psychospiritual pilgrimage aimed at intergrating psychology, psychiatry, religion, and democracy in a total push for self-training in worth and belonging. Through NH, humor (not wit) is approached as a personality variable reflecting self-actualization (or maturity). Humor is seen as an epiphenomenon of the ability to generate self-esteem (SE) and social interest (SI) and to appreciate the paradoxical (mysteries, ineffable, changing) conditions of human existence. NH uses humor to generate encouragement from the most negative circumstances using the same techniques of communication as wit, but humor is encouragement and wit aims for discouragement.

In the spirit of natural high, we need to realize the hidden logic of humor, or it will not only be our pocket books that will be taxed. NH is simple, as is humor, but not easy. A master of natural high realizes the necessity of perpetual (often painful) practice and has a sense of humor when imperfection occurs. For perfection can never be reached, so we must smile even after the tax collectors come.

REFERENCES

Bateson, G. Minimal requirements for a theory of schizophrenia. *Archives of General Psychiatry,* 2:477–491, 1960.

Bockoven, J. *Moral Treatment in American Psychiatry.* New York: Springer, 1963.

O'Connell, W. Teleodrama. *Individual Psychologist,* 6, 42–45, 1969.

O'Connell, W. *Action Therapy And Adlerian Theory.* Chicago: Alfred Adler Institute, 1975.

O'Connell, W. Natural High Therapy. In Corsini, R. (Ed.) *Handbook of Innovative Psychotherapies.* New York: John Wiley, 1981 a.

O'Connell, W. *Essential Readings in Natural High Actualization.* Chicago: North American Graphics, 1981 b.

O'Connell, W. The Natural High Therapist: God's favorite monkey. *Voices: The Art and Science of Psychotherapy,* 16(4), 37–44, 1981 c.

O'Connell, W. The miracle of actualization. In Stern, M. (Ed.) *The Other Side of the Couch: The Faith of Psychotherapists.* New York: Pilgrim Press, 1981 d.

Oliver, W., and Landfield, A. Reflexivity: An infaced issue of psychology. *Journal of Individual Psychology,* 18, 114–124, 1962.

Shaw, G. (1924) *Saint Joan, Major Barbara, Androcles and the Lion.* New York: Modern Library, 1952.

Sterling, P. Psychiatry's drug addiction. *Reflections,* 15(4), 44–52, 1980.

Watzlawick, P., Beavin, J. H., and Jackson, D. D. *Pragmatics of Human Communication.* New York: W. W. Norton & Company 1967.

Chapter 10

PSYCHOTHERAPY AND THE PARADOX OF SERVICE: A TRANSPERSONAL CRITIQUE

MOSHE KROY

INTRODUCTION

Is psychotherapy effective? Does it merit the public expenditure that it incurs in terms of government support for training institutions and of government employment of therapists?

The question seems to be straightforward, and to require a straightforward answer. If a public commission would be appointed to investigate the issue, it would proceed by trying to define *dimensions of effectiveness* and defining costs, and trying to relate the two to each other. However, the question cannot be answered on such a superficial level, as it involves many profound presuppositions. These presuppositions pertain not only to the nature of psychotherapy, but also to the whole issue of *services* in our mode of society. Indeed, similar questions could be asked in societies in which there are no taxpayers — be they societies that are based on the libertarian free enterprise model, where the government does not exist at all, and if it does, it finances itself without taxation, or communistic societies where every person is a state employee.[24,26] Obviously, the parameters of the factual answers given in such respective societies would be different in all respects: one may define differently the aims of psychotherapy if one is in a communist society or a libertarian one, and in the latter case, refer the problem to the supply-demand mechanism of the market to resolve. However, what is really involved in our question goes beyond such sociopolitical differentiations to metaphysical depths. It goes, in short, to a question that relates to the overall perspective on evidence that one adopts. Curiously enough, *the same metaphysical considerations apply*

From *Australian Journal of Transpersonal Psychology*, Volume 8, No. 1, April 1984. By permission of editor and author.

both with regard to the "political economics" of the issue under consideration and to the *psychology* aspect of it. These statements may seem mystifying, but they will be clarified through our progression.

We will commence by examining a paradox that applies to all forms of exchange of services in all societies that presently compete on our political attention. This paradox will then lead to the grounds of its possibility, in the metaphysical preconception that underlies social systems currently in vogue. Challenging these preconceptions will introduce the transpersonal paradigm as the rational grounds that alone can resolve the paradox. This introduction will not be along psychological lines, but rather in terms of the issues of *political economy*. Thus, we will introduce an outline of a transpersonal conception of political economy as a radical alternative to the whole scale of political systems presently competing in public consciousness: democracies and dictatorships, socialistic and capitalistic, communistic and libertarian. In terms of this conception, the task of psychotherapy will be redefined. The new view of psychotherapy will thus integrate both the political economic dimension and the professional dimension into a new radical vision. The incompatibility of the present state of affairs with the requirements of this radical vision will constitute a radical critique too evident to be articulated.

THE PARADOX OF SERVICE

The first observation we may start from is that the issue of the "social utility" of psychotherapy (which is the utilitarian welfare state style of facing our issue) is on par with that of any other profession, organization, or mode of service.[7] Do doctors heal their patients? Do police protect us from crime? etc., etc. It seems that these questions are all separate, specific factual questions that call separately for factual investigations. However, this is not the case. These various questions pertain to one basic issue: the quality and effectiveness of *service* rendered by some human individuals to others, in the context of some relationship of *exchange*.

Let me clarify this point. When A renders service to B in a free market situation, B pays him. The survival of A depends on this payment. Thus, he must continue and find new exchanges similar to the one he had with B, or else he would perish. Similarly, when a state employee serves individuals that come for his help, whatever be its specific nature, he must satisfy *his superiors*. The state that employs him (or more precisely, the state officials who make the decisions, directly or indirectly) must consider his *continued services to be vital*. This consideration may depend on the way his services are perceived by the public (as in a welfare state) or on the way in which they are perceived by political agencies with the government (as in a communist state, or a totalitarian state in general). However, in every particular case, there is a precisely defined exchange involved. It is in the interest of the individual to maintain the conditions for the exchange as long as possible. Indeed, when employed by government, one can see a direct exchange relation as well: the individual sells certain documents recording certain facts covering his service, which the government can use to maintain electoral popularity through their publication. The government pays a salary. Failure to supply such records is failure to maintain the job, as many psychotherapists have discovered. Thus, in all these cases, the service rendered is something that the survival of the server depends on. Thus, he must continue and create *demand for his service*. This applies not just to the free market. A police force, for instance, consisting of individuals that all wish to maintain their salary, and each wants to get a higher salary through a promotion, cannot be content when its efforts produce a crimeless society. A crimeless society is one in which an electoral platform of law and order is not a vote catcher. It is a society in which police forces get, therefore, reduced budgets, and hence have to dismiss personnel and block promotions. A society like that is one that, therefore, would be an anathema to the continued existence of the police force and its employees. It is, consequently, the obvious interest of a police force to maintain a level of crime, while at the same time seeming to be fighting crime valiantly. Indeed, organized crime, which distinguishes bosses and small-time operators, offers the structural solution. Small-time operators are expendable, hence to be detected and persecuted by police.[25] Big bosses can be counted on to keep crime going, to recruit new small operators, and thus to guarantee the sociopolitical necessity, hence the economic viability of the police force. Similarly, medical practitioners cannot survive in a society where they are paid for healing the sick without doing their share to make sure that disease, as such, will not vanish. A society that knows no disease knows no doctors. Once it allows doctors into its boundaries, they would find it their first item of business to change the life-style of the residents so as to introduce disease as a phenomena for which they can cater through *medicine.*

Does the same principle apply to products? Here there is an initial difficulty: products can be tested in separation from producer and consumer interaction. In a genuinely free market economy, competition should allow for the emergence of the highest quality products at the cheapest price. It would seem that the only way the paradox will apply is through the attempt to "stimulate artificial demand by means of advertisement." However, this is not entirely true. Eternal products, e.g. light bulbs that will never burn out, would extinguish both the original producer and his competitors. Such products can be contemplated only by someone who plans to "make a large capital on one big hit" and then fold up his operations. On the other hand, this kind of attitude would encourage precisely the production of low quality products, because there is no reputation to maintain if one does not intend to resell, and since the production of high quality products is normally costlier. Thus, even on the level of products, and even in a free market context (and not one monopolized by state industries or by huge cartels, etc.), there is an aspect of the paradox of service that would apply, beyond the obvious issue of advertisement. For a business that is planned as a long term venture, products must be sufficiently short-lived for the company to resell the product to the same clients. Obviously, if the product is much more short-lived than those offered by competitors at the same or close price, the company will lose its market with its reputation. However, since all competitors are bound by the same consideration, without any need to conspire, a tacit consensus of *maximum allowed quality* would develop.

The only case where one could see the possibility of an exemption, under free market conditions, from the paradox of service, is the production and sale of products that are consumed through use and to satisfy an independently recurring need. A baker can allow himself to provide good bread, because his bread will be consumed and hunger will invite the clients to return. A similar situation applies to typists, etc. Thus, the economics of necessity items that are consumed when used allows some relief from the paradox of service. This, though, does not entirely vindicate even the free market economics (that is easily seen to be superior to any planned economics by arguments developed elsewhere from the transpersonal perspective to be developed later in this paper.[24,25,26] However, we cannot contemplate these issues at full here, because they involve a deviation from our theme.*

However, regarding services where standards are naturally elusive, because the *sold service* cannot be separated clearly from the total interaction between the one that serves and the one that receives the service and thus cannot be inspected in isolation, these exemptions do not apply. The necessity to maintain demand by never solving the problem one is supposed to solve in a permanent or systematic way, or even maintaining the problem at a high level of urgency, can be manifested more directly. It is not an accident that the medical profession and the associated drug industries have fought with all their might any cancer treatment that has proved effective, be it B17 or oregon boxes.[22,23] Cancer patients and other incurables are a regular source of income. They come back for a treatment. Similarly, neurotics can finance a psychoanalyst for his entire life: he can live off the same patients for 30 years, given that analysis is interminable, and only the mortality of patients requires him to renew the search for new patients.[12] These points are not made as a cynical observation on a present situation. Rather, they are made as indications of certain socioeconomic necessities. Insofar as individuals conceive of their survival as depending on their capacity to maintain demand for their services, they must do their best to create this demand. This can be done either by artificial stimulation of demand (advertisement) or, more effectively, by making sure that the problems they specialize in solving are never really solved. In other words, the *paradox of service* is as follows. Every economic unit, whether

---

*The point hinted at is one that will become evident after the conception of economic interaction will be clarified. Given the fact that man's existential goal is revealed within this framework to be a metaphysical necessity of universal application and not a personal whimsical choice, the whole issue of *values* must be considered in a new light. Free market economics presupposes the possibility of complete arbitrariness of individual value systems allowing the market to adjust to whatever is demanded.[25] Thus, hard drugs have always been argued by liberatarians to be morally admissible products, given that the buyer and user chooses freely to use them. However, even given the complete justifiability of the liberatarian arguments against state intervention in the drug trade, the moral issue is not being seriously touched. If man has a necessary existential goal that follows from the very nature of reality, certain products can be produced and offered on the market in order to distract him from pursuing this goal. While it is within his freedom to choose to buy them or ignore them, to offer him temptations is for the seller to deviate from the transpersonal existential ideal. These considerations indicate possibilities of generalizing the concept of the "paradox of service" to deal with all forms of vested interest on all levels, which we will not pursue here.

an individual or organization, private or public, acts in order to create, maintain, and sometimes intensify the problem its functioning is supposed to solve. Thus, every economic unit, if it does not simply sell perishable products at unit cost as above, must function in a manner that is deeply *opposed* to its stated objectives, even though it must cater for these stated objectives on a superficial level, to maintain itself "in business." It must, therefore, operate *hypocritically*. It must operate with a facade of usefulness and an underlying reality of uselessness-destructiveness.

This paradox was conceived of in various terms by economic theorists. Communists argued that the paradox will vanish with universal state employment: when people are free from the "whip of hunger" they will serve effectively and selflessly. However, as they did not challenge the view of individuals as "metaphysical units" in any deep sense, their solution simply produced individuals deprived of their last motive to do anything at all, except the fear of imprisonment in the future if they fail to satisfy their superiors.

Free enterprise economists argue that the problem will be solved through competition. However, while competition maximizes the effectiveness possible under the conditions described, all parties to it are bound within a common consensus to maintain the market. Thus, no matter how fierce the competition, all medical doctors will turn against a practitioner who elevates sick individuals to "permanent wellness." They will see this as a cutthroat operation, and whatever commitments they may have to basic individuals rights will vanish in the face of the very threat to their existence.

The welfare society, of course, has "solved" the problem by covering up through "respectability facades" based on credentials and official reports. State employees must establish their efficacy through records of their activity. Thereby, a system of regularizing and streamlining facade construction is introduced, with an intensification of the tension between underlying motive and surface motive, hence between the apparent and the real objective actually served.*

---

*Thus, the paradox of service implies that those who are involved in service (as well as those involved in producing items that they know full well are damaging or useless for their users) are living inauthentically. They live, as Sartre has beautifully clarified, in *bad faith*. They live a lie, which they avoid ever articulating. When criticized, they will vehemently defend their sincerity, honesty, and integrity, as the attack threatens them with the possibility of an inner confrontation with that which they have always avoided facing.

Thus, it seems that the paradox is insoluble, and that it dooms the very idea of effective service, of whatever nature. But this is not necessarily the case. The paradox in question, like any other paradox, indicates not a fundamental problem concerning the nature of reality, but a false premise. The premise is not only believed, but also *lived*. But this does not change its being a premise. We will expose it in our next section.

TRANSPERSONAL VERSUS "ATOMISTIC" POLITICAL ECONOMY

What are the grounds of the paradox of service discussed above? Under what assumptions does it become inevitable?

Clearly its basic presupposition is that man is a *metaphysical island*. Each one of us finds himself alone facing an indifferent reality. This reality is that of particles whizzing round with no rhyme or reason, but in terms of some mechanical necessities. In this reality, man must work to survive, and he must obtain his survival in a predictable manner, or else he will be destroyed by hunger, cold, etc. To provide for his needs he must, therefore, exchange his product for services with someone or something. This view is not only that of the free market economy, with which many would associate it. Any form of socialism or collectivism simply replaces the major party for exchange. Each individual faces the *state* embodied in his superior, rather than other individuals for his survival. He must serve the state and receive his keep. The parameters of this kind of exchange are vastly different to the free market condition but they share a basic similarity to the "capitalist" case. In all circumstances, the individual is driven to work by an anxiety of survival. He will not survive unless he receives some income from a predictable, regular source, be it his business, his private employment, or his state employment.

The anxiety to survive relates, of course, to the view of oneself as a perishable organism, which is essentially a physicochemical conglomerate. Thus, the scientific or even commonsense view of the universe is naturally presupposed here. The universe consists of metaphysical islands, which are entities of various degrees of complexity and are inherently material. Human beings are such entities, and their survival depends on their ability to exchange their output with the output of other such systems. It is this atomistic materialism which underlies all varieties of political economy mentioned thus far, and which indeed pervades our culture. Indeed, it is the same metaphysics that underlies most methods of psychotherapy, be they psychoanalysis or reconditioning. The psychotherapist helps a system that is essentially material to adjust to a world that consists of plurality of such material systems. Thus, we can observe here a metaphysical *link* between our political economical considerations and those pertaining to psychology and therapy to follow.

Is this a necessary view, though? Is there no alternative to it? The various spiritual traditions of all cultures, be they early Christianity, Taoism, Hinduism, or Buddhism, mystical Judaism, or Zorastrianism, provide us with an entirely different view of existence, and with a corresponding radically different existential orientation.[29] In these terms, focalized by the emerging transpersonal paradigm in psychology, there are no "metaphysical islands," and matter is not the fundamental substance of reality. The view developed by transpersonalists on a variety of grounds, from their interpretation of quantum physics to LSD research and the study of meditation and other altered states, is of reality as a cosmic totality that is, in essence, *one consciousness*. Each individual and entity in the universe seems individual only in view of a profound perceptual delusion, called by the ancient Hindus *Maya* or *Avidya*.[2,8,9,11,13,14,17,18]

Thus, in these terms, each individual has *his place* in a cosmic scheme. He is merely a channel for One energy, One consciousness, One love that pervades all being and *is* all being. His interactions with other individuals are merely exchanges between different channels of what they each receive from the *same source,* the "transpersonal self," or the "Atman" or "Brahman" of the Hindus or, more traditionally, God.

In such terms, service to others is not done in order to obtain anything in exchange from them, though, of course, such exchange may take place as a special case. Rather, all service is done to the *source,* which is perceived in all other entities. As it is the same Self in all beings, serving others is serving the Self, and he who serves the Self finds his correct place in the cosmic scheme if he also fulfills his existential goal on a deeper level. Thus, his survival is not a problem incurring anxiety on two counts: (1) To begin with, survival is guaranteed by metaphysical principle, given that the essential nature of the individual is realized to be his imperishable consciousness, his selfhood, not his physical embodiment. (2) Moreover, as the physical embodiment is used to serve the Source in all manifestations, it is supported by the same Source, in terms of its Cosmic scheme. The tree does not bill the birds who sit in its branches and nest there, nor is he billed by the dogs who fertilize the soil from which he is nourished by their excretions.

The tree is an instrument to serve the birds, who are there to serve other parts of the cosmic totality. The world is not a chaos of causally interacting blind particles, but an ordered unity of purposes, in terms of a cosmic unifying *design*. It is the manifestation of one supermind.[1] Service is not done, therefore, to survive, but as a proper expression of one's *being*. To be what one is is to serve.[4] The essence of individuality is not the *self* (or *I*), because the self is transpersonal and one. Nor is it the ego, because the ego is merely the delusion that the individuality is the self. Rather, it is the *duty* to be fulfilled, the "dharma," as the concept was referred to in the Hindu sources.[5] The dharma differs from individual to individual in society, in the same way that no two trees have the same dharma. Similarly, the mode of preservation of each individual within the cosmic whole and its terms differ, in reflection of the considerations of cosmic design. However, as life is not lived for personal purposes, for pleasure, success, or even survival, but is lived for *service* and toward a goal to be desired beyond life, individuals are not bothered by apparent inequalities or social injustice. They realize that these, like survival-anxiety, reveal a deluded cosmic conception. The original teachings of Jesus (to the extent they survived the church that embodies the above formulated paradox like any other institution) bear witness to this conception. He recommended that a person be like the "roses of the field," which do not care for tomorrow because they exist in *faith*. Faith is the conscious experiential link between the individual and its Source. Faith knows that the fulfillment of duty is all that is required, with no concerns for "fruits of one's action."[6] It also knows that one cannot possess anything, because the Lord, the Source possesses all and is all. Thus Jesus recommended charity and sharing, not because he was in anticipation of Marx, but because he pointed the necessity to give up deluding identifications of Self with individuality, manifested by possessions, in order to experience faith and surrender to one's duty. As the *Bhaghavad Gita* stresses, and Indian saints have illustrated in their lives, he who does his duty with no concern for the fruits of his action, seeing all his actions as done not to gratify ego, to get pleasures or even maintenance but to serve the Lord, is taken care of by the Lord.

It is important not to misunderstand the implications of this conception. It does not imply withdrawal from ordinary exchange relations, but a transformation of the perception of their significance. A labourer paid for his work, or a merchant paid for his merchandise can perceive the payment as the Lord's way of supporting him and the service of merchandise given as their form of service. However, the transformation of *attitude* is crucial. Rather than basing one's existence on reliance on the lacks of others, and on the constant need to maintain such lack through the hidden destructive layers of one's service, one bases one's existence on his direct relation to the Source and the bounty of Being contained in that Source. Thus, the quality of service rendered is not affected by the consideration that one must "hook the client" in some way to want more. A psychotherapist, for example, who is paid for his service, need not keep his patient always needing him, but rather work effectively towards the total independence of the patient regarding his services. He is not haunted by the worry that the loss of patients will mean his starvation, as he trusts the Source of the Cosmic totality to provide him with all that he needs, either through the payment of patients or through any other way, which he may fail to foresee. In other words, the stress is the change from an ego-based concern for personal survival to an attitude of transpersonal service, where personal cares are left over to the One that through His hidden presence constitutes all Being and all consciousness of being. Only with this attitude can one serve without the need to sabotage his own service so as to "provide for tomorrow." Thus, without any need to change his external context, he can switch his economics to become free from the service paradox, and the existential inauthenticity it implies. The last point leads to a clarification of a second possible misunderstanding. The transpersonal conception of economics, as against other approaches, does not require for a societal change on any level, except the deepest level, of individual experience, attitude, and practice. As the transpersonal perspective perceives the Source, the one *I*, the transpersonal transcosmic Self as immanent in all realities, an individual who experiences the truth of this perspective and practices it can switch his own personal economics from whatever system obtains presently to the transpersonal approach. No violent revolutions are required, and no legislative changes. Rather, what is required is an inner change of attitude towards existence, and towards human society as part of this change.

To fully understand how this is possible, it is important to clarify another central aspect of the transpersonal perspective. Other existential approaches always seek for life a meaning within life. One's purpose may be hedonistic, or it may be the fulfillment of ambition. One may seek for "self fulfillment" through creative effort, but all of these goals are still within the context of life, as ordinarily experienced. The transpersonal approach, integrating and reflecting the common core of all great traditions, indicates an ultimate existential goal that transcends the dimensionality of mundane experience. The goal is that of liberation or illumination, namely a total experiential existential transformation where the individual experiences himself totally, on all levels of his being, not as an existential metaphysical island, but as one with the Source, one with the Divinity hidden everywhere. Such transformation has been differently described by those who attest to it from their experience. It can take the aspect of total vanishment of worldly experience and an awareness of only the Self, the *I* in the purity of its consciousness, consciousness now free of contents and centered in its core.[27] It can take the form of a radical transformation of the perception of the world: all that you look at is realized to be one with oneself and to radiate divinity.[21] Whatever the mode of the transformation, it eliminates any form of identification of consciousness with its bodily individualization. It eliminates the "desire for life" as well as the "desire for death."[2] It eliminates all desires, lacks, and concerns towards total peace. It eradicates emotions towards total love and bliss. It eradicates alienation in all forms towards a total sense of cosmic unity.

There is no question of the inherent difficulty of achieving this goal, of the length of the experiential existential path that it requires. All authentic traditions stress that the search for illumination must be frustrated if befuddled with a quest for instant solutions. To be reoriented transpersonally is simply to discover the new vision of the transpersonal meaning and nature of personal existence, to integrate it intellectually, and to start working on its integration on all other levels of one's being. Service to others is part of the path, because through service, done without any personal motive, one realizes that the same Self that he identifies with his own individuality is immanent in all beings. Through compassion and love, which are the condition for any genuine service, be it of a baker or a lawyer, the blindness to the vision of the ultimate truth of cosmic unity is disolved as petty concerns and anxieties of the ego, through more struggle and defeat and struggle and small victories, eventually melt away. Service is a key concept to that achievement, provided that it is done in the sense of pure *duty,* namely total and conscious surrender to one's cosmic role, one's dharma.

Thus, if an individual operating in a social economic context that is not based on this vision finds himself in conflict with others, who perceive his egoless service as a threat for their survival, the agonies of such confrontations are accepted as part of one's path to Liberation. The egoless service of Christ, as a spiritual teacher, clearly threatened the vested interest of the hypocritical and ego serving priesthood that condemned him to crucifiction. However, he perceived his death not as a disaster, but, eventually, as his final step on his own personal path to reach total unity with the Source. Similarly, if a medical doctor starts to realize that the purpose of his work is not to keep his patients in need of him but to serve the Lord, so as to merge eventually in Him, he would risk imprisonment for violating state laws regarding the "legal means of treating cancer." He would perceive his imprisonment as all great martyrs ever did: as a necessary, though painful step on his path to the Lord. Only when a person sees his own personal survival as an ultimate goal must he surrender to official economic and political ideologies in his dealing with others. However, such perception reflects lack of awareness of the transpersonal vision, or a mere rudimentary grasp of it. The more he will proceed on his path, the less be his commitment to ego, and the more his economic conduct will be transformed from that of the "rational agent" of most modern economic theories, or from that of the worker or businessman to that of the servant of the Lord, under whatever circumstances and in whatever capacity. This is the only way to eradicate the otherwise inevitable hypocrisy immanent in the implications of the "paradox of service."

At this point, of course, the transpersonal vision can be challenged, and the grounds for its rational validity questioned. It is impossible within this paper to repeat what has been done elsewhere in meeting this challenge.[15, 16, 17, 18, 19, 20] It is enough to indicate the simple implications of what has been accomplished. If one does not accept the transpersonal vision, then one is committed to the view of man as a metaphysical island. Under such commitment, he will be bound to the paradox of service. Even if a man dutifully serves his country or even his corporation, he still cannot avoid the paradox of service immanent in the existence of these larger entities as metaphysical islands. To serve one's corporation dutifully is to do the best one can to undermine competitors, and to serve one's country or nation dutifully is to under-mine other nations. Any duty conception that does not link man experientially to the Lord rather than to collective egos will result in severe forms of the paradox of service, though perhaps not on the same level as those illustrated above.

Thus, the upshot of this argument is that if the transpersonal vision is rejected, we have an a priori answer regarding psychotherapy, which applies to it in the same way as it applies to all other modes of service offered in any society, free market or communist, capitalist or socialist: psychotherapists must keep their patients hooked to them to guarantee their livelihood. Thus, they cannot be effective, and the money paid to them directly or through taxes is wasted exactly like the money paid to anyone else who is supposed to "help." Moreover, from another perspective still, the metaphysical conception underlying all societies that are not based on some version of the transpersonal vision implies, on the individual level, ineradicable existential anguish.

The point is simple. Given the metaphysical framework of materialis-tic atomism, each individual exists as a material organism, sentenced to a certain irreversible and final annihilation in the form of death. The threat of death, and its impending uncertainty, is thus a given substructure of any experience.[28] Moreover, the repeated experience of *lack*, manifesting through desire, is that of *pain*. Pleasure is only the interval between two pains, as no meal ever eradicates hunger, and no intercourse ever eradi-cates lust.[3] Moreover, moving from birth to death, man lives through periods of necessary decay as well as inevitable losses. He is haunted by his losses and fears as well as by his unfulfilled desires and the emotions attendant on them. Pleasures are passing, but these agonies, as well as the agonies of alienation and loneliness, immanent in materialistic atomism, are permanent. Thus, to live as human is to suffer, and suffering can be only seemingly escaped by distraction, but not eradicated. A psychotherapist sharing this vision of existence, grounded in modern "scientism," with his patients has very little to offer, *even if he, per impossible, genuinely wants the patient to become better in a permanent way*, and not to return to him. He can offer, perhaps, alleviation of certain agonies and "adjusting to the inevitable." Some therapists may also offer distracting entertainment, whether it takes the form of an indulgence in psychoana-lytic interpretation of dreams, delving into archetypes, or some bizarre sexual practices labelled "therapy." However, all this cannot even begin to relate to the existential anguish of he who seeks the therapist's help. His anguish is rooted in his perception of the nature and meaning of his being, as manifested not only cognitively but also emotionally. A therapist committed to the same view is no better off than the patient, and he can offer no relevant qualification to help. It is a cliche that therapists are usually mentally disturbed, and that they always seek therapy. . . . However, the grounds of the truth of this cliché are not usually clarified. A therapist who shares the vision of ineradicable existential anguish with his patient and who, like him, fears death and starvation and desires temporary satisfaction; who, like him, waits for the decay and disintegration of his being, is simply more aware of his existential anguish due to his continual, however vain, attempts to help it in others. Given this fact, the relatively low rates of suicide among therapists (which are apparently higher than most other professions) are an amazing indication of resilience.*

Thus, if one does not grant the validity of the transpersonal approach, one can conclude with safety that psychotherapy must be useless (a) on the general grounds of the paradox of service the therapist cannot afford to have the patient permanently and quickly well, hence independent of his services, and (b) on the specific ground of a lack of genuine awareness of an existential state that is essentially better than that presently of the patient towards which the therapy proceeds. At best, the patient can become an "adjusted person," namely someone who has resigned himself to life as a torture to be clung to ferociously because it is still better than the horror of death.

Obviously, these considerations merely show that the transpersonal perspective is the necessary condition for the possibility of effective psychotherapy. They do not show that it is a valid perspective because it is conceivable that indeed the transpersonal perspective is wrong and that consequently, psychotherapy is a doomed activity, and that all attempts to serve are hypocritical. However, as indicated, the rational-

---

*To see the rationale of the transpersonal perspective is to see its ability to offer a unified account of all facets of human existence and experience. Such perception is sufficient, according to current conceptions of rationality, in order to be convinced rationally of its truth. However, this is not so. Transpersonal phenomenology offers absolute demonstrations of the necessity of the transpersonal insights on philosophical grounds that preclude any concept of theory and reasonableness and require an absolute standard of rationality without premises. Again, the issue transcends our present limits.[18,19,20]

ity and necessary validity of the transpersonal approach have been demonstrated.[18,20] Let us now, therefore, presuppose its validity, either merely as the condition for the possibility of effective therapy or on the preferrable grounds of acquaintance with the rational proofs of its validity. In the first case, all that will be said will be understood *conditionally*. Namely, if psychotherapy is possible at all, that is, if one grants the validity of the transpersonal paradigm, then it is possible under the conditions specified below. In the second case, it can be understood without such qualifying conditions.

THE PREREQUISITES OF EFFECTIVE PSYCHOTHERAPY

The transpersonal perspective is, as we have seen, the necessary condition from the possibility of psychotherapy. What are its implications for the context and nature of the psychotherapeutic interaction?

1. To begin with, the interaction *cannot be conditioned by a financial exchange*, either between the therapist and the individual he works with or between him and the state. The only exchange perceived as taking place is between the therapist and the Lord (the Source), and between the patient and the Lord. Whatever the external manifestations of this exchange, the attitude is the one indicated. Thus, the therapy can be done as charity, within a public institutional context, or within a private practice without its nature and quality being affected.

2. The therapist is himself a self-transforming individual. He seeks, within his own existential framework, to transform himself to become purely a channel, an instrument of service of the Lord. He struggles with his own ego, and relates to the patients' experience from a profoundly personal level — that is the only way to reach the transpersonal one.

3. The therapist does not see himself as responsible to the transformation of the patient. Any such perception involves pride and ego, attributing to oneself what is actually done by the true transforming power of divine presence. Rather, the therapist sees himself as a pure instrument and thus is not concerned with *success or failure*, but only with egoless loving service.

4. The therapist realizes that the condition of the patient, like his

own, is rooted in the delusive ego perception of existence, which grounds the existential anguish of both of them. His major qualification is not a degree that he may or may not have. It is his own authentic effort to become purer channel, and to overcome ego, existential anguish, and metaphysical delusion. This experience has provided him with techniques and insights that he can offer to the patient.

5. The therapist cannot "make" the patient accept anything of what he offers, and as he is unconcerned with success or failure but only with genuine loving service, he does not worry about it. The therapist offers his insights and techniques, thereby confronting his patient with the existential freedom of his own choice: will he use the techniques or will he cling to his anguished condition as a means of serving ego? Will he continue to play the role of a miserable unhelpable wretch? Will he continue preferring this role and its various advantages (making others guilty, subsisting at their expense, etc.) to improvement? His choice is a sacred expression of his freedom, and the therapist cannot be involved in it.

6. The therapist, obviously, aims towards the goal of transformation of the patient. Once the patient has become independent of the technical aid offered by the therapist and starts "working on himself," the therapist withdraws. No one man can bring another to illumination. Only the Lord can grant it.

7. The therapist does not limit his role to "therapy" in any prescribed sense. Philosophical discussion, ethical reflection, recommendations of reading material, and indications of possible life-style changes are an integral part of his activity, not less than experiential exercises of various forms. His offerings are always made tentatively with the only authority he can provide, namely that these approaches have worked for him. Sometimes he may be sufficiently philosophically educated to offer rational demonstrations of the validity of his advice, or at least some accounts of their inherent rationale (which are two different things).[3] In any case, his personal authority plays no role in the therapy. He is, at best, a guide through his own personal experience and transformation.

8. The therapist does *not adjust the goal of the therapy to the declared*

needs of the patient, as he cannot indulge in "ethical relativism." His concern is that of a genuine existential experiential transformation, not the temporary alleviation of suffering. Within the transpersonal context, suffering as such is a blessing. It indicates the need for existential reorientation, it breaks through ego-generated barriers for self-transformation, being a ground of urgency for seeking a change. Sedating sufferers physically or experientially is helping the person to avoid the responsibility of facing the meaning of the suffering and learning whatever is immanent in it as existential guidance.

9. The therapist acts in terms of his own inspiration and experience, not in terms of any dogmatic training. His only genuine goal is to serve, not to satisfy some establishmentarian demands to "appear good on record" or to "hook the patient."

10. The therapist considers his own practice as ground for his own self transformation, as he perceives experiential deviations from these ideal guidelines within himself as indicating aspects of his own being that demand transformation. In the same vein, he encourages the patient to perceive every experience, not only therapy sessions or even self work sessions as guided technically by the therapist, as transforming occasions. The development of a reflective philosophical attitude towards one's experience allows the patient to use a concert, love making, or a meal no less as occasions for self-transformation than clinical sessions. Indeed, it is exactly this attitude that "all of life is a therapy, and that cure lies beyond life, in liberation," which allows the patient to become independent, and the sooner the better.

11. The therapist sees no validity in dogmatic classifications. For him the schizophrenic, the manic depressive, or the compulsive neurotic are simply individuals facing the same universal existential anguish of an identical essence to his own; the anguish of separation, disconnectedness from the source, drowning in ego. Thus, he operates on a purely *experiential* level, not on a technical one. He is not a scientist but a servant of his fellow man.

These fundamental principles follow from the transpersonal perspective as outlined. They undercut any traditional concepts of success, because they do not define success in any external terms, nor do they stress its importance. Success versus failure are relevant categorizations for those bound on serving their ego. On one level, they must succeed to "remain in business." On a deeper level they must still succeed — to maintain the demand that allows them to remain in business.

They are hypocritically torn by the "paradox of service." But for he who serves, the fruits of his action are not his concern, as he really does not see himself as an *agent*, but as a channel for action. If the patient praises him, it is vital for him to avoid attachment to the pride that praise inevitably brings forth in his consciousness, and to redirect the praise to the one to whom it is due, to the source of the love, energy, and wisdom that enabled the therapist to serve as an effective instrument. Obviously, the ultimate therapist is therefore the being who has totally transcended ego and realized that his individuality is merely an expression of the Absolute Source, the Inherent Self of all being, a "wave on the ocean." The *liberated master*, the *guru*, is the best therapist conceivable. He knows from experience the goal towards which he leads his "patient," namely his disciple or devotee. He wants nothing of the devotee. Gurus who sell their services manifest ego and are bound by the paradox of service. The guru's unity with the Source means his inner unity with the one he helps. Thus, he has perfect access to all inner realities of the one helped with no need for verbal exchange, and he utilizes that access for guidance and transformation in the subtlest way possible.

Individuals like Christ, Buddha, Ramakrishna, and Shirdi Sai Baba were the greatest psychotherapists of the past, and so are living masters and saints. However, when one is not in the position to surrender his life to a genuine saint, and has sufficient judgement to avoid a fake saint (one who is "in the market" and "sells enlightenment" or "spiritual progress"), another individual, with or without any official qualifications of any sort, with or without an official context of therapy, may be found to guide him a part of the way, to the point that the guide exhausts his own usefulness, based as it is on his own experience and level of transformation. No guide can guide beyond his own achievement. That is why the ultimate guide can only be He who completed the whole path — or He who was "there" always, forever, eternally. The Lord is the ultimate guide and the only real one, and to find Him one needs not go anywhere outside himself, as He is really the pure *I* or Self.[3,27]

Given these understandings, most existing psychotherapy, especially such that is for purely remunerative motives or on the ground of nontranspersonal perspectives, can be seen through. It is a doomed failure, always conducted hypocritically on some level. However, it is not to be singled out for criticism. Ego-based psychotherapy, like ego-based medicine, or economics, is doomed to fail like the individuals who dedicate their life to the service of ego and the societies that base their working philosophy on ego, in the form of science, political ideology, or dogmatic religion. A transpersonal revolution is a sine qua non to the elimination of the built-in necessity of failure immanent in the paradox of service. This revolution will not take place "in the streets" or in Parliament. If it ever takes place, it takes place *within you and me.* It will not come tomorrow, or in a hundred years. If it will start, let it start *now.* Perhaps it has already started.

REFERENCES

1. Aurobindu, S. *The Life Divine.* Sri Aurobindu Ashram Pondicheri, 1977.
2. Baba, S. S. *Jnana Vahini.* Sri Sathya Sai Baba Education and Publication Foundation, India, 1975.
3. Baba, S. S. *Sadhana: The Inward Path.* Sri Sathya Sai Education and Publication Foundation, India 1978.
4. Baba, S. S. *Geeta Vahini.* Sri Sathya Sai Books and Publications, India, 1980, 4th edition.
5. Baba, S. S. *Dharma Vahini.* Sri Sathya Sai Books and Publications, India, 1980.
6. *Bhaghavad Gita, The Song of God.* Tr. Swami Prabhavananda and Christopher Isherwood, Sri Ramakrishna Math, Madras, 1980.
7. Bentham, J. *An Introduction to the Principles of Morals and Legislation.* Athlone Press, London, 1970.
8. Bohm, D. *Wholeness and the Implicate Order.* Routledge and Kegan Paul, London, 1980.
9. Boucouvalas, M. Transpersonal psychology: Scope and challenges. *Australian Journal of Transpersonal Psychology,* 12, 1981, 136–152.
10. Capra, R. *The Tao of Physics.* Shambhala, Boulder, Colorado, 1975.
11. Fadiman, J. The transpersonal stance. *Australian Journal of Transpersonal Psychology,* 1, 1, 1981, 1–23.
12. Freud, S. Analysis—Terminable and interminable. *International Journal of Psychoanalysis,* xviii, 1937.
13. Grof, S. *Realms of the Human Unconscious.* Viking, New York, 1975.
14. Grof, S. *Principles of LSD Psychotherapy.* Hunter House, New York, 1980.
15. Kroy, M. Parapsychology, phenomenology and the scientific method. *Australian Journal of Transpersonal Psychology,* 1, 1, 1981, 23–41.
16. Kroy, M. Phenomenology, behaviourism and the self. *Australian Journal of Transpersonal Psychology,* 1, 2, 1981, 108–124.

17. Kroy, M. Transpersonal perspectives on psychotherapy. *Australian Journal of Transpersonal Psychology,* 2, 1, 1981, 1–32.
18. Kroy, M. The phenomenological foundations of transpersonal psychology. *Australian Journal of Transpersonal Psychology,* 2, 2, 1982, 83–106.
19. Kroy, M. Psychology vs. phenomenology of religion: A critical approach. *Australian Journal of Transpersonal Psychology,* 3, 1, 1983, 59–76.
20. Kroy, M. *Beyond Being and Nothingness: The Rationality of Mysticism.* In print, 1984.
21. Mahendranath Gupta. *The Gospel of Sri Ramakrishna.* Sri Ramakrishna Math, Madras, 1974.
22. Mendelson, R. S. *Confessions of a Medical Heretic.* Warner Books, New York, 1979.
23. Moss, R. *The Cancer Syndrome.* Grove Press, U.S.A., 1980
24. Rand, A. *Capitalism, The Unknown Ideal.* Signet Books, New York, 1967.
25. Rothbard, M. N. *Man, Economy and State.* Nash Pub. Corp., Los Angeles, 1970.
26. Rothbard, M. N. *For A New Liberty.* Macmillan, New York, 1975.
27. Sankara Acharya. *The Mandukopanisad with Guadapa Karika, Commentary.* Sri Ramakrishna Ashram, Mysore, 1975.
28. Sartre, J. P. *Being and Nothingness.* Pocket Books, New York, 1956.
29. Wilber, K. *The Spectrum of Consciousness.* Quest, Wheaton III, 1977.
30. Yogananda, P. *Autobiography of a Yogi.* Self Realization Fellowship, Los Angeles, 1971.

Chapter 11

DO PSYCHOTHERAPIES
MEET CLIENTS' PERCEIVED NEEDS?

PITTU LAUNGANI

L et us assume you feel there is something the matter with you. You don't quite know what it is. In your own way, you have tried to understand it, tried to locate the cause, and have even tried to do something about it. Hot baths, cold baths, sleeping early, sleeping late, jogging, resting, yogic exercises, strange diets, aspirins, sedatives, "pep" pills, drinking, not drinking—you have tried everything you could think of, or have read about, or have been recommended by your friends, family, and colleagues. You still feel no better, even worse, as though something were slipping away from you, and you were unable to control it. Someone suggests—perhaps, your general practitioner—that you ought to consult a psychiatrist. He or she may be able to sort out your problems for you.

The word psychiatrist creates a feeling of discomfort in you. All kinds of lurid stories come to mind. Cold, damp, soulless corridors in large mental institutions; old, helpless patients in a daze; chaos, confusion, bedlam; electric shocks, drugs, screams; tough, brutal nurses, unfeeling doctors—the images made even more sinister by your recollection of the film *One Flew Over The Cuckoo's Nest*. A cold shudder passes through your spine. Psychiatrists? Oh, no!

How about a psychoanalyst, you ask your doctor in hope? They don't mess around with electric shocks and drugs! They just sit and talk. Or rather, listen. This time, all kinds of funny stories come to mind: they let you look at some crazy pictures, they ask you to examine some inkblots, they persuade you to talk about your mother, they go into your childhood, find out the naughty things you got up to, or more likely, didn't get up to—these images made even funnier by the unsmiling seriousness with which *they* take them.

132

It seems a nice bit of innocent fun to go to a psychoanalyst, you seem to think. But your spirits suddenly plunge when you learn the cost. Four or even five times a week at the going rate, for two to three years *at least!* And twenty years, if you happen to be Woody Allen! Like Woody Allen, you'd need to be terribly well off to afford a psychoanalyst. You probably wouldn't have had any problems if you had that kind of money in the first place, you say to yourself. You could get it for free, you know, your knowledgeable G.P. tells you. On the National Health. There is a slight snag, though. You may have to wait a while. How long? There's no telling, but it could be months. Also—here comes the second snag—you may be interviewed by the psychoanalyst. And he or she might decide you were not quite suitable for his or her kind of therapeutic approach. Oh! Clients are vetted quite regularly. Mind you, you'd have a damn good chance of being accepted for analysis if you're *YAVIS*. A what? Young, Attractive, Verbal, Intelligent, and Successful. If you *were* all that why would you want to go to an analyst, you ask yourself.

What about cut-price therapy, you ask, lowering your sights. Something that doesn't go on for two or three years. You can't wait that long. Besides, you haven't got that kind of money to spare.

And here, an exciting world unfolds before your disbelieving eyes! You are in a consumer's paradise! All kinds of therapies are offered. Tailor-made therapies. Exclusive therapies. Tried and tested therapies. Well-worn second-hand therapies. Individual therapies. Group therapies. Long, elaborate residential therapies. Meditational therapies. Frenetic therapies. Here you can shout, get shouted at, abuse, get abused, scream, get screamed at, insult, get insulted, dance, watch others dance, sing, hear others sing, touch, get touched, massage, get massaged, work yourself into a frenzy, throw tantrums, rest, sleep, dream, have nightmares—all is permitted. Here, you are King, Caliph, Sultan.

It is on these that we shall concentrate. As far as you—by you, I mean the client, the consumer of psychotherapies—are concerned, your main interest, I imagine, is centered on *four* interrelated issues, which are as follows:

1. UNDERSTANDING THE PROBLEM (DIAGNOSIS)
   Your first concern is to find out what your problem is. (Not all clients have an insight into their problems.) The expert you consult should, after an interview (examination) aided by a de-

tailed case history, be able to offer a diagnosis of your problem. He or she should be able to do that accurately, speedily, and with a minimum of fuss, and should also be able to explain to you all this in a language free from needless jargon.

Secondly, you would wish to be assured that had you gone to another therapist instead of the one you have consulted, the nature of your problem would remain *unchanged*. If the diagnosis changes from therapist to therapist, you can't be sure if the first one was accurate. Or indeed any other one. A high degree of consensus among therapists would be quite heartening. Even then, you might be wary. For you know that *a high degree of consensus is nothing more than a statement of reliability*. If a thousand million people tell you the earth is flat, it doesn't make it so! But that, at least as far as you are concerned, is the first step.

2. <u>NATURE OF HELP (THERAPEUTIC PROCEDURES)</u>

It is understandable that you should want to know the kind of help or therapeutic procedures that were going to be adopted by your therapist. You'd want them to be explained to you, you'd want to know if they were going to be painful, and if so, what kind of pain were you likely to suffer, physical, emotional, and for how long. Finally, you would wish to be convinced that the suggested therapeutic procedure, in your case, was the most effective one.

3. <u>PROBABILITY OF SUCCESS (PROGNOSIS)</u>

Should you decide to undergo the recommended therapy, you would wish to know in general terms (a) the duration of the treatment, and (b) its probability of success. Since the concern of most clients is to "return home cured," you would wish for some assurance on your concern. You would certainly want to know if you would become a "better" person, a "different" person, more happy, more creative, more positive, and more complete or integrated as a result of your willing participation in the treatment or training programme.

Another question on which you might wish for a definite answer is the one of relapse. You would want to be told about it and about any other symptoms that you might acquire. You would also wish to be certain in your mind what was meant by being cured. Would there be an objective way of being judged as cured, or would other therapists quibble over the meaning of the word in academic journals?

4. <u>COST OF THERAPY</u>

Not only would you want to know the cost of your therapy but also if you could have had the same (or similar) kind of therapy elsewhere, cheaper.

Also, what would happen if your therapy were not found to be successful? What would happen if your condition were to actually get worse? How far would you go along with the suggestion that you were cured *only when you felt you were cured?*

These, in general, are the four issues with which most clients seeking therapeutic help are likely to be concerned the most. Not very many clients are likely to worry a great deal about other subsidiary problems such as the sex, age, ethnicity, mannerisms, attitudes, and values of the therapist. Some might. Of course it would be nice to relate to a warm, kindly, empathetic, humane, benevolent, understanding, friendly, articulate, good looking, and well dressed therapist who also shared all our values! So would having breakfast in a secluded rose garden! We'd all like that. But an absence of one or two of the above attributes is hardly likely to upset a client to an extent where he or she might feel impelled to terminate the therapy.

Apart from what they expect the therapist to help them to achieve, the clients also cherish at least two private hopes. First they hope that the psychotherapy will help them to overcome their specific problem. This could be anything—an acute phobia, a pattern of obsessive-compulsive behaviour, localised anxiety, addiction of some kind, sexual problems, aggressive behaviour, extreme timidity or shyness, or whatever. Encompassing the first hope is the second. Psychotherapy may help them to find a solution to their "life problems." As a result, they might hope to become better people, certainly *different:* more happy, more kind, more positive, more mature persons who would be able to realise their personality, have peak experiences, and form rich, meaningful, and lasting relationships.

How far do the general expectations of clients match with what is actually provided by the psychotherapists? Is there congruence between expectation and actuality? Or a chasm? Do clients, on the whole, get their money's worth? Or do they return as dissatisfied customers? Are psychotherapists the modern messiahs or yet another breed of false prophets?

To answer some of these questions, we shall examine the growth of psychotherapy from its historical perspective. One would hope that this will give us a clearer view of the problem and will enable us to examine issues that otherwise might have gone unnoticed.

The last forty years have seen what can only be described as a dramatic change in the pattern and practice of psychotherapy and, of course, in the training of psychotherapists. Until the late 1940s, or even up to the early 1950s, the custody of mental patients (as they were then called) and the treatment of their disorders was largely in the hands of psychiatrists and psychoanalysts who, without exception, were medically qualified persons. Naturally, their conceptual framework was based on the medical model. Yet each of them had irreconcilably different approaches in matters related to the definition, etiology, and the treatment of mental disorders. The psychiatrists in general preferred physical methods of treatment that included the use of drugs, electric shocks, and in exceptional cases, psychosurgery. The psychoanalysts, on the other hand, adhered to verbal methods of treatment, and generally confined themselves to the treatment of nonpsychotic disorders.

The definitions of mental illness—such as there were—reflected largely their attachment to the medical model. They were also tautological. "Mental illness is defined as exposure to psychiatric treatment" is one such example. Such anomalies, however, were minor irritants. They did not affect the monolithic structure of psychiatry, which was founded on the medical model. Psychiatry and psychoanalysis—notwithstanding the conceptual divisions that had begun to form in each of them—continued to function as the main professional organisations for the treatment of mental disorders. Occasional voices of dissent, such as that of Wilhelm Reich in the 1940s, hardly made an impact on the prevailing hegemony. The medical model continued to rule, its authority unchallenged.

But the occasional voices of dissent turned into a distinct murmur, which turned into a protest, which turned into a movement. In the mid-fifties, the usefulness of the medical model began to be seriously questioned. The diagnostic methods used by psychiatrists came under sharp attack. They were seen as being tautological. They lacked objectivity and often reflected the preoccupations of the psychiatrists. They were injurious to the interests of the patient (the word patient was being replaced by the word client). They offended the client's dignity, and they stigmatized and invalidated the client. They served no useful purpose other than enabling the psychiatrist to seek shelter behind high-sounding mumbo jumbo. Psychiatry was even seen by some as a form of professionally recognized witchcraft, with the psychiatrist as the witch doctor.

Interestingly enough, the attack on psychiatry and on psychiatrists came from a group of disenchanted psychiatrists. Subscribing to a kind of left-wing, Marxist ideology, the antipsychiatrists looked upon traditional psychiatry as being essentially right-wing. Mental illness, they argued, was used as weapon to degrade, stigmatize, and incarcerate the weak and exploited members of society. This was done with the connivance of the psychiatrist, who even conspired with the Establishment to enforce repressive social control. Many of the criticisms of the antipsychiatrists are without foundation. And since they have been comprehensively discussed elsewhere (see Laungani, 1978), they need not concern us here. The antipsychiatry movement that was popular during the early and mid-sixties has declined considerably. It does not appear to attract a great deal of sensible followers.

Psychoanalytical therapies, too, did not go unchallenged. There was growing disenchantment with them too. They were seen as being mechanical, expensive, time-consuming, they portrayed human beings in unjustifiably pessimistic and negative terms, their effectiveness had not been demonstrated, and the selectivity exercised by the psychoanalysts in the choice of their clients did not make it accessible to all those who needed psychoanalysis.

Dissatisfaction with traditional psychiatry was not an isolated phenomenon. It came from all directions. People searched for alternative approaches to psychiatry and psychoanalysis. Many drifted away from the mainstream of psychiatry to form their own brands of psychotherapies. Many old theories from academic psychology — phenomenology, gestalt theory, instinct theory, exchange theory — were revived, even resuscicated, and given new names. New theories were formulated, and new techniques were introduced. Individual therapy, which was seen as being restricting and time-consuming, gave way to group therapies.

The 1960s witnessed — particularly in California, where there was a spectacular upsurge — an astonishing rise in new methods of treatment, new methods of helping others to achieve their full potential and realise their personality. This new wave of movement swept away the debris of past terms and concepts—mental illness, patient, diagnosis, disorder, treatment, cure, to name but a few. The old order yielded to the new, and terms such as realisation of personality, self-actualisation, authenticity, having "peak" experiences, letting suppressions come to the surface, coming to terms with one's feelings, acquiring holistic changes, acquiring empathy, trust, and being oneself came into popular usage.

The new psychotherapists recognized no allegiance to either Freudian theories, or to traditional psychiatry. In their new found "liberation" they were not restrained by the caution, bordering on paranoia, exercised by their predecessors in terms of periods of training and training requirements for potential analysts. Such stringent measures of the past were seen as being old-fashioned, vapid, and even reactionary. Training procedures were relaxed and in some cases abandoned altogether.

Also, the pecuniary potential of group work that was colossal could hardly fail to go unnoticed! There were fortunes to be made—and quickly. It is hardly surprising that Avis Rent A Car, seeing the business potential of psychotherapies, accelerated smartly into that area. Therapists of all kinds of persuasions grew to meet the growing demands of their consumers. Like fast food, group psychotherapy had at last arrived on the streets to cater *instantly* to the needs of the masses!

Psychotherapy had such a refreshing approach now. Gone was the secrecy, the stuffiness, and the artificiality that had surrounded the psychoanalytical therapies of the past. Gone were the stringent selection procedures of the past to "vet" their potential clients. Here was to be found an almost breathtaking openness! Here the client could come for as many (or as few) sessions as desired. Here the client could drop out of treatment for a few weeks, join another group meanwhile, and return to the fold without loss of face or residual guilt. Here the client was not subjected to the harsh rules of the past, but was liberated and free.

Here the therapeutic atmosphere was easy, informal, and relaxed. So were the therapists. The group members were referred to by their first names, including the therapists, who were sometimes called leaders, sometimes facilitators, and sometimes helping agents. At times the group was persuaded, cajoled, and bullied into doing group exercises suggested by the group leader(s). At times the group was asked to share an individual's emotional experience, thus helping a member to come to terms with his or her own crises. At times the group was shown how to meditate, or practice "pranayanas," in order to attain a state of transcendental tranquility. At times the group members were encouraged to explore their feelings and interact with one another freely—not just with words, but also with their bodies. At times the group was harangued, shouted at, abused in the coarsest possible terms, vilified, and humiliated into believing that *they were* capable of achieving whatever that they might set out to achieve. Everything was possible.

Over time, each group came to acquire its own mould, its own ethos, and its own theoretical orientation. In the midst of such breathtaking variety and free enterprise and zeal shown by therapists in helping their clients to resolve their life problems, how does a client decide where to go and to whom to turn when in need of help? There is *no referral system* with the present-day psychotherapies, as is the case with the more traditional psychotherapies. They are available freely, on the open market. Offers of a variety of therapies are even openly advertised in popular magazines and newspapers. And since it is not always possible for a potential client to distinguish one offer from another in terms of their bonafides, legitimacy, and the professional status of those offering the therapies, it raises the serious issue of *protecting or safeguarding the client's rights* in the matter.

SAFEGUARDING OF CLIENTS' RIGHTS

If therapies operate on the basis of a "consumer-market-economy"—and in a sense they do, because in many of the cases, the client is not *referred to* by any recognized professional channels to the therapist(s)—then it is incumbent upon the "free market" therapists to state clearly and unambiguously the nature and type of services offered. (It should be recognized that one is not necessarily defending a referral system in arguing a case for the protection of clients' rights.) The client has a right to more than vague, platitudinous assurances. It will not do to claim, as is often done, that the process of psychotherapy is one of those rare, rich, unique, mystical, transcendental, existential experiences that can only be shared by members in the group, but cannot be defined. The psychotherapists would need to do better than that. At the very least, the psychotherapists would need to define the conceptual framework within which such "rich and potentially beneficial" experiences emerge. Minimal though the above requirement is, it might not find favour among many psychotherapists. One can even envisage a situation where the more enterprising of the psychotherapists in the near future might well introduce a commercial *caveat emptor* clause to safeguard their rights and interests in the psychotherapeutic transaction! The client, in the future, might be suitably warned! But for now the client needs to be protected from cut-rate entrepreneurial psychotherapists whose professional bona-fides might be just a little suspect.

This brings us finally to the main questions concerning the practice of present-day psychotherapies, questions concerning their *validity, effectiveness,* and *commensurability.* To those practitioners to whom such questions might seem obscene, it is asserted that without informed, objective answers to such questions, the present-day psychotherapies will, in the long run, *be subjected to the same kind of attack* that their proponents have, until now, launched on the traditional therapies.

VALIDITY, EFFECTIVENESS, AND COMMENSURABILITY OF PSYCHOTHERAPIES

All therapeutic practices explicitly or implicitly spring from their respective theoretical framework. A close examination of the literature shows that the theoretical underpinnings of the present-day psychotherapies are, in general, in a state of "epistemological anarchy." This state is aptly summed up by the phrase "anything goes." IF IT WORKS, USE IT appears to be the guiding principle of many psychotherapeutic practices.

Such a refreshingly pragmatic approach would doubtless be welcomed if it could be explained and demonstrated *what it is that actually works* in a given therapy and what are its theoretical links. On this vital point, there does not appear to be a clear answer. It does not help to realise that in many cases, there is not even a faint resemblance or a tenuous link between theory and practice.

When theories from which the practices are supposedly derived are not clearly formulated and are not open to testing and potential (if not actual) falsification, their validity remains a questionable issue. They may be valid, but there is no exact way of telling. And in the absence of such objective knowledge, it raises a moral issue of whether or not one ought to recommend it to a given client. One might be helping the client, or again, one might be doing the client a disservice. The decision to help a client by resorting to a particular kind of therapy whose *unintended consequences* may have far-reaching effects on the mental well-being of the client must be made on more than just a caveat of good intentions. Such decisions must be made, as far as possible, on the state of available objective knowledge. This, sadly, is not always done.

Yet, strangely enough, the evidence—such as there is—seems to suggest that persons who undergo therapy have a better chance of recovering than persons who don't. The figures vary, as do the statistics and the research methods used for evaluating therapeutic outcomes. But the evidence based on studies done in the 1970s, and even in the early 1980s (see Bergin and Lambert, 1978; Luborsky, L., et al., 1975; Rachman and Wilson, 1980; Sloane, R. B., et al., 1975) suggests that therapies do, in general, tend to work. But how therapies work, what are the special features in each therapy, what are the specific identifiable parameters that bring about the reported positive changes in the well-being of the client, have not been clearly articulated. Also, it is not always clear what the investigators mean when they use the word *work* with reference to the effectiveness of psychotherapy. Some rely on the client's subjective reports, some on the disappearance of symptoms, some on changes in test scores and in behavioural measures in the predicted direction, and others rely on the holistic changes manifested in the client's attitudes and values concerning his or her mental health, work, and interpersonal relationships. It appears, however, that the personality factors of the therapist—in particular, warmth, trust, and acceptance—play a crucial role in determining the positive outcome of therapy (Clare and Thompson, 1981).

At present we do not have precise knowledge of how different therapies work. Obviously, not all therapies work with the same degree of success. Some work more efficiently (or inefficiently) than others. Some tend to help more persons than others. But which of the many therapies work 'best' under which conditions, how, with what kind of clients, on what time-scale, with what kind of results are questions which are not easy to answer with a high degree of confidence.

This is so, because most therapies are not easily commensurable. Legitimate comparisons require, among other factors, a clear deliniation of a large set of common parameters, such as the random assignment of cases, severity of life problems or neuroses, use of control (no-treatment) groups, specification of procedures to be followed, agreed definition of cure, period of treatment, the professional expertise of the therapists, and their willingness to allow their work and practice to be examined objectively by others. Such conditions are hard to meet. The few studies (mentioned above) that have been done have not produced unequivocal findings. The practical and methodological difficulties are so daunting that many therapists, weary of the tedium of commensurability, have questioned the legitimacy of commensurability of therapies. It has been suggested that there may be an economic, perhaps even an empirical justification, but is there a rational justification for comparing therapies? Whether there is a rational justification or not is not the issue. The most compelling justification is a *moral* one: it is the moral responsibility of the therapist to ensure that the client who seeks succour is given it, humanely. That is the first consideration. Secondly, any therapeutic procedures that are used to help the client must not be assumed, *but must be seen to be beneficial* to the client. And this can be achieved only when the therapies are put to crucial tests concerning their effectiveness. Otherwise, one is back into a state of epistemological anarchy.

Is it now possible to offer even a tentative answer to the main question posed as the title of this article: Do psychotherapists meet clients' perceived needs? Firstly, one must disregard the psychotherapeutic "cowboys" of the profession who often operate for their own pecuniary gains. Their intentions may be bonafide, but their qualifications and professional training might be, to say the least, suspect. They may even, unwittingly, do more harm than good. The majority of the trained, professionally qualified psychotherapists—considering the uncharitable attitude shown by the Health Services in allocating resources for the promotion of mental health—do not always get the kind of recognition that is their due. The good they do "is oft interred," and occasional scandals get highlighted and come up for public scrutiny.

The uncertainty about the effectiveness of psychotherapies is also, to a certain extent, created by the potential clients themselves. The number of clients seeking some form of psychotherapy or the other has increased significantly, and by the present trend shows every sign of increasing. Why that should be so is a question which, sadly, will have to remain unanswered. The clients have come to expect and, consequently, demand far more than can conceivably be provided by psychotherapists. The present push-button-instant-gratification-technological-Western-society has perhaps beguiled a potential client into believing that happiness too can be obtained instantly. My own feeling, as an Easterner living in the West, is that the Westerner in search of happiness has concentrated on the right to happiness rather than on the right to *pursue* happiness. One has to *work* at happiness. It does not come instantly.

REFERENCES

Bergin, A. E., and Lambert, M. J. The evaluation of therapeutic outcomes. In S. L. Garfield and A. E. Bergin (Eds.), *Handbook of Psychotherapy and Behaviour Change: An Empirical Analysis*, 2nd edition. pp. 139–190. Wiley, 1978.

Clare, A. W., and Thompson, S. Let's talk about ME. British Broadcasting Corporation, 1981.

Laungani, P. Antipsychiatry—A suitable case for treatment. *Bull. Br. Psychol. Soc.*, 31, pp. 388–390, 1978.

Luborsky, L., Singer, B., and Luborsky, L. Comparative studies of psychotherapies: Is it true that "Everyone has won and all must have prizes?" *Archives of General Psychiat.*, 32, pp. 995–1008, 1975.

Rachman, S. J., and Wilson, G. T. *The Effects of Psychological Therapy*, Second Enlarged Edition, Pergamon Press, 1980.

Sloane, R. B., Staples, F. R., Cristol, A. H., Yorkston, N. J., and Whipple, K. *Psychotherapy versus Behaviour Therapy*, Harvard University Press, 1975. .

Chapter 12

EIGHT STEPS TOWARD PROTECTING THE PSYCHOTHERAPY CLIENT FROM "CONSUMER FRAUD"

JAMES K. MORRISON

B ecause it is a repugnant thought to imagine psychotherapists deliber- ately deceiving clients related to services offered, I find it difficult to believe that more than a tiny percentage of psychotherapists engage in real consumer fraud. However, I would like to make the case that unwittingly, and all too often, psychotherapists are guilty of some lesser type of consumer fraud in that they do not do enough to protect their clients from the possible harm caused by their therapeutic interventions. For example, could not psychotherapists be accused of "consumer fraud" when they do not adequately explain the type of therapy contracted by clients? One can imagine therapists who, soon after the initial interview with clients, begin a type of therapy that clients are not expecting and that they do not understand. In this case, are not the consumers fraudulently deceived in some way about the therapy they are contracting? One could, unfortunately, answer in the affirmative.

Are we as psychotherapists not obligated to go out of our way to protect our clients in light of the criticism that psychotherapists are ineffective (Eysenck, 1952; Bergin, 1966; Szasz, 1975) and seriously discriminate against certain groups (e.g., poor, blacks, females: see Breggin, 1975; Brown, 1973; Chessler, 1972; Glenn, 1974; Halleck, 1971; Jones, 1975; Levine, Kamin, & Levine, 1975; Hare-Mustin, 1983; Tennov, 1975), thus fostering a preservation of the *status quo*. In light of the excessive vulnerability of psychotherapy clients to abuses (e.g., seduction by therapists, deterioration of condition by misapplication of techniques, fostering of dependence on the therapist for financial reasons, physical abuse, a staggering and sometimes unnecessary high cost of long-term therapy, dissolution of a marriage without sufficient justification and with the unwitting encouragement of a therapist, and unwarranted verbal rejection by the therapist), it would appear that clients who undergo psychotherapy may not always know what they may be risking when they enter psychotherapy.

One would not be so rash as to assume that more than a tiny minority of therapists knowingly and with intent subject clients to consumer fraud with regard to services offered. However, with some sadness and shame, I do assert that more than a few of us all too cavalierly neglect the rights of clients, and that may border on consumer fraud. At least one can question whether we assume ethical responsibility in protecting consumers from our less than intentional abuse of our positions of authority. Hare-Mustin, Maracek, Kaplan, and Liss-Levinson (1979) state that it "is unfortunate that statements of ethical standards represent more a 'salute to the flag' for therapists than a bill of rights for clients" (P. 3). The remainder of this chapter will be devoted to ways in which therapists can actively protect the rights of the consumers who contract psychotherapy.

EIGHT STEPS TO SAFEGUARD CLIENTS' RIGHTS IN THERAPY

The following are eight ways in which a therapist can assure that psychotherapy does not contain even the slightest hint of consumer fraud. Perhaps no therapist can implement all of these recommendations, at least for every client, but most therapists should be able to find practical ways of using one or more of these.

1. Explain Your Therapeutic Approach More Thoroughly

Most intelligent consumers do not buy most products about which they know nothing. Yet, it still astonishes one how many people contract therapy knowing little or nothing about the process. As psychotherapists, we have the ethical responsibility to teach our clients about our own style of therapy, lest they contract for something quite unexpected. It is a good idea for most therapists—some psychoanalysts and others may disagree—to outline some of their theoretical assumptions and put these down on paper so that the client can see the theoretical bias of each therapist. If, for example, a client does not accept a therapist's assumptions about the impact of early childhood events on a person's personality development, the client can then choose another therapist and the first therapist can save himself or herself from a very frustrating experience.

The techniques used in therapy may also be something therapists want to explain. Certainly any unorthodox procedures should be explained in sufficient detail so that the client can give informed consent. Otherwise, such therapists may leave themselves wide open to lawsuits.

Some therapists certainly may want to surprise their clients with confrontation, role playing, or paradoxical techniques at appropriate times, and believe that to explain these techniques would be to tip off the client and lose the effect of such therapeutic strategies. However, a few words about such techniques in one of the early sessions do not, from my experience, detract from the potency of such interventions. Then, at least, you obtain the consent of the client and further insure protection against lawsuit. In this regard, a written statement, outlining the theoretical and operational assumptions of the therapy (in layman's language, of course), signed and dated by the client, and witnessed by the therapist, would provide some evidence that the therapist had tried to explain his or her procedures to the client and that the client had given consent.

The rule of thumb for the therapist who wishes to avoid even the taint of consumer fraud is: If you are going to do anything that may cause the client any *possible* physical or psychological harm, explain what you intend to do first and obtain written informed consent.

2. Specify Your Credentials

I like to give my new clients a sheet of paper on which I have listed my credentials. It's amazing how few therapists bother to do this. I guess they assume the client can make sense out of the diplomas and certificates on that distant wall in the office.

The kind of credentials that are worth specifying are your academic degrees and the universities where you attained them, years spent in clinical practice, specialized training, list of publications, formal addresses and workshops, professional associations to which you belong, academic affiliations and honors received, and whether you are licensed to practice in your area. You may also offer to answer any questions about these credentials, since many of them may be meaningless to the client. But some presentation of credentials tends to encourage trust in the therapist, something vitally needed for really good therapy.

3. Make Confidentiality Contracts

Although most therapists at one time or another discuss the issue of confidentiality with clients, few of us seem to define it precisely and on paper. One of the ways to insure that both client and therapist understand the limits of confidentiality is to draw up a statement of how the therapist understands it, always staying within the ethical guidelines of one's own profession. It would be a good idea to specify what are the limitations of confidentiality. For example, in many states in the United States therapists seem to be required to report child abuse or a client's intent to murder someone, even though these facts are revealed within therapy. I would also recommend that therapists have their clients sign such statements of confidentiality as evidence that the clients understood and accepted the limitations of the contract.

To date there is a problem with confidentiality in group therapy. According to Foster (1975), if a person makes a statement in the presence of others, there is a presumption in law that such a person does not intend that information to remain confidential. A solution to this problem can be found in "Confidentiality Contracting" (Morrison, Federico, & Rosenthal, 1975). Group clients sign a contract and pledge strict confidentiality in return for an honest discussion of their therapeutic experience. A "liquidated damages" clause stipulates that any offended party can sue for a minimum, agreed-upon amount of money in the event damage to reputation can be proved. In my experience, such contracts have been most effective in preventing breach of confidentiality in group settings. They also increase sooner the frequency of self-disclosures within the group sessions. With such contracts the therapist is protecting clients from damage to their reputations, something few clients think of when joining a group.

4. Draw Up Treatment Contracts

It often happens that clients receive a different kind of therapy or treatment than is expected. Many therapists proceed with the type of therapy they deem most appropriate for the client. I believe not only that the therapy or treatment should first be discussed with clients (see earlier discussion under Step 1), but that the specific treatment goals should be discussed, written down, and properly affirmed by the signature of the clients. Treatment goals often change or have to be revised, but the document does serve as an initial protection for clients, who too often do not agree on what are the problems or the goals of the treatment involved in their transactions with a therapist.

The unspoken acknowledgement of the authority of a therapist often induces clients to accept without question that the therapist is qualified and should dictate the goals and process of the therapeutic relationship (Hare-Mustin, Maracer, Kaplan, & Liss-Levinson, 1979). Specifying both the problem and the treatment seems to make therapists more accountable (Shulberg, 1976) and can prevent misunderstandings concerning methods, responsibilities, and the practical arrangements of therapy. One must be especially sensitive to ethical issues when contracting with the child client, who often cannot give meaningful consent (Robinson, 1974). However, there are some specific ways to ensure the protection of such young clients (see Holdridge-Crane, Morrison, & Morrison, 1979).

A number of examples of therapy contracts can be found in recent literature (Koocher, 1977; Hare-Mustin, Maracek, Kaplan, & Liss-Levinson, 1979; Nevid & Morrison, 1976; Schwitzgebel, 1976). Although the wording varies, the intent is always the protection of the client from some form of "consumer fraud" by the therapist.

5. Form Feedback Groups of Former Clients

As described in detail elsewhere (Morrison, 1980b), therapists can also protect their current clients by periodically meeting with a group of former clients (both successful and unsuccessful in terms of therapy outcome) to discuss their theoretical and operational assumptions — in layman's language, of course. Whenever I have done this, I count such feedback seminars among the most intellectually rewarding experiences of my career. When clients are encouraged to be honest and when they know they will have group support, the information flowing back to therapists can truly provoke changes in their theoretical framework as well as in their therapeutic techniques. Such discussions help therapists to realize how they may be stagnating in their theoretical and operational approach to clients. Such seminars may even stimulate productive research (Morrison, 1980b), research that at least raises important questions for the therapist.

In such group discussions, I use a modified confidentiality contract similar to the one discussed under Step 3 (see Morrison, Federico, & Rosenthal, 1975). Otherwise, former clients might be too afraid to discuss their difficulties with the therapist's theory and techniques in that with such discussion they also often reveal their own psychological problems.

6. Establish Consumer Boards

Therapists may also want to appoint citizens or former clients (or both) to consumer protection boards that overlook their practice. The specifics of such boards can be found elsewhere (Morrison, 1976; Morrison, 1978; Morrison & Cometa, 1979; Morrison & Yablonovitz, 1978) but, in general, such boards can review a therapist's research, initial interview procedures, confidentiality safeguards, continued education and training, legal safeguards for clients, comfort of the waiting room, and a host of other issues. The therapist may even want to make it known to clients who have grievances that they can take these before a board of their peers.

Many therapists seem to fear these kinds of boards. They are afraid that such boards may only "stir up trouble." Such has not been my experience. A board's suggestions and recommendations can be really helpful to the therapist and at the same time quite invaluable to the protection of active clients. If former clients serve on the board, again a type of "confidentiality contract" might be used for their protection (see Step 3).

7. Conduct Outcome Research on Your Therapy

How does doing research on your therapy benefit the client? By insuring that through such research you are doing your best to insure that your armentarium of techniques are the most effective and that you know how to apply the most effective techniques with the type of clients on which they will be the most effective.

Most therapists, especially those in private practice, seem to shy away from doing empirical research. Some think they do not have the time, others that they do not have the expertise, while others yet may fear they will get results that suggest they are not effective therapists. I, however, have been doing empirical research on a modest scale for the eleven years I have been in private practice. It really takes up little time if you find self-report evaluative measures that can be easily understood by the client and easily scored by the therapist-researcher. If therapists feel they do not have the expertise, they can work with academic colleagues who do. The fear of discovering that you are ineffective may be a larger hurdle, but it must be faced for you to continually revise your therapeutic approach so that it grows in effectiveness.

I would strongly urge therapists to engage in outcome research, including follow-up studies of the effect of therapy over time (Morrison, 1977). Perhaps the excitement generated by such studies can prevent "therapist burnout." Therapists who are always learning do not have to worry about boredom with their work.

8. Demythologize Client Attitudes

The mystification of the therapeutic process can only intensify clients' dependence on therapists and lower their ability to assert their rights (Hare-Mustin, Maracek, Kaplan, & Liss-Levinson, 1979). It is my belief that the use of the traditional medical model, with its emphasis on mental illness, correct diagnoses, and physicochemical causes of illness, only perpetuates dependence in a client. I have, over the years, conducted "demythologizing seminars" (Morrison, 1979c) for clients and nonclients and found them to be most effective in changing such attitudes (see review of studies by Morrison, 1979d; 1980a). Such seminars can at times be interwoven into therapy sessions with the purpose of making the client less dependent on the therapist.

This approach is very effective, since I never have clients calling me after hours and seldom during working hours. Furthermore, I seem to have no problems discharging clients. To demystify the therapeutic relationship means that clients feel more independent, less helpless, and are more willing to take charge of their own lives. Thus, the client is protected from being a chronic client who needs medication and periodic hospitalization.

PSYCHOTHERAPY AND THE CONSUMER APPROACH

The consumer-oriented philosophy (Morrison, 1979a) reflected in the above recommendations for safeguarding clients' rights emerged from my own therapeutic approach, emotive-reconstructive therapy (Morrison, 1979b; Morrison & Cometa, 1977). This approach is based on the assumption that the client's perspective on personal problems is of utmost importance to the therapeutic process. Unless the psychotherapist learns to comprehend clients' cognitive processes, the probability of success is greatly minimized. The therapeutic process is centered around a new understanding of clients' imagery processes, which reflect a variety of psychological problems. But, such therapists always use the data (imagery) supplied by clients and seldom their own interpretations alone. In this way, these therapists are probably less likely than more analytically-oriented therapists to "lead" the client in directions that either make no sense to the client or that are actually not in the client's best interests.

Successful emotive-reconstructive therapy emphasizes the dignity and autonomy of the client and provides a perspective that prevents a therapist from allowing therapy to slip into something called "the purchase of friendship" (Schofield, 1964). Client independence is stressed, and dependency on a therapist is discouraged.

SUMMARY

The eight steps toward safeguarding clients' rights in psychotherapy are the following: (1) Explain your therapeutic approach more thoroughly, (2) specify your credentials, (3) make confidentiality contracts, (4) draw up treatment contracts, (5) form feedback groups of former clients, (6) establish consumer boards, (7) conduct outcome research on your therapy, and (8) demythologize client attitudes. These methods of safeguarding a client's rights emerge from an emotive-reconstructive approach to the psychotherapeutic process.

REFERENCES

Bergin, A. E. Some implications of psychotherapy research for therapeutic practice. *Journal of Abnormal Psychology,* 1966, *71,* 235–246.

Breggin, P. R. Psychiatry and psychotherapy as political processes. *American Journal of Psychotherapy, 19,* 369–382, 1975.

Brown, P. *Radical psychology.* New York: Harper & Row, 1973.

Chesler, P. *Women and madness.* New York: Doubleday, 1972.

Eysenck, H. J. The effects of psychotherapy: An evaluation. *Journal of Consulting Psychology, 16,* 319–324, 1952.

Foster, L. M. Group psychotherapy: A pool of legal witnesses? *International Journal of Group Psychotherapy,* 1975, *25,* 50–53.

Glenn, M. (Ed.) *Voices From the Asylum.* New York: Harper & Row, 1974.

Halleck, S. L. *The Politics of Therapy.* New York: Harper & Row, 1974.

Holdridge-Crane, S., Morrison, K. L., and Morrison, J. K. The child consumer's informed consent to treatment: Ethical, psychological and legal implications. In J. K. Morrison (Ed.), *A Consumer Approach to Community Psychology.* Chicago: Nelson-Hall, 1979, pp. 295–324.

Jones, E. Psychotherapists shortchange the poor. *Psychology Today,* 1975, *8,* 24–28.

Koocher, G. P. Advertising for psychologists: Pride and prejudice or sense and sensibility? *Professional Psychology,* 1977, *8,* 149–160.

Levine, S. V., Kamin, L. E., and Levine, E. L. Sexism and psychiatry. *American Journal of Orthopsychiatry,* 1974, *44,* 327–336.

Hare-Mustin, R. T. An appraisal of the relationship between women and psychotherapy. *American Psychologist,* 1983, *38,* 593–601.

Hare-Mustin, R. T., Maracek, J., Kaplan, A. G., and Liss-Levinson, N. Rights of clients, responsibilities of therapists. *American Psychologist,* 1979, *34.* 3–16.

Morrison, J. K. An argument for mental patient advisory boards. *Professional Psychology,* 1976, 7, 127–131.

Morrison, J. K. In praise of psychotherapy follow-up research. *Psychotherapy Bulletin,* 1977, *11,* 31–33.

Morrison, J. K. The client as consumer and evaluator of community mental health services. *American Journal of Community Psychology,* 1978, *6,* 147–155.

Morrison, J. K. A consumer-oriented approach to psychotherapy. *Psychotherapy: Theory, Research and Practice,* 1979, *16,* 381–384. (a)

Morrison, J. K. Emotive-reconstructive psychotherapy: Changing constructs by means of mental imagery. In A. A. Sheikh and J. T. Shaffer (Eds.), *The Potential of Fantasy and Imagination.* New York: Brandon House, 1979, pp. 133–147. (b)

Morrison, J. K. Demythologizing approach to community education. In J. K. Morrison

(Ed.), *A Consumer Approach to Community Psychology.* Chicago: Nelson-Hall, 1979, pp. 57–62. (c)

Morrison, J. K. A reappraisal of mental health education: A humanistic approach. *Journal of Humanistic Psychology,* 1979, *19,* 43–51. (d)

Morrison, J. K. The public's current beliefs about mental illness: Serious obstacle to effective community psychology. *American Journal of Community Psychology,* 1980, *8,* 697–707. (a)

Morrison, J. K. Client-psychotherapist seminars for refining theory and practice. *Professional Psychology,* 1980, *11,* 696–699. (b)

Morrison, J. K., and Cometa, M. S. Emotive-reconstructive psychotherapy: A short-term cognitive approach. *American Journal of Psychotherapy,* 1977, *31,* 294–301.

Morrison, J. K., and Cometa, M. S. The impact of a client advisory board on a community mental health clinic. In J. K. Morrison (Ed.), *A Consumer Approach to Community Psychology.* Chicago: Nelson-Hall, 1979, pp. 113–122.

Morrison, J. K., Federico, M., and Rosenthal, A. J. Contracting confidentiality in group psychotherapy. *Journal of Forensic Psychology,* 1975, *7,* 1–6.

Morrison, J. K., and Yablonovitz, H. Increased clinic awareness and attitudes of independence through client advisory board membership. *American Journal of Community Psychology,* 1978, *6,* 363–369.

Nevid, J. S., and Morrison, J. K. Preventing involuntary hospitalization: A family contracting approach. *Journal of Family Counseling,* 1976, *4,* 27–31.

Robinson, D. Harm, offense and nuisance: Some first steps in the establishment of an ethic of treatment. *American Psychologist,* 1974, *29,* 233–238.

Schofield, W. *Psychotherapy: The Purchase of Friendship.* Englewood Cliffs, N.J.: Prentice Hall, 1964.

Schwitzgebel, R. K. Treatment contracts and ethical self-determination. *The Clinical Psychologist,* 1976, *29,* 5–7.

Shulberg, H. C. Quality-of-care standards and professional norms. *American Journal of Psychiatry,* 1976, *133,* 1047–1051.

Szasz, T. S. The myth of psychotherapy. *American Journal of Psychotherapy,* 1975, *18,* 517–525.

Tennov, D. *Psychotherapy: The Hazardous Cure.* New York: Abelard-Schuman, 1975.

Chapter 13

PSYCHOTHERAPY: CUI BONO?

Thomas J. Nardi

In the comprehensive *Dictionary of Psychology,* (Chaplin, 1968), psycho-therapy is defined as "the application of specialized techniques to the treatment of mental disorders or to the problems of everyday adjustment. In its strictest sense, the term includes only those techniques (psycho-analysis, nondirective or directive counseling, psychodrama, etc.) which are utilized by specialists. More loosely, psychotherapy can include informal talks with ministers, faith cures, and personal discussions with teachers or friends" (p. 402–403). This definition would seem to encompass almost any interpersonal interaction. Could it then be said that whenever one human being talks or listens to another human being that some form of psychotherapy is occurring?

Consider some of the work of Weizenbaum (1976) using "nonhuman psychotherapists." Weizenbaum developed a computer program that could respond to typed questions and statements as would a Rogerian psychotherapist (Rogers, 1951). The computer/therapist "has no mechanism for actually understanding sentences. Instead it seeks out key words that are typed and does some simple syntactical transformations. For example, if the program sees a sentence of the form 'Do you X?' it automatically prints out the response 'What makes you think I X?' When (the computer) cannot match the syntax of a given sentence it can cover up . . . It can say something noncommittal, such as *'Please go on'* or *'What does that suggest to you?'* Or it can recall an earlier match and refer back to it, as for example, *'How does this relate to your depression?'* where depression was an earlier topic of conversation" (Hyman, 1977, p. 34).

So it would seem that "psychotherapy" can even take place between a man and a machine. Perhaps the sine qua non for psychotherapy then lies in the interchange or dialogue between the participants, even if one is a machine.

Unfortunately, this hypothesis must also be discarded when consideration is given to the popularity of self-help audio cassettes. These cassettes include hypnotic and motivational tapes designed to provide some general or specific benefit to the listener. The tapes are directed to a variety of problems and situations ranging from habit control (e.g. smoking, overeating, nailbiting, etc.) to sexual dysfunction to developing financial security. Although the drawbacks, and even the dangers, of the unsupervised use of such tapes has been noted (Nardi & Newman, 1983), there is no doubt that people will continue to use such tapes and some people will indeed derive benefit from them.

Also to be included in this apparently ever-expanding definition of psychotherapy is the self-help book. Recently, a number of self-help books have become major best-sellers. Albert Ellis, the founder of Rational Emotive Therapy (RET), was one of the first professionals to purposely direct his writings to the lay audience. His books on sex (Ellis, 1958, 1960) and general self-help (Ellis, 1957; Ellis & Harper, 1961) have been read by millions of people. It is interesting to note that his books served to gain popular recognition for RET that later led to professional recognition. Professionals became interested in Ellis' methods and theories after his work had already established a "grass roots" validation and popularity. Somewhat ironic by contrast, is the history of the book that achieved recognition for Transactional Analysis, *Games People Play* (Berne, 1964). This book was purposely directed at a professional audience, but became a national best-seller among lay people, much to the admitted surprise of Berne.

Even a cursory (and that is all that space will allow here) review of the recent lists of best-sellers will testify to the current popularity of self-help books. They include advice and information on *How To Make Love To A Woman* (Morganstern, 1982), and if problems arise, *How To Be Your Own Sex Therapist* (Raley, 1980) or, presumably for the less ambitious who want to forget the whole thing, *How To Fall Out Of Love* (Phillips & Judd, 1978). Also included are books on improving one's life by self-hypnosis (Hariman, 1981), relaxation (Benson, 1975), and rational thinking (Dyer, 1976). It also would be appropriate to include two of the oldest self-help books that are still widely read, studied, and consulted: the Bible and the *I Ching* (*Book of Changes*). Both of these texts are quite old and are still venerated for the wisdom and solace they provide to those who *believe* in their teachings. And this factor, *belief,* is perhaps the crucial element in any definition of psychotherapy. Noncritical belief that the "helper" (whether a professional, friend, machine, or book) can and indeed will provide help.

In his classic work, *Persuasion and Healing,* Jerome Frank (1961) analyzed and discussed the similarities between psychotherapy and other social phenomena, including Christian faith healing and shamanism. The key element among these "therapeutic modalities" is the belief that help can and will be provided if one follows a more or less structured model of interaction.

It may be concluded then that various forms of what could be considered "psychotherapy" have existed from earliest times and in various cultures. Each culture and society had its own clearly defined, recognized, and respected form of psychotherapeutic healing. It is only relatively recently, however, that there has developed a myriad of modalities for psychotherapy, each vying with the others for public and professional support. Herink (1980) has identified over 250 forms of psychotherapy currently in use. While some might argue with his criteria for inclusion, Herink's work nevertheless provides evidence that there are probably more types and variations of psychotherapy in existence now than ever before in history. We can only ask "why?" Is the demand for psychotherapy, then, a healthy trend reflecting new self-awareness and a desire to improve one's life while alleviating emotional pain? Does the demand reflect the general acceptance and lessening of stigma associated with seeking help? Or is there some psychological law of supply and demand occurring? Have professionals responded with new and different treatments because people are demanding them? Can it perhaps be, as Frank (1961) suggests, that "the demand for psychotherapy keeps pace with the supply, and at times one has the uneasy feeling that the supply may be creating the demand . . . psychotherapy is the only form of treatment which, at least to some extent, appears to create the illness it treats" (p. 8).

Frank's work serves as a point of departure for the work of Martin Gross. Gross (1978), in a scholarly, scathing indictment of psychoanalysis's stranglehold on current thinking, refers to our Psychological Society. In his meticulously documented and thought provoking book, he shows how Western society has been tyrannized by what may be the greatest intellectual hoax of the twentieth century—psychoanalysis. Citing Freud's long term involvement with cocaine, Gross observes that "no one has yet evaluated the hallucinatory effect of cocaine on Freud's mind during the formative years of psychoanalysis. Without cocaine, could Freud have created such improbable flights of human fancy?" (p. 236). Gross also argues, again with well-documented evidence, that Freud over-generalized about human psychology based upon his own personality.

After detailed documentation drawn from Freud's biographies, auto-biographies, and letters, Gross concludes "We should pose one thought. What if Freud had not suffered from a spastic colon, near-continuous depressive moods, neurasthenia, homosexual tendencies, bad temper, migraines, constipation, travel phobias, death fears, heart irregularities, money phobias, infected sinuses, fainting spells and hostile drives of hate and murder? Would the modern theory of the mind have been more sanguine? Would it instead stress the empathy and concern that people feel for their siblings, their parents, even for all humanity?" (p. 246).

Demand for new forms of psychotherapy may also stem from dissatis-faction with the practice as well as the theory of the psychoanalytically based psychotherapies. For example, Lazarus and Fay (1975) include the belief that "therapy can't hurt you" among their list of "common mistakes that can ruin your life." They make reference to the phenomena cited in the professional literature of "therapist-caused deterioration" and give a case history of a woman affected adversely by a psychoanalyst's so-called "intensive therapy." Lazarus and Fay advocate a more directive, educational model of therapy but note that "many people believe the purpose of therapy is to talk about their problems, rather than devising active means of solving these problems. It is not talk that is important, but action" (p. 26).

In his article, "Iatrogenic Disturbance," Schnideberg (1963) also cites a case in which psychotherapy contributed to a woman's becoming promiscuous, losing her job, and finally needing to be hospitalized for six months. Sadly, iatrogenic disturbance may not be such a rare occurrence. Ellis (1973) notes that "the neurotic (and especially the psychotic) client is frequently overaware of his own thoughts and feelings when he comes to treatment. To spend many sessions making him still more aware of himself, without concomitantly actively depropagandizing his self-condemning tendencies, is irresponsible, and has probably been instrumental in driving not a few psychotherapy patients into more aggravated states of confusion, anxiety, and depression" (p. 134). Ellis later states that "psychotherapy today is, in many instances, one of the most wasteful, ineffective modes of treatment ever invented — mainly because it tries to help most clients function more effectively with their ill-founded philosophies of life instead of compelling them to face reality and give up these views" (p. 145). Ellis (1982) expanded upon this view in a more recent paper, provocatively titled, "Must most psychotherapists remain as incompetent as they now are?"

Is Ellis competent as a psychotherapist? Gross would appear to think so, as Ellis is one psychotherapist who is not critically called to task in Gross's review of contemporary psychotherapists. Gross appears to respect Ellis because "the Ellis philosophy is reminiscent of pre-psychological thought: that Man is responsible for his actions" (p. 317). Indeed, Ellis' RET has emphasized personal responsibility to such a degree that it has been called the "no cop-out therapy." Ellis has always been something of a gadfly stinging the sacred cows of the psychotherapy establishment. RET began as a reaction to what Ellis saw as the wasteful ineffectiveness of psychoanalysis. Today, Ellis still challenges and questions any and all systems of psychotherapy that eschew reason and responsibility in favor of self-indulgence, clinical mumbo jumbo, blaming others, and what he terms "whining," the refusal to tolerate the frustration of an imperfect and at times unfair world. Ellis maintains that no improvement occurs or is maintained without work and effort.

While Ellis and like-minded therapists may be presenting a return to traditional, pre-Freudian values, others are doing just the opposite. Many systems have developed recently to cater to the instant gratification needs of the so-called *Me Generation*. There are some quasi-psychotherapies that offer promises of enlightenment and transformed lives on any given weekend. Such systems avoid legal difficulties by use of disclaimers that what they offer is not "psychotherapy" or "psychological," but nonetheless, in practice, that is what they literally sell in intensive "seminars," "training," and "encounters." Fritz Perls (1970), the founder of Gestalt therapy, gave a prophetic caveat shortly before his death that "we are entering the phase of the turner-on-ers: turn on to instant cure, instant joy, instant sensory awareness. We are entering the phase of the quacks and the con men . . . " (cited in Gross, P. 304).

One could argue passionately yet without resolution as to who is the greater threat — the incompetent or the insincere? The fool or the liar? And perhaps even more importantly, by what criteria should therapists be judged? And by whom?

The answer is not readily nor easily forthcoming. One reason for this rests in the question of the effectiveness of psychotherapy. It appears, to paraphase Lincoln, that any type psychotherapy will help some of the people some of the time, but no type of psychotherapy will help all of the people all of the time. Indeed, the irony lies in the fact that it often appears that no matter how outrageous or nonsensical a theory or treatment might appear, there are those who will attest to having been helped by it. When presented with glowing anecdotal testimonials, enthusiastic clinical reports, and perhaps even media publicity and exposure, how does the professional, much less the lay person, distinguish between legitimate innovation and idiosyncratic nonsense?

As stated previously, psychotherapy is a very broadly defined term, and those offering psychotherapy are an equally diverse group. Perhaps it would be more useful to establish criteria by which to categorize those *seeking* help. Hopefully the following taxonomy will challenge professionals to more closely examine what they actually do and who they actually serve.

The first designation would consist of "patients". Patients would include those with recognized and definable psychological disorders involving true disturbance in thought, affect or behavior. This would include those clinically diagnosed as psychotic or borderline. Patient's disorders often have organic or biochemical etiologies and improve with psychopharmacological therapy (particularly the major tranquilizers or antipsychotic medications) and supplemental talking psychotherapy.

Despite Szasz's (1974, 1976) belief that mental illness is a myth and schizophrenia merely a metaphor, clinical research and experience has proven that some people have such severe mood or thought disorders that they become a danger to themselves or others. For these patients, hospitalization is often required. Many of them show marked improvement with the introduction of medication and psychotherapy in the therapeutic millieu of a hospital or institutional setting. Other patients sometimes have chronic disorders that require long-term treatment and/or maintenance medication. Patients are best helped by highly trained clinicians, including, but not necessarily restricted to, those from the disciplines of psychiatry and clinical psychology. Ancillary and supportive help can often be provided by other professionals (e.g. psychiatric nurses or social workers), paraprofessionals, or friends, but usually only under supervision of a clinician.

The second, and probably the largest group are the "clients." Clients do not have true psychological problems per se, but are experiencing problems in living. They want to alleviate a problem and/or improve the general quality of their life. Problems in living would include difficulty in interpersonal relationships, such as in sexual, marital, and love situations, as well as parent-child and familial conflicts. Oftentimes they have never been exposed to, or have not mastered, certain requisite skills for relating successfully to other people. This category would include, but not be limited to, the adjustment disorders, assertiveness problems, and habitual behaviors such as overeating.

Clients include those who need to learn better ways to negotiate the conflicts, crises, and frustrations that are a part of *normal* daily life. Indeed, many clients "suffer" from immaturity, never having learned or been taught to accept and tolerate the uncertainty and apparent unfairness of life.

For such clients, psychotherapy really becomes an emotional and behavioral re-education with psychotherapists serving as teachers. The lessons taught by the professional are often those that used to be taught by older members of the family. The last few generations have witnessed and participated in a dissolution of the extended family and, to some extent, the nuclear family. Questions and confidences that a few decades ago would have been directed to the patriarch, matriarch, or family elder are now posed to the psychotherapist. People seem to no longer esteem the experiences of the elderly. The elderly are not respected but often, at best, just tolerated by their families.

It is interesting to note that the modern Chinese word for psychotherapy, when translated, literally means "a heart-to-heart talk." And this indeed is what takes place between a psychotherapist and the one seeking help. But it is also what takes place between two good friends. Could it not be that a person often turns to a professional because there is no one else available who will listen or talk to him?

Of course, a professional's training would allow him or her to provide help beyond that which can be offered by a layperson friend. This is expecially true for those who would be included in the "patient" category. But oftentimes those in the "client" category can also be helped by those with less extensive or intensive clinical training, and it is important for the clinicians working with them to realize this fact.

Clients and clinicians alike need to be reminded that periods of indecision and unhappiness are not psychological disorders. Nor is discomfort. Contemporary Americans, in particular, are more likely to seek "psychotherapy" for situations that their more stoic counterparts in some European countries would view simply as something to be endured. Some Americans tend to have less tolerance for hardship and adversity. It is, again, simply an inability to accept the normal difficulties of daily life and not a sign of severe psychopathology.

The above classification of patients and clients is not necessarily unique or original. The categories of patient and client might also be compared to those of "psychotic" and "neurotic and character disorder," respectively. Or, again respectively, to the difference between candidates for "psychotherapy" and "counseling." The categories are by no means intended to be completely exclusive or absolute. Semantic disputes and debates about the terms are invited and could, perhaps, lead to further clarification and understanding of the role of the psychotherapist and the process of psychotherapy.

By way of closing, let us borrow a phrase from Jonathan Swift and consider the following "modest proposal" for a third category. Unlike the other two categories, this one cannot exist in isolation. While there can be patients and clients even if they are not so identified, the third category only comes into existence after they seek help. They are the creation of the merchants of mental health, who transform those seeking help into the category of "customers." Customers are those who fall prey to parasitic psychotherapists who are more interested in cash than cure.

While some patients really do need long-term psychotherapy, when psychotherapists begin to "specialize" in long drawn-out "intensive" therapy, their motivation becomes suspect. Does several sessions of therapy per week over several years give greater benefit to the help seeker's psyche or the therapist's pocketbook?

When the therapist's agenda of highly ambitious and vague, general "goals" take precedence over the more immediate and pragmatic needs of the one seeking help, the one seeking help is transformed into a customer. When the help seeker's complaint that he is not benefiting from therapy is interpreted automatically as resistance and psychopathology, he is transformed into a customer. When the therapist places the onus for improvement totally on the help seeker and does not periodically examine his own skills (or lack of them), he is dealing with customers, not treating patients or clients. Similarly, those with advanced degrees who become complacent and do not continue to update their skills and take advantage of advanced training are dealing with customers.

The client or patient who cannot continue private therapy because he can no longer afford the psychotherapist's fee, and then suddenly finds himself referred to a clinic, while perhaps even being told that his financial difficulties are a reflection of his resistance, has just become a customer.

When clinics and psychiatric centers become more interested in maintaining their census than actually helping people, they are dealing with customers. Some centers and clinics, to maintain their external funding, keep their census high by accepting and institutionalizing people almost indiscriminantly. Other institutions, when criticized for lack of effective treatment, begin to declare people cured and discharge them without true consideration of their ability to function in the community. Similarly, psychiatric hospitals that routinely declare people cured and discharged the day that their insurance coverage expires are dealing with customers.

Physicians who routinely and cavalierly prescribe psychotropic medication without examining the source of the person's anxiety or depression are treating customers. Such physicians have contributed to making the minor tranquilizers Vallium® and Librium® the most widely prescribed drugs in the world. Physicians who routinely renew medication orders over the telephone without even seeing or reexamining the person are dealing with customers. It has been suggested that when physicians prescribe medication without arrangements for monitoring or a follow-up review, and then discover that the person has committed suicide by overdosing, they (the physicians) should be charged as accessories to murder.

Therapists who attempt to treat problems for which they do not have adequate clinical training are working with customers. Those who treat all presenting problems the same way because of the shallowness of their clinical repetoire are also working with customers. Those who take advantage of lack of regulatory legislation to practice "psychotherapy," believing they can substitute "liking people" for formal training, are working with customers. Use of the word "eclectic" to disguise lack of mastery of any particular therapeutic approach, or taking pride in dispensing with any and all theory in favor of "relating," indicates dealing with customers. So, too, does the encouraging of nonsensical screaming and tantrum throwing under the guise of psychotherapy.

Self-proclaimed "experts" who quickly author books to cash in on popular contemporary trends are directing their work to customers. So, too, are those mental health mountebanks who glory in hyperbole and extravagent claims in commercial advertisements, often fancying themselves to be modern magicians performing wizardry.

It is with both irony and optimism that we recognize that customers would disappear if psychotherapists would take responsibility for improving themselves and the profession. Psychotherapists would do well to examine critically and objectively themselves, their motives, and their effectiveness in providing therapy. More research as to the efficacy of various psychotherapeutic approaches is to be encouraged and supported. Parochial and self-serving interests need to be exorcised by the psychotherapists themselves. We must remember that our primary responsibility is to those who, in trust and sincerity, seek our assistance to alleviate their pain. There must be no compromise in the quality of help we provide.

REFERENCES

Benson, H. *The Relaxation Response.* New York: William Morrow, 1975.

Berne, E. *Games People Play.* New York: Grove Press, 1964.

Chaplin, J. P. *Dictionary of Psychology.* New York: Dell, 1968.

Dyer, W. W. *Your Erroneous Zones.* New York: Funk & Wagnalls, 1976.

Ellis, A. *How to Live With a "Neurotic".* New York: Crown Publishers, 1957, Rev. ed., New York: Crown Publishers, 1975.

Ellis, A. *Sex Without Guilt.* New York: Lyle Stuart, 1958, Rev. ed., New York: Lyle Stuart, 1965.

Ellis, A. *The Art and Science of Love.* New York: Lyle Stuart, 1960, Rev. ed., New York: Lyle Stuart and Bantam Books, 1969.

Ellis, A., and Harper, R. A. *A Guide to Rational Living.* Englewood Cliffs, N.J.: Prentice-Hall, 1961, Rev. ed., retitled *A New Guide to Rational Living.* Englewood Cliffs, N.J.: Prentice-Hall and Hollywood: Wilshire Books, 1975.

Ellis, A. *Humanistic Psychotherapy.* New York: McGraw-Hill Books, 1973.

Ellis, A. Must most psychotherapists remain as incompetent as they now are? *Journal of Contemporary Psychotherapy,* 1982, *13*, 17–28.

Frank, J. D. *Persuasion and Healing.* Baltimore, Md.: John Hopkins University Press, 1961, Rev. ed., Baltimore, Md.: John Hopkins University Press, 1973.

Gross, M. *The Psychological Society.* New York: Random House, 1978.

Hariman, J. *How to Use the Power of Self-hypnosis.* Wellingborough, Northamptonshire: Thorsons Publishers, 1981.

Herink, R. (Ed.). *The Psychotherapy Handbook*. New York: New American Library, 1980.

Lazarus, A., and Fay, A. *I Can If I Want To*. New York: Warner Books, 1975.

Morganstern, M. *How to Make Love to a Woman*. New York: Clarkson N. Potter, 1982.

Nardi, T. J., and Newman, M. Dangers of hypnotic tapes: a dissociative mystical reaction. *Journal of The American Academy of Behavioral Medicine*, 1983, *1*(1), 87–90.

Perls, F. S. *Gestalt Therapy Verbatim*. New York: Bantam Books, 1970.

Phillips, D., and Judd, R. *How to Fall Out of Love*. Boston: Houghton Mifflin, 1978.

Raley, P. *Making Love*. New York: Avon Books, 1980.

Rogers, C. *Client-centered Therapy*. Boston: Houghton Mifflin, 1951.

Schnideberg, M. Iatrogenic disturbance. *American Journal of Psychiatry*, 1963, *119*, 899.

Szasz, T. S. *The Myth of Mental Illness*. Rev. ed. New York: Harper & Row, 1974.

Szasz, T. S. *Schizophrenia: The Sacred Symbol of Psychiatry*. New York: Basic Books, 1976.

Weizenbaum, J. *Computer Power and Human Reason*. San Francisco: Freeman, 1976.

Chapter 14

APPLYING ANTITRUST LAWS
TO THE PROFESSIONS
Implications for Psychology

THOMAS D. OVERCAST, BRUCE D. SALES, AND MICHAEL D. POLLARD

ABSTRACT: *The application of antitrust law to the professions raises many questions about organized professional activities that affect market entry, access to third-party payment, and business practices. The Fourth Circuit Court of Appeals decision in* Virginia Academy of Clinical Psychologists v. Blue Shield of Virginia, *holding that the reimbursement policies of Blue Shield restrained competition between psychologists and physicians, establishes the potential for challenging existing restraints on the psychology profession under the antitrust statutes. This article reviews recent legal developments applying antitrust principles to selected professional practices such as accreditation, licensing, specialty certification, restrictions on advertising, and fee setting. The authors present a series of questions about these practices and suggest that psychologists should assess their own professional policies and procedures to see if they could withstand antitrust scrutiny.*

On June 16, 1980, the United States Court of Appeals for the Fourth Circuit handed down a landmark decision affecting the psychology profession. In *Virginia Academy of Clinical Psychologists v. Blue Shield of Virginia*[1] the Fourth Circuit overturned a district court decision that had held that the antitrust laws did not apply to Blue Shield's policy of

From Overcast, T. D., Sales, B. D., and Pollard, M. R. Applying Antitrust Laws to the Professions: Implications for Psychology. American Psychologist, Vol. 37, No. 5, May 1982, pp. 517–525. Copyright 1982 by the American Psychological Association. Reprinted by permission of the publisher and author.

[1]624 F.2d 476 (4th Cir. 1980), *cert denied*, 49 *U.S.L.W.* 3617 (Feb. 23, 1981).

refusing to pay for services rendered by clinical psychologists unless such services were "supervised" by and billed through a physician.[2] The Appeals Court disagreed, holding generally that: (a) the uncontradicted evidence and the district court findings showed sufficient physician control of Blue Shield of Richmond to bring its actions within the purview of Section 1 of the Sherman Act; (b) collaboration between Blue Shield plans in the State of Virginia was not exempt from the Sherman Act under the "Noerr-Pennington" doctrine;[3] (c) defendant Blue Shield was not in the "business of insurance" and thus not exempt from antitrust laws under the McCarran-Ferguson Act;[4] and finally, (d) the reimbursement policies were "in restraint of trade."[5] Blue Shield of Richmond appealed the Fourth Circuit's decision to the Supreme Court, but their petition for review was denied.[6]

The *Virginia Academy* case will have enormous importance for the profession of psychology. It will contribute significantly to the continuing effort by psychologists to achieve recognition as independent mental health treatment providers. At the same time, *Virginia Academy* and the fundamental legal basis on which it was decided — antitrust law — should engender a sense of cautious self-examination and reassessment on the part of the psychology profession. In particular, the *Virginia Academy* case is only one in a series of antitrust cases brought against physicians and

---

[2]624 F.2d 476 (4th Cir. 1980), *cert denied,* 49 *U.S.L.W.* 3617 (Feb. 23, 1981).

[3]In Eastern Presidents Railroad Conference v. Noerr Motor Freight, 365 U.S. 127 (1960), a group of railroads had conducted a misleading advertising campaign designed to influence legislative action that would have placed trucking firms at a competitive disadvantage. The Supreme Court held that this conduct was protected by the First Amendment and therefore exempt from the Sherman Act even though it was plainly anticompetitive. In United Mine Workers of America v. Pennington, 361 U.S. 657 (1965), the Supreme Court found that a collective effort by union officials and mine operators to induce the Secretary of Labor to set a minimum wage so high that only larger government contractors would be able to sell coal to the Tennessee Valley Authority was also exempt from Sherman Act scrutiny, again because of the First Amendment rationale in Noerr.

[4]15 U.S.C. Section 1012(b).

[5]15 U.S.C. Section 1.

[6]49 *U.S.L.W.* 3617 (Feb. 23, 1981). The Supreme Court's refusal to hear the case means that the Fourth Circuit Court of Appeals decision is the law of the land.

the medical profession,[7] and it is part of a recent trend to enforce antitrust laws against a variety of professional organizations.[8] Thus psychology, in its efforts to achieve recognition and equality as an independent profession, could find itself on the defensive in disputes similar to the issues litigated in *Virginia Academy.*

Within this article we cannot address all of the implications of antitrust law for psychology. Rather, our goal will be to identify major issues that the profession ought to address. We will delineate some of the structural, organizational, and professional activities of psychology that may be susceptible to antitrust challenges by other professions, federal and state governments, and even members within the profession.

We will briefly review the activities of other professions, particularly the medical profession, that have been the subject of recent antitrust litigation and draw parallels between litigated activities in other professions and comparable or related activities in psychology. We will begin with a brief overview of the genesis of antitrust litigation directed at professional organizations and then proceed to examine the antitrust implications of particular professional practices.

GENESIS OF ANTITRUST SCRUTINY OF THE PROFESSIONS

Prior to 1975, the antitrust laws were of little concern to the professions.[9] In that year, the Supreme Court struck down a mandatory minimum fee schedule imposed by a local bar association in the case of *Goldfarb v. Virginia State Bar.*[10] The significance of this decision is that the Court rejected the argument that the professions were exempt from the antitrust laws because they were not "trade" or "commerce" as

---

[7]624 F.2d 476 (4th Cir. 1980), *cert denied,* 49 *U.S.L.W.* 3617 (Feb. 23, 1981).

[8]Nat'l Soc'y of Professional Engineers v. United States, 435 U.S. 679 (1978); Goldfarb v. Virginia State Bar, 421 U.S. 733 (1975) (lawyers); United States v. American Soc'y of Civil Engineers, 1972 Trade Cas. ¶73,950 (S.D.N.Y. 1972) (consent decree); United States v. American Inst. of Architects, 1972 Trade Cas. ¶73,981 (D.D.C. 1972) (consent decree); United States v. American Soc'y of Mechanical Engineers, 1972 Trade Cas. ¶74,028 (S.D.N.Y. 1972) (consent decree); United States v. Nat'l Ass'n of Real Estate Bds., 339 U.S. 485 (1950).

[9]But see American Medical Ass'n v. United States, 317 U.S. 519 (1943). This was the only successful antitrust case brought against a professional medical organization prior to 1975. This case involved a criminal conspiracy to stifle competition from a health maintenance organization.

[10]421 U.S. 733 (1975).

defined by the Sherman Act. The Court concluded that Congress had not intended for the professions to be exempt from antitrust scrutiny.[11]

Three years later when asked to rule on an ethical restraint on competitive bidding imposed by a professional society, the Supreme Court reiterated that the professions must comply with the antitrust laws.[12] The Court went even further this time to emphasize that the primary objective of antitrust law is to promote competition and that the sole role of the courts, in reviewing antitrust cases, is to judge the competitive impact and significance of the challenged restraint. The Court said that it is not the role of judges "to decide whether a policy favoring competition is in the public interest or in the interest of the member of an industry."[13] Thus, the Court rejected the argument made by the professional society that competitive bidding would lower the quality of services in the profession. But the Court did acknowledge that the professions may, indeed, deserve special antitrust consideration because they do differ from other business services.

The *Goldfarb* decision, later bolstered by *Professional Engineers,* laid the groundwork for numerous investigations of restraints on professional practice by antitrust enforcement agencies, both at the federal and state levels.[14] The Department of Justice has investigated architects, accountants, civil engineers, mechanical engineers, and physicians' specialty societies. The Federal Trade Commission has reviewed restraints imposed by lawyers, accountants, real estate brokers, physicians, dentists, and veterinarians. States like Ohio, West Virginia, and Arizona have focused their investigations primarily on health professionals.

Antitrust law is founded on the principle that competition is the touchstone for all commercial activity. Competitive markets tend to be more efficient and result in lower prices to consumers. Professional practice has many commercial aspects such as setting fees, establishing office procedures, purchasing equipment and supplies, billing clients, and obtaining referrals. Granted, there may be special characteristics of a profession that may appear to be incompatible with competition, but

---

[11]Id. at 787.

[12]Nat'l Soc'y of Professional Engineers v. United States, 435 U.S. 679 (1978).

[13]Id. at 692.

[14]See note 8, *supra.* See generally Federal Trade Commission (1979a, pp. 32–45).

the cases to date imply that the courts will look with a jaundiced eye on these "special circumstances."

In antitrust litigation involving the activities of professional organizations, the courts are primarily concerned with answering the following question: Have the activities of the professional organization significantly impaired the ability of competitive market forces to determine (a) the price or fee for professional services, (b) who can enter the market, or (c) the degree of innovation within the profession? For certain activities, like price fixing or economic boycotts, the mere fact that a professional association conspired to conduct such an activity would be sufficient grounds for most courts to find an antitrust violation. These activities are so repugnant to our economic system that the courts have found them to be illegal per se, irrespective of intent or effect. For other activities, like denying hospital privileges to a class of practitioners, courts would likely want to review the possible procompetitive and anticompetitive effects before reaching a decision. Here the courts engage in balancing the effects of a restriction and arrive at their decision by using a form of legal analysis referred to as Rule of Reason.

Antitrust action is a two-edged sword: It may, as in the *Virginia Academy* case, be used by psychologists to further organizational and professional ambitions, but just as easily, it may be turned back on certain practices and activities of psychology. The remainder of this article will discuss professional activities that, in light of antitrust enforcement initiated against other professions, should be of concern to psychology.

SELECTED PROFESSIONAL PRACTICES THAT HAVE BEEN SCRUTINIZED BY ANTITRUST ENFORCERS

The Department of Justice (DOJ) and the Federal Trade Commission (FTC) have investigated and, in some instances, challenged a wide range of professional practices. We have selected five activities that seem especially relevant to the psychology profession, and we will describe some of the problems these activities have raised under the antitrust laws.

Educational Accreditation

As early as 1975 the FTC staff began investigating the medical profession's role in the accreditation of physician training in medical schools and teaching hospitals. The impetus for the investigation was the suspicion that accreditation was used to limit the number and size of medical schools and thus limit competition by restricting the numbers of practicing members of the profession. Havighurst (1980), however, has argued that because of increases in federal subsidies to medical schools and students during the 1970s, the medical profession actually has very little control over the supply of new physicians. Accordingly, he contends that concern should be centered on professional control of the *type* of practitioner produced through accreditation standards. By way of illustration, Havighurst points to the strong emphasis in medical schools on "specialization and high-cost acute care, their inattentiveness to cost-effectiveness and efficiency, and their devaluation of primary and preventive care" (pp. 103–104) as evidence of the important areas in which the profession, through accreditation standards, controls the degree of innovation in training and the diversity among graduates.[15]

The analogy for psychology is the American Psychological Association's approval of graduate training programs. The accreditation issue is especially salient for the profession because of the growing number of schools of professional psychology that are seeking accreditation. The primary concern for the APA is to assure that its accreditation criteria are objective, that the standards for review are clearly stated, and that the accreditation procedure affords applicants adequate notice and other due process guarantees. Applicants that fail to meet these standards may allege that they are being "frozen out" or penalized because they use innovative methods. However, accreditation that is fair and objective should survive such allegations and prevail: The courts are unlikely to overturn such a process.

On the other hand, if accreditation is denied for vague or unsubstantiated reasons, unsuccessful applicants may have some grounds for challenging

---

[15]Shearn (1971) notes that in order to receive accreditation, Kaiser-Permanente's medical residency program must be structured conservatively, so physicians cannot be trained easily in accordance with Kaiser's emphasis on health maintenance.

the accreditation process. For example, a denial based on the judgment that graduates of the program being reviewed were inferior to graduates of other programs might be the target of a successful challenge. Justifications for denials based solely on quality grounds would be shaky under the ruling in *Professional Engineers.* The likelihood of success for this type of challenge also would be enhanced if reinbursement or other economic benefits for graduates were conditioned on accreditation of the training program.

It is worth noting that accreditation does not appear to be a priority for the antitrust enforcement agencies at this time. If the accreditation practices of a professional organization were challenged, the most likely route would be through private lawsuits.

Professional Licensing

Traditionally, professional practices conducted pursuant to state licensing statutes, and the regulations promulgated to flesh out those statutes, were considered to be immune from antitrust scrutiny under the state action doctrine.[16] This doctrine holds that the antitrust laws apply to "individual not state action,"[17] thereby exempting certain anticompetitive conduct as long as it has received the imprimatur of a state. The core for the exemption is the concept of state sovereignty, whereby deference is paid to state regulatory initiatives. The doctrine has been progressively narrowed over the years.[18] The Supreme Court's most recent opinion concluded that two requirements must be met before a state regulatory scheme can be immune from federal antitrust scrutiny: (a) the challenged restraint must be "clearly articulated and affirmatively expressed as state policy," and (b) the policy must be "actively supervised" by the state itself.[19]

Important questions remain concerning the goals and activities that constitute legitimate state policy and the degree of scrutiny by the state

---

[16]See Parker v. Brown, 317 U.S. 341 (1943).

[17]*Id.* at 352.

[18]Compare the decision in Parker v. Brown, 317 U.S. 341 (1943) with City of Lafayette, Louisiana v. Louisiana Power and Light Co., 435 U.S. 389 (1978) and Cantor v. Detroit Edison Co., 428 U.S. 579 (1976).

[19]California Retail Liquor Dealers Assoc. v. Midcal Aluminum, Inc., 445 U.S. 97, 105 (1980).

necessary to qualify as "active" supervision. The FTC's studies of occupational licensing have identified several restraints on the commercial aspects of professional practice, but have not been focused on antitrust enforcement.[20] The only enforcement action taken by the FTC was adoption of a trade regulation rule in 1978 allowing truthful advertising for eyeglasses and vision care services.[21] This rule invalidated conflicting state licensing laws that restricted or banned advertising. The rule was in effect for 18 months but was subsequently overturned by the District of Columbia Circuit Court of Appeals and remanded to the FTC.[22]

Since psychology is regulated by licensure in most states, these statutes and regulatory schemes may be vulnerable to challenges brought by other professional groups. For example, most statutes limit independent private practice to the PhD or PsyD and withhold this right from the MA. But what if such statutes were challenged as monopolistic and as fostering restraint of trade? We believe that many boards could meet the two-pronged test laid down in the *Midcal* case. State boards that don't meet the test should be examined and perhaps reconstituted. At a minimum, state licensing requirements and procedures for psychologists should be reviewed and the necessary steps taken to bring them into compliance with current law.

Specialty Certification

Although specialty certification has been a longstanding practice in medicine, it has only recently been discussed as a possibility within psychology and other nonmedical mental health professions. In 1979, a task force composed of representatives from APA's Education and Training Board, Board of Scientific Affairs, Board of Professional Affairs (BPA), and BPA's Committee on Standards for Providers of Psychological Services was appointed and subsequently recommended initiation of specialty designation in psychology. The Board of Professional Affairs then created a subcommittee, the Subcommittee on Specialty Criteria, to evaluate and operationalize the criteria and procedures proposed by the

---

[20]See, generally, Federal Trade Commission (1980a, 1980b).

[21]16 CFR Part 456, June 2, 1978.

[22]American Optometric Ass'n, et al. v. FTC, 626 F.2d 896 (D.C. Cir. 1980).

task force to accomplish the specialty designation task.

Antitrust case law[23] recognizes that the professional certification of practitioners may be a valuable source of information for consumers and other individuals interested in the delivery of quality professional services, such as third-party payers. On the other hand, if interested parties (such as hospitals) are controlled by certified specialists, the certification process could become a mechanism for restricting access to the specialty and to the institutions necessary to practice the specialty.[24]

In medicine, control exerted by the medical staff of a hospital over the admitting privileges of other practitioners can be a substantial barrier to entry. The problems chiropractors and osteopaths have had in gaining admission of their patients to hospitals illustrates this point. Similar problems might arise if adherents of a particular psychological specialty were to gain control over the admissions policies of a clinic or long-term care institution. They might then restrict access to other persons within their specialty, excluding those professional psychologists who may be competent to provide services but who are not members of that specialty.

Several important considerations need to be kept in mind in the development of specialty certification procedures in psychology. Any such procedure should be carefully reviewed concerning such matters as: (a) the objectivity and fairness of specialty standards, (b) the procedural fairness with which standards are applied, (c) the division of potential markets among categories of specialties, (d) the method by which "grandfather" provisions are applied when speciality standards are initiated or changed, and (e) the degree to which alternative certification procedures are available to practitioners. A careful review of professional activities in support of specialty certification, in light of these factors, would help to ensure that consumers receive the highest quality psychological services at the lowest cost and might help to minimize the possibility of antitrust litigation against the profession.

---

[23]Marjorie Webster Junior College, Inc. v. Middle States Association of Colleges and Secondary Schools, Inc., 423 F.2d 650 (D.C. Circuit), *cert. denied* 400 U.S. 965 (1970).

[24]At one time, the FTC staff investigated an allegation that plastic surgeons were trying to exclude board-certified otolaryngologists from the practice of facial surgery unless they also sought and obtained specialty certification in plastic surgery. This investigation sparked considerable controversy among the plastic surgeons. See Paxton (1979) and Randall (1978).

Professional Organization Restrictions on Advertising

One of the most prominent antitrust cases following *Goldfarb* was an FTC complaint against the American Medical Association and two state medical societies charging them with unfairly restricting professional competition by imposing a ban on practitioner advertising.[25] An agreement not to advertise, or an ethical sanction against such activity, is clearly a violation of antitrust law and is an obvious point of attack against any profession. The First Amendment also prohibits professional organizations and associations, at both state and national levels, from placing undue restrictions on the ability of member professionals to advertise their availability and the cost of their services.[26]

Although most psychologists might not opt for newspaper, television, or radio advertising, they might find informational brochures or business cards helpful, particularly for purposes of referral from physicians or hospitals. Activities designed to attract or steer patients to a particular practitioner were, at one time, forbidden by the AMA. The FTC's decision in the *AMA* case reviewed these restrictions and held that they were unreasonable and had significant anticompetitive effects.[27]

The *AMA* decision does allow the professional association to formulate and adopt ethical guidelines governing the conduct of its members regarding representations that would be false or deceptive within the meaning of Section 5 of the FTC Act.[28] Thus, the profession still retains considerable latitude in setting standards for its members. However, the outer limit of those standards is the case law defining what is false and deceptive, not some vague notion of what is "appropriate" for professionals to say in advertisements or solicitations. Consequently, ethical standards (to the extent they exist in the psychology profession) governing advertising that are based on what is considered to be "tasteful" or "in the best interests of the profession" are probably unenforceable.

In response to issues arising out of the restriction of advertising by

---

[25]American Medical Ass'n v. FTC, 94 F.T.C. 701 (final order, Oct. 12, 1979).

[26]Bates v. State Bar of Arizona, 433 U.S. 350 (1977).

[27]American Medical Ass'n v. FTC, 94 F.T.C. 701, at 1005 (1979), *aff'd* 638 F.2d 443 (2d Cir. 1980), *cert granted*, 49 U.S.L.W. 3954 (June 22, 1981).

[28]*Id.* at 1037.

professional associations, the APA Council of Representatives, at their January 1979 meeting, approved a rewording of Principle 4 of the Ethical Standards of Psychologists, which deals with public statements. The principle specifies what information may be included in an advertisement of professional services. Following a list of specifics, the principle states that "(a)dditional relevant or important consumer information may be included if not prohibited by other sections of the Ethical Standards." Section b of Principle 4 pertains to information that is prohibited in advertising by a psychologist, including the normal prohibitions against false, fraudulent, misleading, deceptive, or "unfair" statements. In addition, however, Section b prohibits statements concerning the comparative desirability of advertised services or statements directly soliciting individual clients. In light of the *AMA* decision, this section should be reviewed and perhaps revised.

Without having a specific example of a psychologist's advertisement, it is difficult to determine what might or might not be acceptable. Using attorney advertising as a model, however, many of their televised and print advertisements would be objectionable under Principle 4 of the APA's standards. Although the full extent of permissible advertising activity has not been tested in a court and thus it is not possible to determine whether the restrictions imposed on psychologists by Principle 4 would stand under an antitrust challenge, it is clear that this is one area where further scrutiny of the profession's policies on advertising is essential.

Fee Structures

Following *Goldfarb's* condemnation of minimum fee schedules as a price-fixing device, two elements of fee structuring in the medical profession were obvious targets for antitrust litigation—relative value studies[29]

---

[29]For background and detail on relative value studies, see Committee on Governmental Affairs (1979); Havighurst and Kissam (1979). Several consent orders have been signed by professional groups agreeing not to enforce relative value scales. *See* California Medical Association, 93 F.T.C. 519 (1979); Minnesota State Medical Association 90 F.T.C. 337 (1977); American College of Radiology, 89 F.T.C. 144 (1977); American College of Obstetricians and Gynecologists, 88 F.T.C. 955 (1976); American Academy of Orthopaedic Surgeons, 88 F.T.C. 968 (1976). The Massachusetts Nurses Association has also agreed, in settlement of a lawsuit filed by the State of Massachusetts, to stop publishing suggested rate schedules for private duty nursing services. Commonwealth of Mass. v. Mass. Nurses Ass'n., 1980–2 Trade Cas. ¶63,304 (Mass. Super. Ct. 1980).

and the medical profession's control of Blue Shield.[30] The Although psychology has no comparable methods for determining practitioner compensation, it may be nonetheless instructive to understand their implications for planning the future of psychology.

Relative value studies result in a series of numerical weights attached to a variety of medical procedures. The weights indicate the proportional value of each procedure to all others included in the study. Such tables are not fee schedules, but can easily be converted to them by multiplying each proportional value by a dollar conversion factor. Federal regulatory agencies immediately saw the relationship between relative value studies and the pricing formulas subject to sanction in other industries, and as a result, many such procedures have been enjoined or are subject to consent decrees.[31] In a recent case,[32] however, a federal district court rejected the argument that a relative value study was a per se violation of the Sherman Act. After considering the "special circumstances" of the profession and the manner in which the relative value guide was adopted and used, the court held that the guide withstood judicial scrutiny under per se rules. However, it is not clear how the case would have been resolved had the Department of Justice introduced evidence on the adverse economic effects of the scheme and the court had based its decision on the Rule of Reason.

Professional medical control of Blue Shield was another obvious target for federal regulators taking a careful measure of the health care industry. At one time, it looked like the federal government would attempt to severely curtail the medical profession's influence over the policies of Blue Shield (Federal Trade Commission, 1979b). Forewarned

---

[30]The states of Ohio and West Virginia brought and settled cases to end medical control of Blue Shield plans. *See* Ohio v. Ohio Medical Indemnity, 1978–2 Trade Cas. ¶62,154 (S.D. Ohio 1978). The state of Arizona challenged a medical-society-sponsored insurance plan as price fixing, but the Ninth Circuit held that the allegations had to be judged under the Rule of Reason. Arizona v. Maricopa County Medical Society, 1980–1 Trade Cas. ¶63,239 (9th Cir. 1980). Forty-four states, stating that antitrust enforcement is important in holding down health care costs, joined Arizona in seeking to persuade the Supreme Court to hold that such conduct is per se illegal.

[31]*See* note 29, *supra.*

[32]United States v. American Society of Anesthesiologists, 473 F. Supp. 147 (S.D.N.Y. 1979).

of the possibility of such close scrutiny, other medically dominated organizations (e.g., Joint Commission on the Accreditation of Hospitals) have taken at least token steps in the direction of nonmedical representation on governing boards.

Although the use of relative value studies and professional control of a health insurer are practices that at this time have no analogy in psychology, as the profession matures and becomes a larger force in the field of mental health care, it is not inconceivable that pressures might develop to utilize similar approaches. Before this occurs, the lessons from the past must be carefully considered. Mechanisms such as the relative value study appear to have been used to facilitate price fixing in cases where it would otherwise not have been possible. However, they also are useful to third-party providers and for self-regulatory efforts at cost containment within a profession. The structuring and implementation of such a mechanism should be undertaken only after a very careful consideration of the purposes for which it is intended, balanced against the illegal activity for which it can so easily be used.

, Similar cautions are appropriate with respect to professionally sponsored prepaid treatment plans. They should be structured and governed to provide for diverse representation of interested professional and consumer groups. Even the appearance that a prepaid plan restricts competition among professionals or operates to advance the self-interest of the sponsoring group may be sufficient to trigger time-consuming, expensive, and professionally embarassing antitrust litigation.

DISCUSSION

The application of antitrust doctrine to professional self-regulation raises serious issues. The traditional basis for professional self-regulation was that consumers should look to the profession rather than to competitive forces to ensure the highest level of quality in practitioners and services. Traditional antitrust doctrine, however, flatly rejects this premise. A fundamental assumption of antitrust law is that industry-wide groups *cannot* serve as unbiased arbiters of price or quantity of services. Instead, the market is the final arbiter of these economic issues. Even if it is unclear whether market forces in the provision of professional services can adequately regulate such matters, antitrust doctrine requires that decisions be made on a competitive basis, by professionals whose ability to further their own interests is checked by the need to compete for consumer dollars.

The point is not that the professions are prohibited from any form of self-regulation for the purpose of ensuring the quality of the services offered by member professionals. Again, the FTC's decision in the AMA case makes it clear that peer review is an important function for professional societies to perform. Many federal and state agencies encourage (and in the case of Professional Standards Review Organizations, mandate) professional organizations to take action to monitor the quality and cost-effectiveness of services. The dividing line between prohibited and permitted professional group activity under the antitrust laws is whether it substantially lessens competition, measured primarily by its economic effects. Therefore, even apparently well-intentioned professional restraints may be struck down if they result in a net loss in competition. Of course, competition is measured in terms of price, quality, convenience, and the like. Competition is not a simple concept, nor does it fail to take into account *real* differences in quality.

It should be apparent that the threat of antitrust litigation places psychology in a quandry. It is no longer a simple task to attempt, through self-regulation, to ensure that the quality of psychological services remains at a high level and at the same time to avoid opening those same self-regulatory activities to possible charges of antitrust violations. There is a real need for a detailed examination of current professional activities to determine where such troublesome issues may arise.

The recent trend in antitrust law enforcement against the professions, exemplified by the recent decision in the *Virginia Academy* case, may result in a mixed blessing for psychology. On the one hand, *Virginia Academy* will surely help the profession to be recognized as independent from the medical profession in the delivery of mental health services. From this perspective, *Virginia Academy* and related reimbursement cases in other states may represent only the beginnings of a major movement in that direction. On the other hand, the antitrust laws could be used as a weapon against psychology by other professional groups if it, in turn, tries to dominate the mental health services market the way physicians did until quite recently.

Our goal here is to raise many more questions than can be answered within the limited framework of this article. Answers, however, can be derived from a systematic review of the directions and goals that psychology sees for itself in the future. Such an analysis needs to be undertaken to provide the knowledge upon which significant organizational policy decisions will be based and should incorporate such fundamental questions as those which follow.

General

What is psychology's position with respect to the general dictates of antitrust law? To what extent does psychology believe that competition among psychologists and between psychologists and other mental health professionals is possible? What organizational initiatives have been undertaken by psychology to encourage or restrict the development of innovative and competitive treatment and service delivery alternatives? What role should the government and the public play in monitoring or limiting self-regulatory efforts? What policies have national and state psychological organizations adopted concerning the status of non-PhD practitioners? What is the rationale for these policies and what evidence supports that rationale? Do these policies represent valid efforts at self-regulation or do they really organize efforts to exclude lower-priced competitors?

Accreditation

What degree of control should psychology, as a professional organization, have over the the training of practitioners? To what degree does psychology enhance innovation in research and training by virtue of graduate training program approval standards? Are existing standards compatible with the legal and political climate and are they consistent with the goals of the profession? To what extent does the process of approval/accreditation contribute to the increasing cost and availability of mental health care?

Licensing

What degree of control should the national and state organizations exert over the licensing process? To what extent should national and state organizations promote restrictive licensing provisions and examination procedures? To what degree does a national licensing examination help to ensure the quality of services provided by professionals and the integrity of the profession, and to what extent does it serve as a mechanism to limit access to the profession and to reduce competition among members of the profession?

Specialty Certification

Given the nature of the field of psychology, is specialty certification a viable alternative? What reasons are put forth in support of it and what purpose would it serve? What lessons can be learned from existing models of specialty certification regarding the practical and professional implications of such a mechanism?

Restrictions on Advertising

Are national and state-level policies on psychologists' advertising consistent with recent trends in case law? Do organizational policies reflect strictly professional concerns or do they encompass economic and commercial concerns as well?

Fees and Compensation

Should national and state-level organizations seek to influence decisions about fees or should such decisions be left to individual practitioners, thirdparty payers, or government health benefit programs? Should psychology continue to rely on Blue Shield and other insurers or should it establish its own system of prepaid services? If a separate system is contemplated, what form should it take to avoid antitrust charges like those now being directed against physicians and Blue Shield?

CONCLUSION

Antitrust enforcement within the context of the professions is a reality. We feel that the psychology profession is presented with an opportunity to actively deal with potential conflicts between professional activities and the antitrust laws in advance of legal challenges. By systematically examining the existing structure of psychology, the resulting knowledge can be used as the basis for possible change in organizational policy to avoid antitrust allegations and also can be used to formulate preventive action to reduce the likelihood of such suits. More importantly, however, the knowledge gained can be used to formulate policy for the future direction of the profession. We believe that organizational policy and strategy affecting competition always should be formulated with an eye to their antitrust implications.

REFERENCES

Committee on Governmental Affairs. U.S. Senate, 96th Congress, 1st Session, 1979. *Staff report on the California relative value studies.* Washington, D.C.: Government Printing Office, 1979.

Federal Trade Commission. *Health services policy session briefing book.* Washington, D.C.: Author, 1979. (a)

Federal Trade Commission. *Staff report on medical participation in control of Blue Shield and certain other openpanel medical prepayment plans.* Washington, D.C.: Author, 1979. (b)

Federal Trade Commission. *Staff report on effects of restrictions on advertising and commercial practice in the professions.* Washington, D.C.: Author, 1980. (a)

Federal Trade Commission. *Staff report on state restrictions on vision care providers: The effects on consumers.* Washington, D.C.: Author, 1980. (b)

Havighurst, C. C. Antitrust enforcement in the medical services industry: What does it all mean? *Milbank Memorial Fund Quarterly: Health and Society,* 1980, 58, 89–124.

Havighurst, C. C., & Kissam, P. C. The antitrust implications of relative value studies in medicine. *Journal of Health Politics, Policy, and Law,* 1979, 4, 48–86.

Leibenluft, R., & Pollard, M. Antitrust scrutiny of the health professions. *Vanderbilt Law Review,* 1981, 34, 927–963.

Paxton, H. T. As trustbusters see it, everything doctors do is wrong. *Medical Economics,* 1979, 56, 37–59.

Pollard, M. Fostering competition in health care. In A. Levin (Ed.), *Regulating health care: The struggle for control.* New York: Academy of Political Science, 1980.

Pollard, M. The essential role of antitrust in a competitive market for health services. *Milbank Memorial Fund Quarterly: Health and Society,* 1981, 59, 256–268.

Randall, P. The FTC and the plastic surgeons. *New England Journal of Medicine*, 1978, 299, 1464–1466.

Rosoff, A. Antitrust laws and the health care industry. *St. Louis University Law Review*, 1979, 23, 446–490.

Shearn, M. A. Professional education in a service system. In *The Kaiser-Permanente medical care program: A symposium*. Palo Alto, Calif.: Commonwealth Fund, 1971.

Weller, C. D. Approaches to health care problems: Antitrust. In National Association of Attorneys General (Ed.), *Attorneys General's approaches to problems of health care*. Raleigh, N.C.: National Association of Attorneys General, 1978.

Chapter 15

CAN THE TAXPAYER AFFORD TO HAVE THE MEDICAL ESTABLISHMENT GO ON IGNORING CLINICAL ECOLOGY?

VICKY RIPPERE

. . . when I stress that I am looking for still further improvements in perform-ance that should not be taken as a criticism of the Service. What I am stating is that it is our clear duty constantly to seek to improve the quality of the service we provide for patients, and for the taxpayer who finances it.

The Rt. Hon. Norman Fowler, addressing the
National Association of Health Authorities (cited in Scrutator, 1983).

INTRODUCTION

Clinical ecology is a developing branch of medical-behavioural sci-ence that is concerned with elucidating some of the environmental causes of human illness, mental as well as physical (i.e. Dickey, 1976; Mackarness, 1976, 1980, 1982; Bell, 1982). Practitioners of clinical ecology maintain that many symptoms and syndromes arise from unsus-pected hypersensitivity to environmental agents, and there is now an abundance of good published evidence to support their claim (some of it reviewed in Rippere, 1983a).

Ecological treatment differs from conventional allopathic treatment in that it does not aim at suppressing symptoms by means of drugs but at preventing symptoms either by identification and avoidance of exposure to their precipitating environmental agents and/or by fortification of the affected individual's own biological defences in order to reduce his or her excessive reactivity. The means used in this effort include protracted or spaced avoidance of noxious substances, desensitization to specific allergens, enhancement of immune tolerance and/or digestion by vaccines, drops, nutritional supplements, digestive enzymes, and general diet

183

reform to ensure adequate nutrition, among many other techniques. Ecology techniques may be used in conjunction with other treatment modalities such as acupuncture, homoeopathy, meditation, relaxation, etc., and also allopathic drugs, but these latter are normally only used to terminate acute, life-threatening reactions. In addition, ecological treatment may also be used alongside psychological or behavioural treatment in cases whose difficulties have both ecological and psychological components (Rippere & Adams, 1982).

Now what has clinical ecology to do with improving the cost-effectiveness of health care in the developed world? Simply this: in the long run, it is not only cheaper but also more humane and more effective to discover and remove the causes of chronic disease than to stop at suppressing the symptoms with costly drugs which themselves may cause further illness. And discovering and removing the causes of chronic disease are what clinical ecology is about. While the initial diagnostic phase of ecological intervention *may* be (but is not necessarily) labour-intensive and highly technological, the implementation of treatment, in all but severe cases, normally is not: the patient makes relevant changes in diet and physical environment, takes supplements and/or enzymes, and, after settling into a regimen, may be discharged from further professional attention. Moreover, the experience of supervised ecological diagnosis and treatment may equip the patient with the knowledge and skills needed to cope on his/her own with any further ecological problems that may develop, or indeed, to prevent further problems from developing. Thus, undergoing ecological treatment may reduce not only the need for extended professional involvement but also further avoidable morbidity. Furthermore, as Strickland (1982) has noted, the application of ecological knowledge at the level of society may make possible primary prevention of environmental illness on a very wide scale, thus promoting still further savings for the taxpayer.

THE ARGUMENT

This essay takes its point of departure in the juxtaposition of two facts. The first is commonplace, viz, that throughout the developed world the costs of allopathic health care are soaring. In Britain, per capita health expenditure rose from £141 in 1978 to £162 in 1979 (Office of Health Economics, 1981, Table 8). By 1983 it had reached

£280 (Scrutator, 1983), doubling in only 5 years. In the United States, the comparable figures for 1978 and 1979 were £389 and £405, respectively (Office of Health Economics, 1981, Table 8). And in the majority of 11 developed countries for which data are available for both years, there was a higher percentage increase over previous year for health expenditure than for consumer prices generally (Office of Health Economics, 1981, Table 8). These figures appear to speak for themselves and we needn't argue about them.

The second fact from which we depart is the observation that practitioners of clinical ecology (especially those who work in the public sector) are commonly ostracised and even persecuted for their efforts to develop their relatively inexpensive, relatively safe, and often definitive form of treatment. The widespread resistance on the part of the medical establishment to clinical ecology has been well documented (i.e. Society for Environmental Therapy, 1982; Adams, 1983; Forman, 1981 a, b).

Now my argument may be stated as follows: especially in a publicly-funded health care delivery system, the authorities who decide how medical funds are to be deployed are responsible for making efficient use — in Cochrane's (1972) sense — of the available financial resources. They are obliged to deploy these funds in such a way as to obtain the greatest benefit for the most people for the least cost. Since for the increasingly widespread modern diseases of adaptation clinical ecology (which has been developed specifically to deal with these diseases) is, as the only available rational treatment, potentially the most cost-effective approach, the authorities may be considered irresponsible for neglecting to investigate what clinical ecology has to offer and, instead, allowing its proponents to be persecuted and driven out of the public sector. The current policy of treating clinical ecology as an off-colour joke is causing a considerable proportion of the taxpayer's health expenditure to be wasted on conventional allopathic treatments that are often demonstrably short-sighted, dangerous, and ineffective (see, for example, Weitz, 1981).

RELATIVE COST–EFFECTIVENESS OF CLINICAL ECOLOGY

At the present time, we have no systematically gathered comparative objective data on the cost-effectiveness of clinical ecology versus allopathic treatment for diseases of adaptation. However, some self-report data from a sample of eighty-five British members of allergy self-help groups have recently appeared (Rippere, 1983b). Respondents in this open-ended questionnaire survey were asked to indicate which kinds of treatment they had received for their condition from all outside sources, and how much they had been helped by these treatments. They mentioned conventional investigations and treatments, alternative medical treatments (such as homoeopathy, acupuncture, Gerson therapy, radionics, etc.), and clinical ecology. Content analyses and frequency counts were performed on their responses. Their evaluations of treatments were classified not evaluated, little or no benefit, some or transient benefit, moderate benefit, great benefit, adverse reaction, and a synthetic category representing the sum of responses rated either moderate or great benefit. The results are shown in Table 15-1. (data from Rippere, 1983b)

Table 15-1.
Comparative Effectiveness of Conventional, Alternative
and Clinical Ecology Treatments as Evaluated by Survey Participants

Type of treatment	Not Evaluated	Little/No Benefit	Some/Transient Benefit	Moderate Benefit	Great Benefit	Adverse Reaction	Moderate and Great Benefit
Conventional	29.7	29.7	16.2	15.3	8.1	12.2	23.7
Alternative	27.8	44.4	2.8	11.1	13.9	5.6	25.0
Clinical ecology	21.6	—	24.3	16.2	37.8	5.4	54.1

On the basis of this evidence, which is all we have to go on, it appears that from the personal point of view of ecological casualties, clinical ecology outperforms both conventional and alternative medicine by a comfortable margin and is also associated with an appreciably lower rate of adverse reactions than conventional medicine.

One important feature of these data not evident from the table is that the majority of conventional treatment interventions and investigations mentioned were obtained in the public sector, whereas the majority of alternative and clinical ecology interventions were obtained in the private sector. If patients who have failed to benefit from conventional help wish to try clinical ecology, they normally have to go outside the NHS (which they are already paying for out of their taxes) into the private sector (at further and often considerable expense). Thus, they have to pay twice for their care because they have the misfortune to suffer from a condition that the authorities who deploy public health money neither acknowledge nor make adequate provision for.

While this state of affairs is manifestly unfair to the ecologically-afflicted taxpayer, it has further implications for *all* patients that may not be so obvious. Specifically, if less than a quarter of the conventional medical care expended on ecological casualties is of any use to them, it follows that over 75 percent of such interventions are wasted, since they lead to no discernible benefit for the recipients. Not only does the taxpayer have to fork out for all these wasted investigations and treatments, he also has to endure shortages of *other* medical services that the system cannot afford to provide because it is pouring so many resources down the drain of treating ecological casualties allopathically and creating more illness in the wake of its refusal to appreciate that these people are not suffering from Valium® deficiency. With the increasing need for community geriatric services, the chronic shortage of community facilities for the mentally ill and physically and mentally handicapped, the increasing lack of suitable residential places for chronically sick children, and all the other major, pressing service demands that one reads in the newspapers are not going to be met because of cutbacks in public health expenditure, can the taxpayer, whether or not he himself suffers from an ecological disorder, afford to let the medical establishment go on persecuting its few intrepid clinical ecologists and driving them out of the public sector?

A CASE HISTORY

The potential savings that might be expected to accrue to the taxpayer as a result of the wider use of ecological methods are probably best illustrated by detailed examination of an individual case. To anyone who is acquainted with the ecology literature, the story of Bob will have a familiar plot.

Bob first experienced intrusive, unwanted recurring thoughts at the age of eleven. He continued to experience obsessions intermittently over the next eight years until he began a university degree course. When he moved from his home to the hall of residence, Bob's obsessions became worse. His concentration was so impaired by his ruminations that he failed his first year exams and was forced to withdraw from the course. After a series of short-term clerical jobs, in which he was also disabled by his obsessions, he took a manual outdoor job, where concentration was not so critical. But being a highly intelligent and sensitive young man, he was unhappy and socially isolated in his work and became increasingly depressed.

During this period, Bob was treated with a succession of minor tranquillizers and antidepressants, initially by his general practitioner and subsequently by a series of local psychiatrists at the district general hospital psychiatric outpatient department. In due course, when he was still just as bad as he had been when he started, and had taken several overdoses, had several admissions, and developed hypertension (for which he was treated with more drugs), he was referred, at the age of twenty-six, to a psychiatric teaching hospital in London, a three and one-half hour journey from his home.

Bob was initially seen for assessment by the consultant psychiatrist and his registrar (resident), had his drugs changed, and was told that he would be referred to the psychologist for further assessment for behaviour therapy, which is generally considered the treatment of choice in obsessional disorders. When the day of his first appointment with the psychologist arrived, he appeared with his mother, who was in a more distressed state than he was. On the verge of tears, she was adamant that Bob had to be admitted to hospital because she was ill and could no longer cope with having him at home. She was suffering from severe hypertension and Crohn's disease, and was not up to the strain of looking after a suicidal son. It transpired that since his recent appointment with the psychiatrist, Bob had taken yet another overdose—with his new tablets—and had been briefly admitted yet again to his local psychiatric ward. After an emergency consultation with the firm's senior registrar, admission was arranged for the following day. Bob agreed not to try to kill himself again that evening and returned home with his mother to pack his case. The following day, he returned to the teaching hospital and was admitted. This was in November 1978.

On admission, Bob's complaints included the obsessions, depression, and hypertension already mentioned and also acne, constipation, and panic attacks. His antihypertensive medication was eventually changed from diuretics to beta blockers because of their anxiolytic properties. He was also treated with various antidepressants throughout his stay, but the mainstay of treatment was psychological and behavioural. His admission to the teaching hospital lasted nine months at an estimated cost to the taxpayer of £280 per week, a total of around £10,000. It would be pleasant to be able to report that this massive outlay on the regimen of intensive, prolonged multiple psychological, behavioural, and pharmacological treatments effected a significant improvement in Bob's disabling chronic obsessional ruminations. Unfortunately, however, they didn't. His obsessions resisted many drugs, thought stopping, satiation, relaxation training, counselling, Gestalt techniques, ward group therapy, occupational therapy, and amytal abreaction, undertaken at his own request. In addition, he had weekly interviews with his registrar, multiple physical investigations, and a full psychometric assessment. Apart from his IQ and memory quotient, both of which were considerably above average, all investigations were normal. In view of his refractoriness to treatment, he was, as a last resort, referred for assessment to a consultant who specialises in behavioural treatment of obsessional disorders. The consultant reviewed his treatment history to date and, after interviewing him, said he had nothing to add.

Eventually it became clear that the teaching hospital had no further resources to offer Bob as an inpatient. He was discharged to outpatient follow-up in both the registrar's and the psychologist's clinics. He returned to his manual job and took days of annual leave to come to London for his six weekly appointments. His obsessions were no better than they had been on admission. If anything, they were somewhat worse, but at least he no longer seemed to be actively suicidal.

After a year of follow-up in the registrar clinic there were no further drugs to try, so Bob was discharged to the care of the psychologist, who continued to see him at intervals of from two to three months. Their discussions centred on *learning to live with your problems if they aren't going to go away*. Towards the end of 1980, Bob's local psychiatric services, who were also still involved, mooted a leucotomy. Bob was, to say the least, not keen on the idea. As a last resort, the psychologist proposed a clinical ecology approach to banish his obsessions. She had been using dietary and ecological treatment with a few outpatients since around the time Bob had started in treatment, with encouraging results, but she had not tried clinical ecology with an obsessional patient before. All the indications in the literature seemed to point against there being any hope of a good outcome. But on her recently developed screening questionnaire, Bob came out positive for probable masked allergy, chemical sensitivity, and hypoglycaemia, so there seemed no harm in trying, although neither had much confidence that the approach would work where so many others had failed so miserably.

In December 1980, Bob kept daily baseline self-ratings of all the symptoms he had endorsed on the questionnaire, in order to enable them to evaluate the outcome of ecological treatment. In January 1981, Bob commenced an elimination diet that had been devised by Dr. Richard Mackarness (1980) of Park Prewett Hospital, Basingstoke. His *Stone Age Diet* eliminates all the modern foods that are most commonly implicated in the modern diseases of adaptation: cereal grains, milk, dairy products and eggs, refined sugar, chocolate, coffee, tea, alcohol, manufactured, tinned, preserved, or adulterated products, and foods containing additives. It consists of fresh meat, fish, and poultry, fruit, vegetables, nuts, olive oil, sea salt, fresh ground pepper, herb teas, dandelion coffee (not instant or with lactose), and bottled spring water. Bob was also instructed to eat a high-protein breakfast and to take an all-purpose multinutrient supplement.

During the first month of treatment, Bob experienced a withdrawal reaction with worsening of many of his symptoms, followed by a gradual and patchy improvement. In February, at a meeting the psychologist discovered that he was still not eating any breakfast and firmly enjoined him to eat a high protein meal (i.e. a 4–6 oz. portion of animal protein and a piece of fresh low carbohydrate fruit) in the morning. He began this practice and within two days experienced a dramatic improvement of his obsessions. The results of his treatment for most of the first 7 months are shown in the graph of his daily self-ratings in Figure 15-I, from Rippere (1983d).

The graph shows that within 48 hours of starting the high-protein breakfast, Bob's obsessions declined in severity from level 7 on a subjective scale running from 0 to 10 (with 10 representing maximum severity) to a level of 2, where it remained for the rest of the month. At this point, he stopped continuous ratings, but 6 weeks later he recorded an average rating of one for the intervening period. After continuing with his regimen for the next 2 months, Bob decided on his own initiative to undertake the much more stringent Longcroft Clinic elimination diet, which consists solely of fresh lamb, pears, and bottled spring water (described in Nathan Hill, 1980). Starting this diet produced a small-scale withdrawal reaction, more manifest in Bob's mood than in his obsessions. Thereafter, he began systematic reintroductions of individual foods on a trial basis. Individual provocative tests for eggs, pork, and

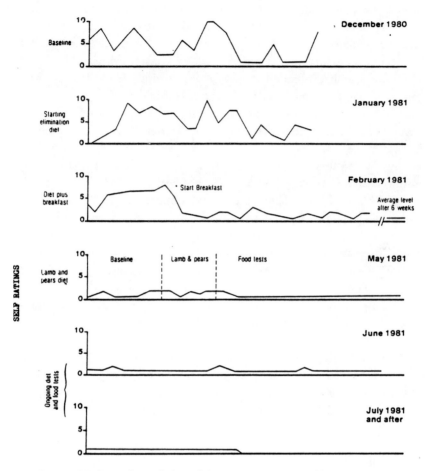

Figure 15-I. ° British Psychological Society, 1983, reprinted by permission.

tiger nuts produced the transient, mild worsening of his obsessions, shown in the graph for June 1981. The following month, some 7 months after he had started the original elimination diet, 25 months after starting treatment at the teaching hospital, and 18 years after first experiencing obsessions, Bob awoke to freedom from his persistent and disabling affliction. At the time of writing (September 1983), Bob has remained obsession-free for over 2 years and has been discharged from follow-up for 8 months, though he has remained in touch with the psychologist informally.

Bob's other presenting symptoms also improved on ecological treatment. His acne and constipation were relieved shortly after he started the elimination diet. It is not entirely certain when his hypertension vanished, but its disappearance was discovered before he started the lamb and pears diet. Because he intended to use pulse testing (Coca, 1956) when reintroducing foods on a trial basis, the psychologist wrote to his general practitioner to ask whether he could suspend his beta blockers for the duration of the trial since the drug, which prevents the sort of pulse rate increases used to detect reactive foods, would interfere with Bob's testing. When the drug was withdrawn, it was found that Bob was now normotensive without it, and he did not return to taking it when he finished his food tests. The panic attacks stopped before the obsessions, and as his problems melted away, his mood lifted to a great extent. At the end of his formal attendance at the hospital, Bob's only residual problems were a host of social difficulties resulting from the severity and chronicity of his former obsessions: underemployment, social isolation, and lack of professional opportunities due to his truncated higher education. He is now trying to obtain a university place to resume the academic career he was forced to interrupt over a decade ago.

One question left unanswered by Bob's recovery on his ecological regimen was: why? He declined to return to his former eating habits en masse to see whether this maneuver would provoke a return of his obsessions, so our answer to this question must be tentative rather than definitive. From the dramatic decrease in the severity of his obsessions following the introduction of a high-protein breakfast, it seemed likely that hypoglycaemia, probably secondary to the multiple food addictions that caused him to experience a withdrawal reaction when he started the elimination diet, was responsible for the obsessions (Philpott & Kalita, 1980). To test this hypothesis, his GP's help in obtaining an extended glucose tolerance test was enlisted. Because of a mix-up at the laboratory where he had the test done, only the two-hour test was conducted. However, on this test, his blood glucose values fell to hypoglycaemic levels at two hours, as shown in Table 15-2.

Thus, the hypoglycaemia hypothesis appears to have been confirmed. Although Bob's one off early morning test results do not show fasting hypoglycaemia, it seems quite likely that this condition, having its onset at midmorning, was responsible for a state of cerebral inefficiency that prevented the operation of the normal inhibitory mechanisms by which

Table 15-2.
Bob's Two-Hour Glucose Tolerance Test Results

Time	Blood Glucose mmol/l
Fasting	4.3 (NR fasting 3.3–6.1 mmol/1)
30 min.	6.8
60 min.	3.9
90 min.	2.3
120 min.	1.9

means obsessional ideation must be screened out of awareness. Further support for the hypoglycaemia hypothesis comes from Bob's recent report that he has been able to reintroduce all foods except alcohol with impunity. After a protracted period of total avoidance, it would be expected that most of his food addictions would diminish. He now takes care to vary his diet and his various somatic problems have not recurred.

DISCUSSION

In the context of the present economic argument in favour of wider dissemination of clinical ecology, two features of this case history require our attention. First, if we consider the comparative performance of orthodox treatment versus clinical ecology, there is no doubt that clinical ecology proved more effective than all the orthodox pharmacological, psychological, and behavioural treatments combined in relieving the patient of his multiple afflictions. In a word, clinical ecology worked and the rest didn't. Second, if we consider the comparative cost to the taxpayer of Bob's orthodox versus his clinical ecology treatment, there is also no doubt that clinical ecology, administered on an outpatient basis for a total of around 12 one-hour sessions (including the baseline period and over a year of follow-up) by a nonmedically trained clinical psychologist, also worked out considerably cheaper than all Bob's previous local admissions and general practitioner treatment and a nine-month teaching hospital inpatient admission and a year of psychiatric and psychological follow-up, multiple drugs, physical and psychometric investigation, and sickness benefit from the Department of Health and Social Security. That is to say, in case there are still any readers who need to have the point belaboured, clinical ecology was both more effective and more efficient than any of the first or even second and third-line conventional treatments that were attempted, producing considerably greater benefit to the patient at considerably less cost to the taxpayer. A small spin-off from his eventually successful treatment was that when the next ecological obsessional patient to come the psychologist's way was referred for treatment, he was offered clinical ecology in the first instance, rather than after all else had failed, and it may be said that when he adheres to his regimen, his obsessions are appreciably less marked than when he fails to comply. Alcohol is a particularly troublesome substance for him, as it is for his predecessor. The savings in efficiency in his case that has resulted from applying knowledge derived from Bob's treatment must also be reckoned in the calculations. And it is unlikely to be the only case to benefit from this knowledge.

Because there are at present no systematically gathered objective group data on the comparative cost-effectiveness of clinical ecology versus orthodox treatment, the reader will have to take on faith that Bob's case of longstanding disability relieved by simple environmental intervention is not atypical of ecological patients' histories. Because there are as yet no epidemiological data on the overall prevalence of ecological disorder amongst the general run of psychiatric patients, the reader will have to make do with a simple, operational study conducted in 1981 in the writer's clinical unit at the Maudsley Hospital in London. During this year, the writer attempted to screen all new cases referred to her clinical unit for assessment for treatment, a predominantly very chronic group of treatment resistant patients, numbering 46 in all. For various reasons, 4 could not be screened (two refused and 2 were discharged before they could be seen and did not respond to follow-up enquiries). The 42 screened patients were subdivided into so-called "routine referrals," in whom no suspicion of ecological disorder was raised at the time of referral, and "suspects," who were specifically referred for investigation of possible ecological involvement. There were 23 routine cases and 19 suspects. Using the criteria normally applied in clinical practice for identifying ecological cases, some 95.7 percent of the routine group (22 to 23 cases) and 94.7 percent (18 to 19 cases) of the suspects were found to be positive (Rippere, 1982a, b). Although we should expect to find the rate of ecological involvement somewhat lower in a population of acute cases referred to the psychiatric services for the first time, these findings suggest that ecological disorders are not uncommon among psychiatric patients seen in a general adult clinical psychology practice in the public sector. The fact that the patients in the group were predominantly very chronic suggests, further, that the presence of an unsuspected ecological disorder may be an important factor contributing to chronicity under conditions of routine allopathic treatment.

Returning now to my argument, we may appreciate that, given the increasingly high cost of providing the population with psychiatric services and the undoubtedly high rate of ecological disorder (for which the conventional allopathic services are generally irrelevant) in the population requiring psychiatric care, the potential savings to the taxpayer that might be expected to result from the wider use of ecological methods in psychiatry alone are enormous. It follows, too, that the result of failure to disseminate the use of ecological methods in psychiatry can only be an equally enormous waste of the taxpayer's money. Under these circumstances, I would argue again that the taxpayer simply cannot afford to have the medical establishment go on ignoring clinical ecology and systematically driving its few clinical ecologists out of the public sector.

THE COST OF SAVINGS

Now we come to another important issue that must be considered before closing this chapter. We need to examine the immediate and long-range costs of the savings I am advocating. It is necessary to acknowledge that widespread adoption of ecological methods in public sector psychiatry (as well as in nonpsychiatric branches of medicine) would entail capital expenditure in the short term and running costs in the longer term. Because many ecological victims are extremely sensitive to low-level chemical exposures, new clinics would have to be provided or significant structural and chemical alterations made in existing facilities so that the more seriously affected patients would not be poisoned by the physical premises of the clinic. Hospital pathology laboratories would have to extend their offerings to include faster and more comprehensive immunology services (Rippere, 1983c), extended glucose tolerance tests, and other relevant ancillary investigations. Catering budgets would need to be expanded to allow for additional training of staff in biological dietetics (Randolph, 1976) and rotating diets (Corwin, 1976) and for provision of ecologically suitable food and water obtained and prepared for individual patients. Suitably uncontaminated inpatient facilities, as well as outpatient clinics, for diagnosis and initial treatment of the more severe multiple allergics would also have to be laid on: there is no point in trying to admit seriously affected patients with chemical involvement to contemporary psychiatric wards, where the air is laden with tobacco smoke, residues of floor polishes, air fresheners, antiseptic, bleach, natural gas fumes from the ward kitchen, outgassing from paint and plastic floors and seats, *inter alia*. If such patients are to be treated, proper facilities must be provided.

These innovations in physical premises and operational practices represent an investment that would be expected to yield long-term savings in improved diagnosis and treatment of the rising numbers of ecological casualties, for whom orthodox allopathic methods, applied in ecologically unsafe surroundings, cannot be expected to produce significant benefit.

Initially, the magnitude of operational changes required and their costs may seem prohibitive when compared to the running costs of dishing out Valium® in a preexisting outpatient clinic. But when we consider that highly technological medical procedures such as preoperative care for patients who have had, say, organ transplant surgery require even more extensive and costly modifications and more and more intensively trained staff to implement them, and that they benefit a considerably smaller number of patients, the magnitude of the changes necessary to enable fully adequate clinical ecology services to be offered falls into perspective. Given the projected degree of benefit, the introduction of such services would be cheap at the price. Objections to the cost must be seen as special pleading *contra*clinical ecology.

Now it may be argued that since the majority of practising clinical ecologists do not have access to comprehensive inpatient environmental control units, such units are not necessary to the practice of clinical ecology. Indeed, it is true that some of the less severely affected cases can be dealt with reasonably satisfactorily on an outpatient basis with little or no equipment or technological backup. But, as anyone who practices under these conditions will be quick to realise, the service that can be offered and the population of sufferers to whom such services are relevant are rather limited: the most severely affected cases are automatically excluded because the setting itself will make most of them ill and a proportion, perhaps as high as a third, of the less severely affected will prove to be unable to muster the self-discipline and, in some cases, the financial resources, necessary for the long-drawn-out and costly elimination diet and food testing procedure that can be offered. It is one of the great paradoxes of life in the developed world today that, all things being equal, the *fewer* expensive chemicals with which a food is adulterated, the more it costs, and food testing needs to be done with unadulterated foods. Thus clinical ecology, practised without appropriate facilities, becomes a treatment reserved for the elite of well-motivated, financially secure, middle-class patient who is not totally disabled by his or her allergies. The arguments concerning the limited relevance of psychotherapies for patients who benefit from them in proportion to their lack of absolute need for them are too well known to bear repetition here, but the analogy is too compelling to pass over in silence. But just as the taxpayer cannot afford to have long-term psychotherapy available at the public expense as the main line of treatment for psychological disorders, it seems an inescapable conclusion that the same taxpayer cannot afford not to have clinical ecology services be more widely available to the same population.

CODA

It should be noted that I am not (repeat not) proposing clinical ecology as the *sole* modality of treatment available for mental disorder. Drugs do sometimes have their uses; behaviour therapy is of proven effectiveness in many cases of maladaptive learning; cognitive therapy, counselling, and even sometimes psychotherapy all have their place. But to the extent that patients' symptoms are not due to genetically transmitted tendencies to develop biochemical imbalances, enzyme deficiencies, congenital structural defects, endocrine disturbance, maladaptive conditioning, childhood trauma, misleading cognitions, lack of social support or social skills, excess stress, bereavement, drug or heavy metal poisoning, brain injury, poverty or *Weltschmerz* among others, but rather due to hypersensitivity to the physical or chemical environment, with or without interaction of nutritional deficiencies and imbalances, then clinical ecology needs to be granted its rightful place in the clinical armamentarium. If it is not, ecological patients will continue to have a large amount of public money wasted on their ineffectual allopathic treatment and the taxpayer, as well as the patients, will be the losers.

REFERENCES

Adams, N. (1983) An alternative meaning of "Action Against Allergy," *Newsletter of the Society for Environmental Therapy,* 3(1), 17–18.

Bell, I. R. (1982) *Clinical Ecology. A New Medical Approach to Environmental Illness.* Bolinas, California: Common Knowledge Press.

Coca, A. F. (1956) *The Pulse Test.* University Books: New York.

Cochrane, A. L. (1972) *Effectiveness and Efficiency. Random Reflections on Health Services.* The Nuffield Provincial Hospitals Trust.

Corwin, A. H. (1976) The rotating diet and taxonomy. In L. D. Dickey (Ed.) *Clinical Ecology,* Charles C Thomas: Springfield, Illinois, pp. 122–148.

Dickey, L. D. (Ed.) *Clinical Ecology.* Charles C Thomas: Springfield, Illinois.

Forman, R. E. (1981a) Medical resistance to innovation. *Medical Hypotheses,* 7, 1009–1017.

Forman, R. E. (1981b) A critique of evaluation studies of sublingual and intracutaneous provocative tests for food allergy. *Medical Hypotheses,* 7, 1019–1027.

Mackarness, R. (1976) *Not All in the Mind.* Pan: London.

Mackarness, R. (1980) *Chemical Victims.* Pan: London.

Mackarness, R. (1982) Mental health and the environment. In A. R. Rees and H. J. Purcell (Eds.) *Disease and the Environment,* Chichester: John Wiley, pp. 131–135.

Nathan Hill, A. (1980) *Against the Unsuspected Enemy.* New Horizon Press: Bognor Regis.

Office of Health Economics (1981) *OHE Compendium of Health Statistics.* 4th Edition. Office of Health Economics: London.

Philpott, W. H., and Kalita, D. K. (1980) *Brain Allergies: The Psycho-Nutrient Connection.* Keats Publ. Co.: New Canaan, Connecticut.

Randolph, T. G. (1976) Biologic dietetics. In L. D. Dickey (Ed.) *Clinical Ecology,* Charles C Thomas: Springfield, Illinois, pp. 107–121.

Rippere, V. and Adams, N. (1982) Clinical ecology and why clinical psychology needs it. *Bulletin of the British Psychological Society,* 35, 151–152.

Rippere, V. (1982a) Prevalence of ecological disorders in psychiatric patients. I. Historical features. *Newsletter of the Society for Environmental Therapy,* 2(2), 18–24.

Rippere, V. (1982b) Prevalence of ecological disorders in psychiatric patients. II. Symptoms, prevalence and pointers. *Newsletter of the Society for Environmental Therapy,* 2(3), 7–13.

Rippere, V. (1983a) Nutritional approaches to behaviour modification, *Progress in Behaviour Modification,* 14, 299–354.

Rippere, V. (1983b) *The Allergy Problem: Why People Suffer and What Should be Done.* Wellingborough: Thorsons.

Rippere, V. (1983c) Some problems with NHS food allergy tests, *Newsletter of the Society for Environmental Therapy,* 3(2), 18–21.

Rippere, V. (1983d) Dietary treatment of chronic obsessional ruminations, *British Journal of Clinical Psychology* (in press).

Scrutator (1983) This week. *British Medical Journal* (16 July), 287, 227.

Society for Environmental Therapy (1982) Symposium on Medical Resistance to Innovation, *Newsletter of the Society for Environmental Therapy,* 2(4).

Strickland, B. R. (1982) Implications of food and chemical susceptibilities for clinical psychology. *Int. J. Biosocial Res.* 3(1), 39–43.

Weitz, M. (1980) *Health Shock.* Newton Abbot: David & Charles.

Chapter 16

EVOLUTIONARY REQUIREMENTS ON MODELS OF PSYCHOTHERAPY

NOLAN SALTZMAN

I

Two close friends, Paul and Thomas, go for a walk. Paul is distressed over a recent parting of the ways with a woman he hoped to marry.

P: I used to feel relieved when an affair broke up.

Th: But now you just sound hurt and anxious. What are you worried about?

P: I don't know. Maybe that nothing will last, no matter how good it seems to be at first.

Th: You're afraid nothing will last. So, if nothing lasts, then what?

P: Then *what?* Then I wind up all alone is what!

Th: Hey! What are you getting angry at me for?

P: Sorry.

Th: That's all right. But you were always blowing up at Liz, weren't you?

P: Sometimes. Most of the time I was depressed. When we got together it would take me an hour to warm up to her. Then I would be fine for a while. Whenever we had to split, like towards the end of our vacation, I got grumpy.

Th: As though it was her fault; the way you got angry at me just now.

P: Yes, I felt resentful. I don't like to feel resentful, but I do a lot. Especially towards women in my life.

Th: You feel resentful towards women in your life. Paul, suppose you couldn't work it out with any of them, what would that say to you? About yourself?

P: That I wasn't good enough, somehow. Doesn't make sense, I know, but I'm always on guard for the first sign a woman doesn't think I'm good enough.

Th: But they usually think you're a terrific guy, don't they? Where did you get that feeling of not being good enough?

P: It's in my mind. After my father died, I thought my mother wouldn't leave if I did everything right, but I could never figure out what it was I was supposed to do.

Th: Your mother did leave you, didn't she? But Liz isn't your mother. How could you respond *now* when you and Liz or your next woman friend have to separate in the daily course of things?

P: Well, I could say to myself, this doesn't mean she thinks I'm not good enough.

What happened in this talk? Thomas observed his friend's feelings, elicited their expression, even drawing onto himself some of the emotional charge; examined the significance of these feelings with Paul, who was able to connect them to the anxiety-provoking climate of his childhood; and suggested to Paul there might be a healthier resolution of his feelings.

How does this differ from what might transpire between therapist and patient? First of all, the consultation would take place by appointment, in an office. There would be formalities of seating and behavior emphasizing the difference in status between professional and client. An amount of money would pass from patient to therapist, which the latter would regard as meager remuneration for his years of study, experience, and skill. To the patient, the same fee would seem like the first ransom payment for a kidnapped banker.

What else? Alas, the rest of the comparison would show some professional therapists to be less able than Thomas. Many therapists are out of touch with own feelings and the feelings of their patients. Furthermore, many therapists are burdened by cumbersome models of therapy that prevent a simple sharing of feelings.

Thomas learned how to be a friend not from textbooks, but from his own loves, his marriage, and discussions of his feelings with many friends. By contrast, let us take, as a horrible example, a psychoanalyst who has gone the conventional route through medical school, psychiatric residency, and postgraduate training in psychoanalysis. He has not had much time for his feelings, for he has been studying for the next exam since his early teens. He has learned and mostly forgotten a staggering amount of material of little relevance to emotions or behavior. He never quite figured out how to talk to young women, but after he became a doctor, he didn't have to; they pursued him. He never had to express his needs to them, certainly never to put his soul on the line with any of them.

The young analyst enters private practice. A patient is sent to him by her physician, a classmate in medical school. The patient is his age, thirty-two, but she has had a far richer emotional life than he has. Now her marriage is falling apart, and she is weeping on his couch. To the psychiatrist, her face and her pained breath are reminiscent of physical casualties he treated on his tour in the hospital's emergency room. What is he to do? What does he know about emotional pain? Write a prescription? (Much of his training was in prescribing for patients on the hospital's psychotic ward.) Then, some months or years down the road, "when she is ready for it," he will help this woman discover that her life is a shambles because she wanted to sleep with her father, and because she envied her brother's penis. Let us call this, "Weird Interpretation Therapy." It is still taught in prestigious schools.

Not to pick on the poor psychoanalyst, there are people doing things in the name of therapy that make one nostalgic for the good old couch. When I was already an established therapist, I took courses in the leading contemporary methods to keep current. One teacher had her students run around her in a circle. After a few laps she took to hitting them in the belly. As I came around I indicated by flexing an arm that I would give blow for blow. "Don't act out!" she said. "Don't you act out!" I retorted cleverly. "Why are you being defensive?" she asked. "Because I'm being threatened!" I exclaimed.

Later, she explained that the belly whacks "brought up feelings." Noticing my thick lenses, she volunteered that I had trouble seeing what people were like. This was not her unaided judgment; her school of therapy simplistically linked physical defects to psychic ones. "I see people as well as anyone," I said, a bit stung, "but mostly I listen to tones of voice. You, for example, have difficulty showing anger in your voice. I would not be surprised to learn that you admire your father very much" (this from her carriage and style of dress), "and that you may find yourself involved with men you are contemptuous of" (No inference is so safe as that which is occurring before one's eyes). "I do—I did—I do," she gasped, and let me alone after that.

By contrast to "Weird Interpretation Therapy" or "Belly Whack Therapy," let us grant that the conversation between **p** and **Th** is intuitively agreeable with what we would like therapy to be. Let us call it, "Friendly Therapy." Part of the problem is that the therapists who offer weird interpretations or belly whacks might not agree that "Friendly Therapy" is better for mind and belly.

We need psychotherapists who are whole, open emotionally, warm, and friendly. Instead of emotional health, we too often get academic skills and/or quirks of character such as emotional sadism, which has a charismatic appeal to many masochistic patients. How shall we get healthier therapists? It cannot be legislated. I doubt it can be arranged. Perhaps the most we can hope for is that, in time, the patient population may come to demand emotional soundness in therapists.

While waiting for the millenium, I would like to suggest two evolutionary criteria for the validity of any model of psychotherapeutic intervention. These criteria have the merit of passing "Friendly Therapy," as we shall see, while rejecting "Weird Interpretation Therapy." The premises of "Belly Whack Therapy" have to be made more explicit before the criteria can be applied.

The first, or *selectivist* criterion, requires theoretical consistency with the principle of natural selection. As is true for all living creatures, human beings are the result of modes of operation that proved most reproductive in ancestral populations. Such modes, "selected" by the fact of their reproductive success only are based on genetic variation that originally occurred without respect to whether it would help its possessor reproduce (or in any other way). Whatever an ancestor of ours did or experienced in his life cannot have affected the content of his genes at all.

The second, or *phylogenetic* criterion, is that a particular mode of operation postulated as an inheritance from our primate or prehistoric hominid ancestry must be compatible with our knowledge of the actual conditions of our ancestors' lives. The selectivist requirement is clearer in application, because it is theoretical. The phylogenetic criterion concerns adaptation to past environments and sociocultural constraints, and in its "historical" nature lie many problems. Our lack of knowledge of our hominid past invites fantasies ranging from "savage hordes" to images of contemporary families in loincloths. Almost any trait an author wants to put forth as fundamental to our natures can be justified by postulating conditions at some early stage in our ancestry, where such a trait would be reproductively advantageous. However, the "almost" is significant. Some uninformed speculations about our past are excludable.

It is not that psychologists have ignored evolutionary theory; rather, they have often invoked it in casually incorrect ways. Thus, Freud (1939) wrote that we inherit "not only dispositions, but also ideational contents, memory traces of the experiences of former generations," although he was not certain whether one overwhelming experience or many repetitions were necessary to leave a trace. Jung spurred Freud on with his notions of the "collective unconscious" and "archetypes," which "are systems of preparedness that are at the same time images and emotions. They are inherited with the structure of the brain. . . . " (Jung, 1928). Thus, Jung explained a child's fear of his mother when there was no rational cause for it as a reenactment, a phylogenetic relic.

Freud and Jung (whose own educations preceded the modern understanding of evolution assembled by Fisher, Haldane, and Wright by the early 1930s) produced reams of pseudobiological psychology that fail the selectivist criterion. Nothing that the primordial horde of brothers (Freud, 1918) lusted after, killed, ate, or regretted, nor any other experiences of our animal or hominoid ancestors, could have left a trace in their genes! Yes, a child can be afraid of his mother "for no rational reason." No, it cannot be a "phylogenetic relic," because there is no way such an allegedly inheritable emotion could enhance reproductive success in its possessors.

Freud's (1933) *Death Instinct,* "whose aim is destruction," is another example of a psychological postulate inadmissible in terms of evolutionary theory. Such an "instinct" could not increase reproductivity in its possessor relative to nonpossessors. More recently, psychologies that regard anger as essentially disruptive of human operation are invalid on related grounds. An individual's vocal expression of anger is a useful biological capacity, helping defend his vital interests in confrontations with others; it is the suppression of anger that leads to hostility and destructiveness, effects Freud explained by postulating a Death Instinct.

Let us now consider an evolutionary basis for a therapy based on the conversation of friends.

Evolutionary Basis of "Friendly Therapy"

The human mind evolved largely as a mechanism for interpersonal learning through emotional sharing. We are social primates: we need each other. It makes us feel better to share our emotions, and to feel that they are validated by our peers. What we learn, initially through emotional rapport with our mothers, is how to express our feelings so as to get our needs met. Later, this learning can be modified through emotional exchanges with family and others. "Friendly Therapy" enhances the communication of human beings so that, on the whole, they feel better after each meeting than before.

II

Here is a similar framework for my Bio Psychotherapy, which I like to regard as an intensification of "Friendly Therapy," because it involves direct elicitation of intense emotions and spontaneous validation of them. I include postulates that may be corroborated when the physiology of emotions is studied in the context of free climactic expression.

Evolutionary Basis for Bio Psychotherapy

The freedom to express one's emotions is essential to healthy human operation. One who possesses such freedom chooses the extent to which he expresses himself according to the risks and opportunities of the circumstances. He isn't rigidly programed, for example, to suppress his anger when provoked, or to show it when it wouldn't be practical. He is not afraid or ashamed to express his need for love.

For most of the past fifty million years our ancestors shared with other arboreal, social primates an abundance of food, including leaves, roots, seeds, fruit, insects, lizards, smaller mammals, birds' eggs and nestlings, and freedom from predators, since nothing catches a primate in the trees. Thus, the sculpting edge of evolution that shaped our line was selection for the capacity to communicate, between mother and infant, and among the members of the social band. What was communicated was *emotion*, the readiness to behave in some major mode, such as to give or receive an embrace, to fight or flee. Our ancestors evolved a physiological urgency to express their emotions vocally, giving samples of the state of the body (its readiness to engage in fighting, fleeing, and embracing).

Among our primate ancestors there was selection for ability to learn through emotional communication in infancy how to operate socially. Reproductive success depended upon rapport with members of the band. Capability in attracting desirable mates, dealing with jealous confrontations, and interacting with offspring so that they learned to be socially operative, were conducive to leaving more descendants; therefore, over generations, these capabilities increased. Rapport was maintained by the communication of the emotions. Eventually, because it is safer, more efficient, and more flexible, expression of the emotions partly superseded overt action. Communication—crying out, roaring, shrieking whatever was felt in the moment—became the primary social behavior of our ancestors.

In our ancestral line there was also selection for a capacity we regard as essentially human: *Conscious choice* of one's behavior, including extent and form of emotional expression. The capacity for conscious choice involves loss of many inherited fixed behaviors—including rigid responses (which may also be regarded as choices, though not conscious ones) after an initial period of learning. The greater freedom of choice, the greater selective value assignable to intelligence. The more intelligence and awareness, the greater rewards for conscious choice. Greater intelligence includes capacities to abstract, to generalize, eventually to represent through arbitrary signs. The evolution of human capacities for society, language, and culture during the Pliocene and Pleistocene epochs, that is, the past five million years of prehistory, have been considered by Washburn (1961) and others. These human capacities are emergent phenomena, that is, they cannot be well understood on the basis of biology.

Patterns of susceptibility to social dominance and emotional control, evolved among our primate ancestors, were extended and redesigned during hominid evolution. One must be cautious in suggesting this or that genetically-based behavioral mode would have been advantageous (more reproductive for its possessors as opposed to nonpossessors) in the very different societies developed under the varying conditions our ancestors encountered during millions of years on the plains of Africa, skirting Ice Age glaciers northwest along the Mediterranean basin, or eastward across Asia.

Since the last glaciation, that is, in the past ten thousand years, agriculture and the rise of cities made transactions as common among strangers as among members of the extended family or tribe. It fell to increasingly hierarchical societies to regulate impersonal transactions. One consequence may have been the tightening of cultural constraints on emotional expression. Free expression may have suffered, not only between members of different castes, but among intimates and ultimately between mother and infant. The preceding two sentences describe nothing more than a guess about a significant phase of the war in our natures between emotional freedom and emotional control. There are signs of the conflict in primate behavior, so the usurpation of the human operative apparatus by emotional control may have been well established much earlier. Emotional control also may have gained increasing ascendance at later stages of civilization.

Emotional control retains considerable functional value in contemporary life, but *excessive* control of emotional expression is the underlying source of human misery. Like a cultural virus, excessive emotional control propagates itself from generation to generation. Those whose emotions were suppressed or distorted in infancy often act as though they have an investment in defending against emotion. When they become parents, they tend to treat their infants as they were treated. Often they ally themselves with the more repressive and distorting elements of our civilization.

Yet, deep layers of the human psyche derive from the emotional apparatus of our social primate ancestors. Human beings retain a chemical urgency to express their emotions in biologically-given patterns of vocal resonance. Free climactic expression of emotion discharges the system of tension, pain, or anxiety, allowing a return to the steady state towards which physiology is directed. When emotions are suppressed, the chemicals that urge expression linger in the body, causing emotional distress, dysfunctional behavior, and psychosomatic illness.

The psychobiologic apparatus of the human newborn is labile. He must learn how to fulfill his needs by relating to others in his society. The process entails hazards, especially at the damaging extremes of parental responses in a society that exacts repression or distortion of emotion as the price of membership. Rejection of a child's expression of his need for love, of his good feelings, angers, or fears, associates pain to the physiological mechanisms that urge vocalization. Anticipating this pain, he may respond to his own emotional state—as though to an external danger—in fear or anger, or some disorganized version of these emotions. One way of regarding neurotic behavior and character disorder is as the patient's attempt to avoid the pain of expressing emotions he feels are unacceptable.

A fellow human being can be reeducated to feel good towards all his emotions through spontaneous loving response to their free vocal expression. He has a sense of himself as lovable, then. When his needs are no longer a source of helplessness and pain, he relates to others in mutually fulfilling ways that bring happiness.

REFERENCES

Freud, S. (1913) *Totem and Taboo.* Std. Ed., Vol. 13. London: Hogarth Press, 1955.

Freud, S. (1932) *New Introductory Lectures on Psycho-Analysis.* New York: W. W. Norton, 1933.

Jung, C. G. *Contributions to Analytical Psychology.* New York: Harcourt Brace, 1928.

Saltzman, N. "Facilitating Cycles in Free Emotional Expression," *International Journal of Eclectic Psychotherapy,* December, 1982, 1-19.

Saltzman, N. "Results of Bio Psychotherapy," In J. Hariman (Ed.), *The Therapeutic Efficacy of the Major Psychotherapeutic Techniques.* Springfield, Ill.: Charles C Thomas, 1983.

Saltzman, N. "Paracatastasis and Exorcism in Bio Psychotherapy: Treating Shame, Guilt, and Bad Feelings about the Self," *International Journal of Eclectic Psychotherapy,* May, 1983, 14-30.

Saltzman, N. "Dealing with Rage and Killing Feelings in Bio Psychotherapy," *International Journal of Psychotherapy,* in press, 1983.

Washburn, S. L. (Ed.) *Social Life of Early Man.* Chicago: Aldine, 1961.

Williams, G. C. *Adaptation and Natural Selection.* Princeton, N.J.: Princeton University Press, 1966.

Chapter 17

CONTEXT AND CONSIDERATIONS OF
THE EDUCATION OF PSYCHOTHERAPISTS

PHILLIP SMITH

What can be, what could be, what should be the education of psychotherapists? To reach a conclusion to the question inherent in the title of this chapter, three general areas will be looked at. The raison d'être for psychotherapy, its historical antecedents, and a number of contemporary issues all need examination. However, it is not proposed to treat the exotic or nontraditional therapy extensively. In any case, the breadth of the contemporary traditional field prohibits anything but global references to the major issues involved in psychotherapy. The value of this chapter should lie in the questions that a reading of it provokes: questions that are relevant to the significant question of the education of psychotherapists. Perhaps therapists still practise somewhat as an elite priesthood, alone possessing secret knowledge, but as the medical or illness model is relinquished, as McNeil (1970) has observed, that may change.

HELP!

First, why psychotherapy at all? What kinds of justification may be found for intervention by one individual in the life of another? Although the environment can drive an individual to neurosis or worse, to psychosis, prime and major responsibility for an individual's psychic welfare must rest with that individual. Although Tennov (1975) argues that

> Structuring the social environment to contain more opportunities for positive reinforcement and fewer aversive contingencies will further reduce the inclination toward individual psychotherapy.

The need, or the indication, for therapy may typically occur at the lowest common denominator, when an individual is vaguely unwell or feels uncomfortable. (Preferably, he/she will have been checked by a competent medical practitioner.) His/her lack of ease has been found to have no organic basis, so he/she acquires the status of possessing a functional disorder. With this status, an individual may approach a traditional therapist or solicit help from one of the fringe groups. If there are signs of physical disorder such as gastric or duodenal ulcers, some form of psoriasis, and most forms of obesity, for example, which have an agreed psychological etiology, a medical programme could well include psychotherapy. These psychosomatic disorders carry clear indications for treatment: they are inherent in the appellation of psychosomatic. Psychotherapy is indicated also for an anxious individual whose anxiety is expressed in his/her daily activities of driving a motor vehicle, sleeping, or relating to his/her friends. Frequently, such individuals are referred by their concerned medical practitioners for appropriate treatment. Or the case arises where an individual has a clear-cut habit disorder such as smoking, nail biting, gambling, or drinking. Either he/she comes to realise that these are detrimental to his/her health, or signify his/her declining health, or he/she is persuaded by associates or medical practitioner to seek psychotherapeutic help to resolve or dissolve this habit. A second group of issues relates to a rather more serious form of psychological disability.

This disability is manifest as an interruption to the individual's work life, sex life, ability to relate to family effectively or friends: or it is expressed in frequent divorces or failure to maintain relationships before marriage. Either the individual is referred by his/her medical practitioner or is motivated by the degree of discomfort he/she feels to obtain some form of help to alleviate his/her felt lack of ease. On the same continuum, although to a more acutely severe degree, where, in the opinion of responsible and informed persons, if the individual is likely to endanger himself or cannot care for himself/herself, or is likely to endanger others, then he/she is not only advised to enter psychotherapy but may be legally committed or scheduled to do so under appropriate laws of the country in which he/she is residing.

That is a different sort of consideration to that of etiology; and on etiology it is less possible to be dogmatic than it used to be. Anderson, Rotter, and Zonana (1978) show that in some diseases with implications for behavioural problems of interest here:

Thus, environment can influence the expression of what appears to be primarily
a genetic disorder, and the genetic background influences the susceptibility to
environmentally caused disease.

These are the issues to which the therapist must address himself, and
consequently any programme of education of the therapist must express
cognisance of and reflect the need for those skills and techniques
indicated in treatment. There can be, there must be only one general
aim of therapy. The therapist must assist the patient to become master of
his/her own destiny within the constraints of the individual's unique
talents and abilities. What is more, there will be differences in therapy
between societies. However, there will be trends in societal responses as
Tygart (1982) showed in his assessment of opinions on mentally retarded
felons.

HISTORICAL TRENDS

The cultural context or social context in which psychotherapy has
been carried out has always been relevant. It has determined the type of
therapist and possibly the kinds of psychic disabilities that have been
treated. In the time of Hippocrates, treatment reflected the cultural
context of the ancient Greek civilisation. As Christianity became the
dominant factor in the general ideology that characterised European
civilisation for the next 1500 years after the Greeks, it is quite apparent
that the religious context with the priest as the major therapist was the
distinctive feature of this era. Then, as the religious aspect waned, so
secular guides became prominent. In this secular movement, it was
tacitly assumed that comfort was gained by observance of rules of good
living—discomfort was avoidable and irresponsible. Benjamin Franklin
was as noted for his guidance about living as for his scientific pro-
nouncements. There was an underlying movement too, which had
begun about this time, of Freemasons, who combined the religious and
the civic in their precepts for successful living. It is of interest also, that
by the end of the 19th century, when the waning of the church and
religion had become obvious to almost everyone, that the waxing of
hypnotism and, later, psychoanalysis occurred.

At this point, it is worth noting that in the time of Hippocrates
treatment of the mind was inseparable from the treatment of the body.
To Hippocrates, the division of mind and body was not an issue.

Unfortunately, following the rise of Judeaism and then Christianity, mind and body became increasingly separated. The tendency was reinforced with the development of physical medicine, with an accompanying development of physics and chemistry, which led ineluctably to an emphasis on the treatment of the body, rather than the whole person. This trend had occurred during the 1500 years or so of Christian dominance and was expressed in the medicine inherited from the Arabs and disseminated through the medical schools of the great mediaeval universities.

It is thought that the physical emphasis in medicine was greatest as the religious process began to approach its nadir in the 19th century. However, at this time, curiously, an interest in mind and body relationship was reawakened. This became obvious from the work of James Esdaile, the Scottish surgeon and physician who performed many operations, including amputations with the use of hypnosis, when he was an army surgeon in India. It is helpful to an understanding of the crescendo in psychological thought to note the impact of William James in the United States and elsewhere. It was enormous.

At the end of the 19th century, Pavlov and others came into prominence by showing how it was possible to precisely change behaviour. Successful application of their work and those who followed them was strikingly apparent in the brainwashing of prisoners by North Korea during the Korean war. The approaches of Freud and Jung and the discovery of the unconscious in the clinical treatment of various supposed functional disorders had been helpful also in reemphasising the position of mind in the control of behaviour. Underpinning the contribution from hypnosis, and from Freud and Jung, was the deliberate and very systematic development by Thorndike of a proper scientific method in psychology. That work provided a rich harvest almost half a century later, when Skinner took one of Thorndike's ideas and developed it to its logical conclusions within the propitious context of behaviourism. However, despite the work during the last forty years or so by Eccles and others, who have unravelled the complexities of the functioning of the central nervous system, comparatively little has been achieved in defining the behavioural correlates for particular neurological states. Nevertheless, the point has been reached where it can be easily demonstrated that the mind can control the body, following the work of Miller in the 1950s. To some extent, the beliefs and prognostications of Mrs. Eddy of

Christian Science appear, therefore, to have reasonable foundations. If the mind can control the body, and the mind can be controlled, then the logical question is, "If the mind is to be altered, why shouldn't it be altered?"

CONTEMPORARY ISSUES

Perhaps the answer to this would appear to lie in the cultural context within which psychotherapy is practised today. This is an age, in the western world, of instant gratification; therefore, pain relievers and mood alterers have achieved a preeminence that would have been unthinkable eighty years ago. (It is obvious that alcohol, a significant mood alterer, has been with us for thousands of years; however, there have always been certain prohibitions and certain side effects from the use of it, so that it has not always enjoyed widespread use.) Of necessity, the widespread use of mood altering drugs and pain relievers has led to a search for methods that did not rely on chemotherapy at all, and hence there has been an increasing movement toward the substitution of behavioural methods.

It is well that there has been this movement, because overall it would appear that the cultural context in which people live is becoming less propitious for optimum human development. About eighty years ago Durkheim, the eminent French sociologist, pointed to a state of anomie as the basis for the perturbation and felt inability to cope that individuals in western society experienced. The complexity of modern technology, which leads to increasing demands on the individual, must inevitably increase the stress and difficulties in coping that many individuals experience today. Undoubtedly, there are two possibilities suggested by this dilemma. One is to have a number of centres operating in communities and schools that propound the principles and practice of mental hygiene or prophylaxis against stress and other psychological discomfort. Undoubtedly, programmes such as Relationship Enhancement, developed and propounded by Guerney (1977), would be of great value in that educational effort. The other possibility is to produce a stress-free environment, and probably this is the proper task of ecological psychology, which is rather in the infancy stage at present. It will be helpful if at this point the contemporary psychotherapeutic scene is surveyed. Who are our psychotherapists today?

Psychotherapists have varying academic backgrounds, qualifications, and expertise. Clinical psychologists, for example, are university trained practitioners holding a bachelor's degree, a master's degree, or a doctorate. The doctorate in psychology may practice in a general manner or as a specialist in a general area, such as the mentally retarded or the physically handicapped. Psychologists do not necessarily practice in all of the areas for which their training has fitted them. Some practice as psychometricians, some as diagnosticians, and others as learning consultants, for example. These variations would appear to arise from the nature of the therapy on the one hand and from the relationship between the therapist and the patient on the other. Of course there is considerable variation between patients, and there is variation between the response of patients to the same therapist. Therapists may come to differ less and less.

It is indeed likely that more and more in the future that the dynamic, with other related groups, will in fact share common grounds with the behavourist. What is shared is their common basis in the new ecological approach to human behaviour. It will be helpful to remember, too, that Freud commenced his professional life as a neurologist. Analysts have argued that they have an advantage over the behaviourists inasmuch as they are not intruding their own hangups into a therapeutic situation. They have also claimed that there is not enough respect paid to the integrity of the individual by behaviourists who alter the behaviour of an individual rather than letting the individual alter his own behaviour. Focus of control appears to be external rather than internal. Behaviourists have claimed, in defence, that they only alter the behaviour of those whom they love. There have been some real and large difficulties between these views, which may or may not need to be solved. As Miller, Galanter, and Pribram (1960) suggest in the epilogue to their discussion of plans and behaviour, there should be a decline in the necessity to distinguish between introspectively derived and behaviourally derived concepts. They anticipate a point where human experience and human behaviour will be understood in the same terms.

The problem that confronts the psychotherapist is whether he is to treat the symptomatic behaviour or the mechanism underlying the behaviour, or to describe it alternatively, is a temporary or an abiding change to be induced. Is the psychotherapist to produce a superficial change in behaviour or is he to assist the individual to attain some degree of change within his unique personality configuration? Is the psychotherapist to do this quickly or is he to work slowly? Is psychotherapy to be practiced for a short term or for a long term?

Inevitably, it appears that psychotherapy must rest more and more strongly on an understanding of the neurological basis of behaviour, and the major problem will be to specify or define the behavioural correlates of specific neurological states. For as Eibl-Eibesfeldt (1970) has noted:

> Only the exact knowledge of the determinants of our behaviour will lead to its eventual mastery.

Yet, as Tourney (1970) concludes in his paper, those determinants are lacking.

It will be readily apparent that the mind, which it is generally agreed is a production of the central nervous system, will be affected by the kind of nutrition that an individual enjoys. It is for this reason that some reference in the training of psychotherapists must be made to the practitioners best qualified to cope with this aspect of human development and maintenance. At the present time, these are medical practitioners. They are conversant with the effects of vitamins and other features of diet that enable individuals to maintain an adequately functioning nervous system. It would seem unreasonable to expect psychotherapists to do everything.

Reflection about the foregoing matters provide the indications for selecting psychotherapists who can effect an approved therapeutic result, although it would be unrealistic to expect psychotherapy always to succeed. As Erickson (1964) noted in a discussion of the burden of responsibility in psychotherapy:

> There are other patients whose goal is no more than the continuous seeking of therapy but not the accepting of it. With this type of patient hypnotherapy fails as completely as do other forms of therapy.

Initially, it needs to be decided whether males or females or both are to be selected for training as psychotherapists and whether, in fact, a male therapist is requisite for male patients and a female therapist for female patients, or vice versa. Other questions that merit answers are whether the therapist should be young, middle-aged, or elderly. It needs to be resolved whether therapists will be shown to be more effective who have been drawn from other professions or who come from a trained background. Whilst a necessary level of intelligence is a prerequisite to training, the effective expression of intelligence must be ascertained in candidates for training. Attributes of personality required to practice effectively obviously have yet to be sufficiently defined if the contemporary rate of therapeutic failure is borne in mind.

When these matters are considered, it will be helpful if the attrition of trainees of the practice of medicine is noted. This attrition has been attributed to a reliance on high intelligence and high entrance marks in the prerequisite qualifying examinations or prerequisite degrees rather than a primary reliance on the dedication and the personality of the applicant for training in medicine. A further problem stems from the matter of "brainwashing," or socialisation (referred to by Brim and Wheeler), which appears to be very necessary in inducting any individuals into a new organisation or to a profession. It is quite obvious that the remuneration, the ultimate remuneration, of medical practitioners will be a factor in determining the kind of applicants and the attitudes of those applicants who wish to enter medicine. We have to bear in mind that in the present changing society, the values that motivated professional and independent practitioners twenty, thirty, or forty years ago may now no longer be relevant. It would be well to note that these considerations apply to psychotherapists.

Undoubtedly, the inculcation of the appropriate values, attitudes, skills, and techniques, as they are applied in a particular and special relationships, which is psychotherapy, will depend considerably on the mentors, the guides, the trainers of the candidates, who offered themselves for training as psychotherapists. At present, in the orthodox or traditional training of psychotherapists there is an emphasis either from academics or clinicians and often from the former. Psychologists are mostly trained by academics, albeit some of the trainers possess considerable clinical experience. Psychiatrists, on the other hand, after they have undergone their initial medical training, are trained by clinicians. It is suggested that in the future training of psychotherapists that, without argument getting bogged down in the useless, it would seem helpful to consider in the controversy between theory and practice, the contrast that needs emphasising is that between a clinical approach or a research-oriented approach. This issue is brought forward here to emphasise it rather than resolve it. Naranjo (1973) is convinced that results in psychotherapy are inseparable from a personal ingredient in the therapist. It is assumed that this personal ingredient can be inculcated in training.

Finally, it is clear from the foregoing discussion that there is a strong case for eclecticism by implication. Perhaps the consideration of the matter of eclecticism would assist the resolution of the question that has just been raised concerning clinical or research-oriented training for psychotherapists.

One of the final questions remains, and that has been partly answered in the more immediate discussion: where are psychotherapists to be trained? One point that may be raised before particular places and institutions are discussed is the question of whether that training should be full time or part time. If it is to be part time, are psychotherapists to practice in the context or a similar context to the one in which they work or in which they will work? That question is relevant to the place and hence, type of training. With the explosion of knowledge in the latter part of the 19th century, and the 20th century, institutions of advanced studies other than universities have arisen to meet specific needs. It is therefore relevant at this point to ask whether the training of psychotherapists could properly be undertaken in a university. It could well be that an institute of technology is a far sounder place to conduct training for psychotherapists, rather than universities with their academic emphasis.

That medicine has survived and possibly prospered on a basis of university training is no argument for the training of psychotherapists in universities, as medicine has a completely different history. Indeed, it has an ancient and honourable history that the polyglot psychology cannot match, and that is a handicap in the training of psychotherapists. It will be important, therefore, for whichever institution psychotherapists are to train in to determine what kind of environment they should experience as they train. Should they be trained in an institution in the middle of a large city where they have access to a large number of cases exhibiting various conditions? Or should they undergo training in parochial or rural institutions that could, more hopefully, provide an environment that is necessary to nurture the very special person that psychotherapists appear to need to be? If the distinction between psychologists and psychiatrists made earlier is borne in mind, it may be seen to be in the best interests of all psychotherapists if their training followed the psychiatric model. That is, training would proceed initially with studies leading to the acquisition of a related and basic qualification. Followed by an internship of five years or so, supervised by a collegiate body that represented the profession of psychotherapy, an examination by clinicians would determine the fitness of candidates to practice.

CONCLUSION

In the foregoing discussion, some major aspects of the problem of the education of psychotherapists have been raised. In effect, discussion has illustrated one or both of the two major problems of training or education: the aims, and the means of obtaining those aims. No firm answers can be given. In fact, by implication, firm answers should be avoided. Whether the education of psychotherapists should proceed by traditional or nontraditional means will depend on the definition of the aims that groups or individuals have or the kind of person they wish to see practice psychotherapy. May quotes with approval William James's comment that those who would make the world more healthy had best start with themselves. Once concerned bodies have specified the attributes of those kind of persons, they can then more intelligently and more rigorously (because that is sorely needed) work to ascertain the means for producing the kind of person who will be the most effective psychotherapists that our western society can produce. It seems unlikely that if that paradigm were accepted that traditional or nontraditional means of educating psychotherapists would be followed. Something else is indicated!

REFERENCES

Anderson, C. E., and Zonana, J. Hereditary Considerations in common disorders. In M. M. Kaback (Ed.) *The Paediatric Clinics of North America.* 25,3, 1978. Philadelphia: Saunders, 1978.

Eibl-Eibesfeldt, I. *Ethology, The Biology of Behaviour.* New York: Holt, Rinehart & Winston, 1970.

Erickson, M. H. The burden of responsibility in effective psychotherapy. In J. Haley (Ed.) *Advanced Techniques of Hypnosis and Therapy.* New York: Grune & Stratton, 1967.

Guerney, B. G. *Relationship Enhancement.* San Francisco: Jossey-Bass, 1979.

McNeil, E. B. *The Psychoses.* Englewood Cliffs, New Jersey: Prentice-Hall, 1970.

May R. *Man's Search for Himself.* New York: Delta, 1953.

Miller, G. A., Galanter, E., and Pribram, K. H. *Plans and the Structure of Behaviour.* London: Holt, Rinehart & Winston, 1970.

Naranjo, C. *The Healing Journey.* London: Hutchinson, 1975.

Tennov, D. *Psychotherapy: The Hazardous Cure.* New York: Abel-Schumann, 1975.

Tourney, G. Psychiatric therapies. In T. Rothman (Ed.), *Changing Patterns in Psychiatric Care.* New York: Crown, 1970.

Tygart, C. E., Effects of religiosity on public opinion about legal responsibility for mentally retarded felons. *American Journal of Mental Deficiency,* 1983, 86,459–464.

INDEX